# THE ROAD NOT TAKEN

# *The*
# ROAD NOT
# TAKEN

*Early Arab–Israeli
Negotiations*

Itamar Rabinovich

*New York   Oxford*
OXFORD UNIVERSITY PRESS
1991

Oxford University Press TALLAHASSEE, FLORIDA
Oxford   New York   Toronto
Delhi   Bombay   Calcutta   Madras   Karachi
Petaling Jaya   Singapore   Hong Kong   Tokyo
Nairobi   Dar es Salaam   Cape Town
Melbourne   Auckland

and associated companies in
Berlin   Ibadan

Published by Oxford University Press, Inc.,
200 Madison Avenue, New York, New York 10016

Oxford is a registered trademark of Oxford University Press

Library of Congress Cataloging-in-Publication Data
Rabinovich, Itamar, 1942-
The road not taken : early Arab-Israeli negotiations / Itamar
Rabinovich.
p.   cm.   Includes index.
ISBN 0-19-506066-0
1. Israel-Arab War, 1948–1949—Diplomatic history.
2. Jewish-Arab relations, 1949–1967.   I. Title.
DS126.92.R33 1991
956.04'2—dc20   90–22368

9 8 7 6 5 4 3 2 1

Printed in the United States of America
on acid-free paper

# Preface

"All history is contemporary history," wrote the Italian historian-philosopher Benedetto Croce to describe the complex relationship between the historian's craft and the political and social context in which he or she lives and writes. Croce correctly maintained that there is no such thing as totally objective historiography, that even a historian concerned with a remote period and society also brings to bear both personal baggage and current issues. It can thus be safely assumed that an Italian historian active in the 1920s or 1930s who was writing on, say, Julius Caesar could not have avoided at least an implicit comparison between him and Mussolini and consequently between the rise of the Fascist movement in modern Italy and the transition from a constitutional republic to an imperial dictatorship in ancient Rome. This close relationship between past and present becomes all the more evident when dealing with contemporary history and even more so when writing about processes and developments that affect our own lives.

The Arab–Israeli conflict continues to be an important international problem. The issues discussed in this book are still nourishing intense political debates and academic controversies: the nature of Arab–Israeli relations; the risks and opportunities inherent in Arab–Israeli negotiations in regard to the threat of another Middle Eastern war; the delimitation of Israel's borders and the definition of the state's character; the Palestinian problem and questions that arise therefrom (for example, whether it is the core of a larger conflict or whether the Arab–Israeli dispute is primarily one between states); the relationship between the West Bank and the Gaza Strip; and Jordan's role and the importance of the policies pursued by foreign powers, particularly the United States.

The striking similarity between the present political configuration and the one obtaining during the early years of the Arab–Israeli conflict understandably leads many observers to interpret the events of 1948–49 in the light of the positions they hold in current political debates. The first chapter of this book analyzes this pattern. This pattern also can, of course, be reversed; that is, contemporary issues can be illuminated by the knowledge and perspective provided by an examination of their origins. For example, those familiar with the Jordanian demand for and subsequent negotiations on a corridor linking the West Bank to the Gaza coast were probably not surprised when soon after the declaration of Palestinian independence in November 1988 Yasir Arafat demanded that the idea of such a corridor be considered. Likewise, those who studied the Jordanian–Israeli negotiations of 1949–50 might have expected that Abdullah's grandson twenty or thirty years later would also have a hard time trying to persuade the Jordanian political system to support a controversial agreement with Israel. And yet it is erroneous to conclude, as some moderate Israelis did in the mid-1950s, on the basis of the failure to achieve peace in 1949 and 1950, that the Arab political generation formed by the defeat of 1948 will similarly be incapable of making peace with Israel.

Indeed, any analysis that draws on the continuity and similarity of the major issues and forces at work that have shaped Arab–Israeli relations during the past forty years must necessarily be incomplete.

But these obvious parallels should not obscure the changes that have taken place over the years: Israel's increasing power in absolute terms; the transformation of the Palestinians into a more significant, autonomous actor; the Soviet Union's acquisition and subsequent loss of its central position in the region; Israel's later control of all of Palestine west of the Jordan River; and the Israeli political system's transformation in the 1970s. But the purpose of this book is not to compare Arab–Israeli relations in 1949 and 1990 and to explore the ensuing political ramifications. Rather, its purpose is to reexamine Arab–Israeli relations in light of recently available archival materials. These new documents have enabled us to reevaluate the nature and state of the conflict at that time and to try to understand how and why it so quickly became one of the world's thorniest problems. This book focuses on the three sets of negotiations that Israel held between 1949 and 1952 with Egypt, Jordan, and Syria. The negotiations were, as a rule, held directly between Israel and its Arab neighbors and dealt with issues of both principle and practice, thus providing insights into the various parties' positions. To provide a background, I shall describe and analyze other dimensions of Arab–Israeli relations at that time, such as the role of the international players in mediation efforts and attempts to impose a solution.

I was fortunate to find a title for this book that expresses in such a vivid fashion the core of the problem. Robert Frost's poem "The Road Not Taken" begins by suggesting that the choice when reaching the fork in the road "has made all the difference." But later in the poem this choice becomes more ambiguous when, having made a choice and having made progress, the poet discovers that it is impossible to know whether his choice was the right one:

> Though as for that
> the passing there
> Had worn them really about the
> same

To return to the subject of our book, this is where we stand now. The lives of Israelis and Arabs in 1990 have been shaped by the decisions made by their leaders in 1948 or 1949. Although important decisions were made regarding Arab–Israeli relations in earlier and later years, those made during the first Arab–Israeli war and its immediate aftermath were crucial. We can look back from the vantage point of 1990 at the events and decisions of 1948 and 1949 and evaluate the choices made then. But we can never know whether they have "made all the difference." Indeed, another aspect of Robert Frost's choice of words is its failure to identify who decided not to take the road. The choices of 1948–49 were made by Arabs, Israelis, Americans, and others. And credit and responsibilty for them belong to all.

It is a pleasant duty to thank all those who helped me in researching and writing this book. The Dina and Yona Ettinger Chair in Contemporary Middle Eastern History at Tel Aviv University and the Littaver Foundation of New York City provided the resources. The staff and faculty of the Moshe Dayan Center for Middle Eastern and African Studies at Tel Aviv University provided a professional home, a research infrastructure, general support, and camaraderie. Among my friends and colleagues at the center, I am particularly grateful to Uriel Dann, Martin Kramer, Asher Susser, Edna Liftman, and Amira Margalith. Special thanks should go to Lydia Gareh, who typed the manuscript in both Hebrew and English and whose blend of talent and goodwill has spoiled us all for many years.

Many friends and colleagues were generous with their knowledge, advice, and private collections: Michael Apel, Gabriel Cohen, Mordechai Gazit, Bruce Maddy-Weitzman, Yoram Nimrod, Elhanan Oren, Michel Oren, Shabtai Teveth, Moshe Zak, and Eyal Zisser. Avraham Biran, Ziama Divon, Josh Palmon, Gideon Rafael, Moshe Sasson, Ya'acov Shimoni, Yael Vered, and other participants who prefer to remain anonymous shared their memories wih me. Yehoshua Freundlich and Yemima Rosenthal, senior staff members at Israel's state archive who researched the same period, were most helpful. Uriel Dann and Bernard Lewis read the manuscript and offered criticism and advice. Fouad Ajami suggested the book's title.

And I am particularly grateful to my research assistant, Tikva Bracha, for her talents and devotion.

Finally, a technical note: In order to simplify matters, Arabic and Hebrew names were rendered on the basis of phonetic rather than strict academic transliteration. Whenever possible, therefore, the spelling used by the Columbia Encyclopedia was followed.

*Tel Aviv*                                                      I. R.

*November 1990*

# Contents

# THE ROAD NOT TAKEN

# 1

————————————

# Introduction

The real as well as semantic transition from the Arab–Jewish conflict
in Palestine to the Arab–Israeli conflict was the product of the war
in 1948 that the Israelis call the War of Independence and the Arabs
named the Palestine war. The creation of the state of Israel established
it as one of the protagonists in this ongoing story, serving in this
capacity as the successor to the Zionist movement and the Jewish
community in Palestine. The 1948 war also completed the transformation of what had originally been a clash between two nationalist
movements in and over Palestine into a more complex dispute between Israel and the Arab world. Before 1948 when the conflict in
Palestine was principally a struggle between the Zionist movement
and the Palestinian Arab nationalist movement, the Zionist movement
and the Yishuv, the Jewish community in Palestine, were also con-
tending with Arab nationalism in a broader sense. This contention
derived not only from the solidarity of other Arabs with the Palestinian Arabs and their political considerations but also from the fact
that the Arab nationalists regarded the Zionist effort in Palestine as
a particularly significant test and challenge. The 1948 war then made

this far more important. The challenge became more concrete, and was compounded by the humiliation of the Arabs' defeat at the hands of Israel, only a small state. And if the struggle against Zionism was seen as a test of the Arab world's ability to cope with the West and modernity, the establishment of the state of Israel and the war that united it were a painful demonstration of the distance that had yet to be traveled.[1]

From Israel's perspective this situation had far-reaching ramifications. If the establishment of a state meant conflict with the whole Arab world—possibly an irreconcilable one—the young state was doomed to live in insecurity. It was in this spirit, therefore, that David Ben-Gurion wrote in his diary in the summer of 1949:

> It should be assumed that the war is over . . . but as far as the fundamental geopolitical facts are concerned, the position is grave, and security is a cardinal concern of the state. . . . [We] should take into account our neighbors, first and foremost the Arab world, and they constitute a great danger. It is a unified world in terms of language, religion, and culture; we are an alien element. There may also be a desire for revenge, and the association with the crusaders will be at work; our victory is not an index for the future.[2]

With this in the background, the armistice agreements that were signed in 1949 with four Arab states were considered at the time to be a great achievement. The illusion of a breakthrough that these agreements created in Israel, at least for a brief moment, and the subsequent disillusion were well described in 1949 by Moshe Sharett, the foreign minister, in a bitter lecture he delivered in 1957:

> This is how things developed: The state was created. There was the War of Independence. Whatever happened happened. There were the armistice agreements. We regarded their signature as a great thing. Our position was not bad at all . . . [T]he end of the War of Independence left us in the following state: The Arabs had 20% of the country's territory, and we had 80%, a contiguous territory, not divided, in which the Arab population hardly amounted to 15%. This was the outcome of the War of Independence, and for this reason the armistice agreements that confirmed this state [were] a

tremendous achievement for Israel. It was a complete revolution; more than that, it was a very significant political fact; the Arab states had explicitly signed a revolutionary agreement with the state of Israel, in their own name and as an act of state. And this agreement was perceived as a transitional phase toward arrangements of peace. This agreement decreed progress toward a peace settlement.

We all lived in the belief that peace was around the corner; that the Arab world was resigned to the outcome; that it was a question of time, but not a long time, a few years. I will exclude no one; we all believed that the psychological stage in the Arab world had been set for peace; that the issue of peace was to crystallize further and consolidate. At this point [however], our policy suffered its greatest disappointment. The vision did not materialize; it turned out that we had failed to read the future correctly. We are facing this question as if no progress had taken place, as if a retreat had occurred."[3]

## Various Views of Arab–Israeli Relations

This book will discuss the disappointment referred to by Moshe Sharett, the failure to transform the armistice agreements into peace agreements and a state of peace, and instead the evolution of the full-fledged Arab–Israeli conflict of the 1950s. In its academic and political context this issue has preoccupied many. Was the course of events inevitable, or would different results have been possible if different policies had been adopted by Israel, the Arab states, and the external actors—the United States and Britain in particular? In later years, Moshe Sharett became the implicit founding father of the dovish school in Israeli politics, and he has been depicted as representing an approach to Arab–Israeli relations different from that of Ben-Gurion, the "activist."[4]

The issue of the Ben-Gurion and Sharett "schools" of Israeli foreign and national security are discussed later. But it should be emphasized that Ben-Gurion's and Sharett's paths diverged in the 1950s. Sharett replaced Ben-Gurion as prime minister when Ben-Gurion temporarily retired, and he returned to his post as foreign minister in Ben-Gurion's subsequent cabinet. In both capacities Sharett grew increasingly critical of the activist security policy that culminated in the Sinai campaign launched by Israel against Egypt in coordination with the Anglo-French Suez campaign. But between 1948 and 1952, Sharett, temperamental differences notwithstanding, shared Ben-Gurion's outlook on the fundamental issues of war and peace. From the perspective of 1957, despite his bitterness and the exacerbation of policy differences since 1953, Sharett stated that peace had not been and was not possible because of the Arab position. Israel's mistake was not so much a matter of its policy but a

> failure to penetrate the psychological essence of the problem. The question of peace will not be resolved according to interest or logic. It is from the beginning to end a question of will. . . . [T]he shock caused to Arab consciousness by the establishment of the state of Israel was far deeper and more powerful than we had thought . . . [and consequently] we are dealing here with a change whose maturation is not a process of years but of decades. . . . I say that as long as the generation that has encountered this shock as a direct, personal experience is alive, active, and influential and is making decisions, there is almost no prospect, or there is but a dim prospect, that the mental reconciliation will come, without which peace is not possible.[5]

Sharett's statement was a typically eloquent articulation of the prevailing establishment outlook, which viewed the modulation from the 1948 war to the Arab–Israeli conflict as a deterministic development generated by the underlying causes of the war and the Arab–Israeli political dispute. Israel wanted a peace predicated on the status quo, whereas the Arab world, according to this view, either was not interested in peace or insisted on terms that would have further eroded the Israeli state's fragile existence and therefore were unacceptable.[6]

This view was dominant but not free from criticism and challenge. Political critics on the Left had challenged it from the outset, and by the 1950s academic literature began to appear that argued, though not necessarily for political reasons, that peace might have been achieved in 1949 or 1950. Rony Gabbay, in a book published in 1959, contended that Israel had missed an opportunity to make peace with Egypt in January–February 1950.[7] David Forsythe, in his book on the Palestine Conciliation Commission published in 1972, asserted that such an opportunity existed in 1949 but did not blame Israel in particular for missing that opportunity.[8]

The distinction among academic analysis, political conviction, and advocacy of a certain policy line was never clearly drawn in the discussion of this issue. Accordingly, in 1975 my late teacher, Malcolm Kerr, published an introductory essay in an edited volume that contained a critique of U.S. policy (as too lenient toward Israel), policy recommendations for peacemaking in the Middle East, and a sharp criticism of Israel's policies. Kerr saw a remarkable continuity in Israel's policies from the 1948 war to the mid-1970s, of which he clearly disapproved:

> Israel's obsession with security, its preoccupation with territorial possession and military advantage by *faits accomplis*, its great distrust of outside intermediaries and its reluctance to take initiatives or show restraint . . . all this has been clearly illustrated since the 1967 war; but it has also been true for many previous years. In many respects, the 1967 war and its aftermath constituted a replay of 1948–9.[9]

In recent years a series of developments exacerbated the challenge to the dominant Israeli view, fully or in part. First the changes in perspective and the erosion of the firm consensus on questions of national security that had been achieved in Israel during the state's first two decades. This consensus was also reflected in the accepted view of the nature and evolution of the Arab–Israeli conflict. The breakdown of the consensus led to a review of positions and measures that in the past had been considered above questioning. It also contributed to the rise of revisionist historiographic schools, on both the Left and the Right, that seek to link the domestic Israeli debate of the 1970s and 1980s to the crucial events of the establishment of the state.

Second, the signing of the Israeli–Egyptian peace treaty in 1979. This breakthrough and the fact that the most important Arab state (Egypt) accepted Israel as a legitimate political entity were projected back into the past and prompted many to question whether the same could not have been accomplished thirty years earlier. After all, contrary to Moshe Sharett's assertion in 1957, it was Anwar al-Sadat, who had served as an officer in the Egyptian army in 1948, who signed the peace treaty with Israel.

Third, the opening of diplomatic archives and the availability of thousands of documents concerning Arab–Israeli relations in the late 1940s and early 1950s. These documents have revealed previously unknown facts and have exposed a political reality far more complex than that portrayed by traditional scholarship. But the opening of some archives has also presented a challenge to the historians whose task is to place the new material in the proper context and proportions. This challenge is made all the more serious by the fact that although Israel has opened its diplomatic archives and pursued a rather liberal policy of declassification, its Arab counterparts have not opened their archives. Historians working on the documents available in Israeli, American, and British archives in order to reconstruct Arab policies and positions must resort to papers written by Israeli and Western diplomats and to such Arab sources as memoirs and press accounts. Nonetheless the danger exists that such accounts might inflate the importance of Israeli actions and statements, thereby distorting the historical reality. A history of diplomatic negotiations written essentially on the basis of one party's archives is thus liable to imply that it made the major decisions while the other party or parties stood by passively.

The thrust of the new school that blames Israel, explicitly or implicitly, for failing to resolve the Arab–Israeli conflict at the end of the 1948 war is exemplified by Avi Shlaim's essay on the initiatives taken toward Israel in the spring of 1949 by Husni Zaim, Syria's first military dictator. We shall discuss in detail this episode in Chapter 3, but for the purposes of this chapter, here is the final paragraph of Shlaim's essay:

> In retrospect it might be tempting to dismiss Zaim as an unstable and unpredictable military dictator, as a corrupt and unprincipled opportunist and as a megalomaniac whose removal from the scene

made very little difference to the prospects of solving the Arab–Israeli problem in general or the refugee problem in particular. But as this article has tried to demonstrate, despite Zaim's undeniable defects of character, he was a serious proponent of social reform and economic development and regarded peace with Israel and the resettlement of the refugees as essential for the attainment of these greater goals. What might have happened if Zaim had managed to prolong his hold over power, there is, of course, no way of telling. But during his brief tenure of power, he gave Israel every opportunity to bury the hatchet and possibly lay the foundations for peaceful coexistence in the long term. If his overtures were spurned, if his constructive proposals were not put to the test and if a historic opportunity was frittered away through lack of vision and obsession with minutiae, the fault must be sought not with Zaim but on the Israeli side. And the fault can be traced directly to that whole school of thought, of which Ben Gurion was the most powerful and short sighted proponent, which maintained that time was on Israel's side and that Israel could manage perfectly well without peace with the Arab states and without a solution to the Palestinian refugee problem.[10]

This book does not seek to defend any of the actors or to allocate blame. Nor is it my purpose to focus on the ever-intriguing issue of "missed opportunities," although the actions taken and the decisions made by leaders at crucial points in history do require analysis and assessment. My purpose is to use the abundance of fresh sources in order to reexamine the evolution of the Arab–Israeli conflict in its early and formative phases, to measure its depth, and to examine the conduct of the various parties to the conflict in its larger context. To this end, we shall study in detail the attempts to conduct negotiations between Israel and three of its Arab neighbors—Syria, Jordan, and Egypt—in the aftermath of the 1948 war. The endeavor to generate Syrian–Israeli negotiations for a comprehensive settlement was made while the two countries were actually negotiating the armistice agreement. We shall look at this in the next chapter. Chapter 4 examines a particular phase of the long-standing Jordanian–Israeli relationship—the effort made by both sides between November 1949 and March 1950 to create a relationship beyond that of the armistice agreement. In regard to Israel's relations with Egypt, Chapter 5 will examine the series of attempts to resolve, regulate, or at least discuss the Israeli–Egyptian conflict that were made between the signing of the armistice agreement in February 1949 and the Egyptian revolution in July 1952. That revolution launched a new era in the politics of the region and in the history of the Arab–Israeli conflict and so provides an appropriate terminal point for the transitional phase examined in this book.

Before considering these three cases we shall look at the context in which they occurred: the political developments in the Middle East, the early years of the Arab–Israeli conflict, the Arab and Israeli political systems, and the first efforts to find a political solution to the conflict.

## The Middle East, 1949–1952

In the contemporary history of the Middle East, the years between 1949 and 1952 marked the end of the order that had ruled in the Middle East since 1920. At the close of World War I Britain was the hegemonial power in the region, drawing on its own power as well as the fact that for different reasons, the United States, the Soviet Union, and Germany were absent from the Middle East or played only marginal roles in its affairs. Both Britain and France ruled directly or indirectly over most of the region and exerted influence over states enjoying varying degrees of formal (as distinct from real) independence. One consequence was that between 1920 and the post–World War period the question of relations with the dominant external power was the principal issue in the domestic politics of the region. The socioeconomic and political changes that took place during these decades became apparent only at a later stage when these countries had achieved full independence and the imperial powers had left.

In this respect World War II had a lasting effect on the Middle East. It produced the age of decolonization, thereby diminishing the power of Britain and France, and placed the two superpowers, the United States and the Soviet Union, and the conflict between them at the center of the international stage. The effect of these developments was felt in the Middle East only gradually. France was the first to be evicted, from Syria and Lebanon, and more as a result of its own decline and the influence of the other powers than because of the pressure of local nationalist movements. Britain lost its control of Palestine, failed in its attempt to replace its 1930 treaty with Iraq with one conforming better to the times, and found itself fighting to preserve at least some presence and influence in Egypt.

The cold war crept into the Middle East from several directions. The Soviet Union, like czarist Russia in the nineteenth century, took advantage of its territorial contiguity with the region and applied direct pressure to Turkey and Iran. Unable at that stage to obtain influence in the Arab world, the Soviet Union therefore extended support to Israel in the 1948 war, primarily in order to dislodge Britain from its imperial position but possibly also in hopes of acquiring assets in a state dominated by socialist parties. The Soviet Union—like Germany and Italy in the 1930s—was a model for the region that those aspiring to national power might be expected to find attractive. In the early 1950s after Israel had abandoned its nominally neutralist policy and openly joined the Western camp and after the Soviet Union's Josef Stalin had changed his country's policy toward the Jews and had achieved the first Soviet successes in the Arab world, the Soviet Union officially moved to support the Arab side in the conflict with Israel.

America entered the region only reluctantly. To some extent this reflected Washington's ambivalent recognition of its position of responsibility and leadership during and immediately after World War II. In the Middle East the United States' new position was complicated by the need to ease out—however gently—the British, who acknowledged their need to rely on the far superior power of the United States and yet were reluctant to give up the role of the mature and experienced tutor that they had played earlier. At the war's end Britain was forced to call on the United States in order to stand up to the Soviet Union in Iran and Turkey and Greece but were incensed when Washington forced its own position on the Palestine question and tried to shape the Western strategy regarding the construction of a Middle Eastern defense system according to its own taste and priorities. Indeed, it was this effort to establish a defensive system against what was perceived as a Soviet quest to gain control of, or at least acquire influence in, the Middle East that stood at the center of Western policy in the region in the late 1940s and early 1950s.

France was the junior partner in this Western policy. Although it was a party to the Tripartite Declaration in 1950, which sought to demonstrate the West's hegemony in the region, it was excluded from the private American–British consultations and was not invited to join most of their ensuing moves. Britain still maintained a considerable military presence in the Middle East and was assigned the principal role in waging a land war in the region, a prospect that in the late 1940s appeared quite likely. This task led Britain to try to preserve or develop military bases at key points in the region and to guarantee efficient communication among them. This was the main consideration underlying Britain's effort to deny Israel the Negev, or at least the southern Negev, so as to provide an easy and secure "land bridge" between Britain's bases in Egypt and its forces in Jordan. For the same reason the British government tried in January 1951—during a particularly difficult crisis in its relations with Egypt—to obtain bases and lines of communication in and through Israel.

Finally Britain concluded that all attempts to preserve a residual position and influence in such countries as Egypt and Iraq, through the traditional mode of bilateral treaties, were futile. Britain therefore sought to form a regional defensive organization tying the Arab states to the United States and itself against the Soviet Union. The British assumed that a multilateral arrangement would enable the Egyptian and Iraqi governments to make concessions that were not conceivable in a bilateral treaty. This line of thinking was translated for the first time into a concrete policy in 1951 in the form of the Supreme Allied Command Middle East (SACME).

The United States was less than a full partner to this effort. It was, of course, interested in an effective defense organization in the Middle East but less so in the preservation of Britain's traditional position in the region. In fact, an element of hostility can be discerned among some American policymakers and diplomats with regard to an ally perceived as an imperial power of the old (indeed antiquated) school whose style and interests encumbered the Western alliance with an unnecessary load of Arab hostility. These Americans felt that they represented a fresh force and that there was no objective reason for disharmony between them and the Arab world and its nationalist movements. They thus advocated a policy of distancing the United States from Britain and France and, in a different fashion, from Israel.

The United States was guided by the concern that the Soviet Union, banging on the doors of the Middle East, would be able to exploit the instability in the region in order to obtain the presence and influence that until then it had been denied. There were three such focal points—the Arab–Israeli conflict, the social and political ferment in much of the Arab world, and the Anglo-Egyptian dispute—and the United States sought to neutralize all three. It tried openly to resolve the Arab–Israeli conflict and the Anglo-Egyptian dispute. It also tried discreetly to influence political developments in several Arab countries. This attempt, which will be discussed later in regard to Syria, is one of the most intriguing aspects of Washington's Middle Eastern policies in this period.[11]

Middle Eastern oil constituted another focus of American interest in the region. American–British rivalry in this field surfaced after World War I, and the United States maintained its interest in the region's oil when it withdrew from playing an active role in its affairs. This essentially economic interest was reinforced after World War II by strategic considerations, that is, the need to guarantee the free flow of oil to Western Europe. In the late 1940s, U.S. oil interests were concentrated in the Persian Gulf and Arabian peninsula, but the decision to lay a pipeline to carry Saudi oil to the Mediterranean through the territories of Jordan, Syria, and Lebanon added a new dimension to the United States' interest in the Levant.

## Regional Politics: Inter-Arab Relations

Although Turkey and Iran had played a crucial role in the region's earlier history, they had only a marginal role in its politics during the period that we are discussing. As a result, the regional politics of the Middle East centered on two issues: the Arab–Israeli conflict and inter-Arab relations.[12]

Inter-Arab relations have been shaped on one level by the integration of a political doctrine with the political reality and, on another level, by the relations and balance of power among the various Arab states. After the dissolution of the Ottoman Empire, pan-Arab nationalism became the dominant political doctrine in the Arab world. This doctrine maintained that all Arabs constituted one nation, that the Arab world's partition was artificial and ephemeral, and that all Arabs should be united in one political framework. But it so happened that the doctrine of pan-Arab nationalism established its supremacy simultaneously with the Arab world's partition into a number of states that, in time, acquired considerable staying power. The Arabs' desire for unity could not, in any event, be realized as long as Britain and France ruled any part of the Arab world. But then when they left, two significant obstacles still stood in the way: In the new states, ruling establishments and vested interests were created that in practice were opposed, even if they stated otherwise, to dismantling the existing entities. The other problem was who should lead the campaign for Arab unity and the great united Arab states once they were formed. It was evident that the candidacy of any state or ruler for this role would engender fears and opposition among the others and that it would be difficult to distinguish personal and dynastic ambitions from the idealism in which all such ambition was bound to be cloaked.

This dynamic formed in the 1930s the basic pattern of inter-Arab relations. Two rival blocs emerged: the Hashemites versus the Egyptians and the Saudis, with the weak Syrian state and the Palestine problem providing the chief arenas in which the struggle was waged.

These patterns crystallized and took their final form after 1945. The "formative" or "dynastic" phase of inter-Arab relations lasted until 1954 when Gamal Abdul Nasser seized power in Egypt and ushered the whole Arab world into a new political era.

The Hashemites were the main agitating force in inter-Arab relations between the two world wars. As a family they could not become reconciled to the loss of the Hejaz and the Saudis' control of the Arabian peninsula, and into the 1950s, some of them still dreamed of returning. The Saudis, in turn, felt the need to defend against these ambitions. Individually, both Faysal and Abdullah were unhappy with the domains that they were allotted. Both wanted Syria, and Abdullah also cultivated an interest and an investment in Palestine west of the Jordan River. During World War II, in anticipation of the ensuing changes, both branches of the Hashemite family published unity plans: Abdullah's "Greater Syria" and the "Fertile Crescent" plan of Nuri al-Said, the prime minister of Iraq. Both plans were rejected, and the notion of Arab unity was embodied for the time being in the looser framework of the Arab League that was formed in 1944–45. Furthermore, Egypt—which in earlier decades had been hesitant to embrace Arabism—enthusiastically did so in the 1940s and, by bringing its full weight to bear, assumed the hegemony in the Arab League. In managing the Arab system through the league, Egypt relied on Saudi Arabia's cooperation against its rival Hashemite bloc.

Abdullah continued to seek the formation of a Greater Syria, or, in more concrete terms, to have himself crowned in Damascus, but the focus of inter-Arab activity had clearly shifted to the Palestine question, concerning which several important changes had taken place. On an ideological and emotional level, the Palestine question had become the centerpiece of Arab nationalism, a litmus test for loyalty to the Arab cause and the effectiveness of those claiming Arab leadership. The commitment of the Arab states to the Palestinian Arabs was reinforced and formalized in a series of summit conferences. Another of these changes was the Palestinian Arabs' loss of control over their own fate, which had been turned over to the Arab collective. This collective, in turn, conducted itself according to a familiar pattern as various states and rulers sought to promote their particular interests.

Abdullah played a key role in this context as well. It was an open secret that he was seeking to annex Palestine west of the Jordan River, or at least its Arab segment, and that he was trying to obtain Britain's and the Jewish community's support for this policy. Abdullah's Arab rivals intensified their own involvement in order to preempt him while he himself promoted the notion of Arab military intervention in Palestine so as to create an effective and legitimate mechanism for dispatching his army to the areas he was striving to annex. He was ultimately successful in realizing his dream, albeit tortuously and at a very high cost. For the Arab collective the Palestine war was a traumatic failure. If until 1948 the Arab–Jewish conflict in Palestine was considered a challenge and a test of the highest order for Arab nationalism, the Arab states' military defeat gave it additional depth and importance. Their inability to overcome Israel became a cardinal symptom of the crisis in Arab society, and the evolution of the conflict with Israel became an important index of the Arab world's general state. On a different level the Arabs' military defeat reflected the inefficiency of their collective and of the Arab League as its institutional embodiment. Rivalries and the lack of coordination among the Arab states took their toll in their defeat, and the defeat, in turn, exacerbated the existing rivalries. The Egyptian–Jordanian conflict during the war and its transformation into a conflict over the fate of Arab Palestine at the war's end provide an excellent illustration of this point.

In 1949, Arab rivalries were once again conducted along the two familiar channels. In regard to the Palestine question—now the question of Israel—the intra-Arab conflict centered on the settlement issue. The 1948 war was terminated by a series of armistice agreements, three of which were negotiated on the island of Rhodes during the early months of 1949. One of the main factors accounting for the success of the Rhodes armistice negotiations was the determination and ability of Ralph Bunche, acting as the United Nations mediator, not to deal with the Arabs as a collective but to enable the individual Arab states to obtain separate agreements serving their own particular interests. But later, when Abdullah tried to conclude a comprehensive agreement with Israel, he encountered a solid wall of Arab opposition to a move that would have broken the unity of their ranks. Resentment of the personal achievements that Abdullah expected reinforced his Arab rivals' opposition to his separate deal with Israel.

At the same time, the Syrian question was reopened when Syria's Husni Zaim led a coup on March 30, 1949. Until it became known that Zaim had not acted on Abdullah's behalf, it was widely assumed that he had acted on behalf of the Jordanian king's Greater Syria plan. But a few weeks later it became clear that this was not the case and that Zaim was drawing closer to Egypt and Saudi Arabia by securing their support against the Hashemites' efforts to bring him into their camp. This was just the beginning of a long period of instability in Syria during which the warring blocs in the Arab world tried to undermine those Syrian rulers that they considered hostile and to replace them with their own supporters.

To these familiar patterns the Anglo-Egyptian conflict and the effort to establish a pro-Western defensive pact in the region were added as new and interrelated issues. As a rule, Egypt sought to mobilize the broadest possible Arab front against Britain and also to persuade the United States and Britain that without Egypt's agreement, as the main Arab state, it would be impossible to organize the Arab world, or even parts of it, into a regional pact. This policy presented the other Arab states, particularly Egypt's rivals, with an ever-present dilemma: the need to choose between the promotion of their own interests and the maintenance of Arab solidarity, which in this case, at least, served the interests of their senior sister-state.

## Arab Politics

The period that we shall examine in this book began with Husni Zaim's coup and ended with the Egyptian revolution in July 1952.

The three Syrian coups in 1949 and the Free Officers movement in Egypt indeed helped shift Arab politics from its traditional pattern to a new, revolutionary phase. During the years immediately following World War II several political systems in the Arab world entered a state of paralysis because the traditional, yet bankrupt, establishments nonetheless retained sufficient strength to ward off the attacks mounted by new and not very effective forces.

The rules of the game in the pseudoconstitutional systems built or left by the West enabled the royal houses, the patrician politicians, and the traditional parties to foil the efforts of the new groups and parties to win power or a share of it and to launch social and economic reforms once independence had been achieved. At that stage or soon thereafter the broad coalitions that were behind the nationalist struggle in the 1920s and 1930s disintegrated along class lines: The new social groups, particularly the salaried middle classes and the professionals, voiced demands for an appropriate share of power as well as for such social and economic measures as agrarian reform. As a rule, the traditional politicians resisted any measure likely to diminish their power or to affect its social and economic underpinnings. They thus were perceived by the opposition as a fossilized fixture preoccupied with preserving its privileges and failing all national tests, particularly vis-à-vis the West and Israel. In this state of affairs, rage and frustration were manifested in political violence, such as the strikes and demonstrations that broke out in Egypt and Syria in the late 1940s, and in a particularly strident form on "Black Saturday" in Egypt in January 1952.

The Gordian knot was cut by the army officers in Syria and Egypt who toppled the old establishment and opened the door to new leaders. The instigators of the coups, Zaim and Hinawi in Syria and Nagib in Egypt, seemed to have no ideological baggage, but it soon became clear that behind them stood younger officers—Shishakli in Syria, Abdul Nasser and the Free Officers in Egypt—who had received their political education in the ideological parties that had taken root in the region in the 1930s. These officers wanted a new order in both their own countries and the region as a whole. The proximity of the coups to the Palestine war was not accidental, but it would be erroneous to present them as largely a consequence of the Arabs' defeat. As Abdul Nasser wrote in *Philosophy of the Revolution*, the defeat provided a painful demonstration of the ancien régime's bankruptcy. It also aggravated, as in Husni Zaim's case, the rivalry between the civilian and the military leadership. In these respects the war expedited the changes but did not produce them.

## Politics in Syria

Syria had been governed since 1943 by politicians and factions that originated in the National Bloc, the mainstream of the nationalist movement in the interwar period. The bloc did not emerge from the war as a victorious and cohesive nationalist movement but, rather, as a weary and corrupt cluster of politicians and their retinues. Because they found it difficult to hold on to power, they were increasingly forced to rely on the army's support. The army, in turn, was headed by officers who had been trained and cultivated by the French Mandatory authorities and were estranged from the leaders of the nationalist movement by an attitude of mutual contempt. These frictions between the military and the civilian elites finally drove the army's commander, Husni Zaim, to stage his coup on March 30, 1949.

Husni Zaim had no ideological commitments, but he did view himself as a Syrian Ataturk, destined to institute reforms and build up his country's national power. Before staging his coup Zaim, uncertain of the international reaction, took care to coordinate his moves with the United States as well as to inform the British. He had no civilian supporters of his own to rely on and his regime rested on an uneasy alliance with part of the old political establishment. During Zaim's first months in power, Adel Arslan, one of the better-known Arab nationalist activists of the interwar period, was, as Syria's foreign minister, the most prominent civilian member of his government. But in July 1949 Zaim reorganized his regime, had himself "elected" president, and appointed Muhsin Barazi, a second-rank nationalist politician, as prime minister. Zaim's earlier attempt to cooperate with such new political forces as the Ba'ath party had failed.

As we mentioned earlier, Husni Zaim was not tied to the Hashemites, and as his relations with both branches of the Hashemite family continued to deteriorate, he drew closer to their Arab rivals. The Hashemites, in turn, encouraged the domestic opposition to Zaim's rule and played a role in staging the coup by Sami Hinawi that overthrew Zaim on August 14, 1949. By then Zaim had lost the support he had gained soon after his own coup, when he was still perceived as a man who wanted reform and was capable of effecting it. In time, however, he became increasingly viewed as a power-hungry and corrupt megalomaniac. Although Zaim's special relationship with the United States remained concealed, his rapprochement with both France and Turkey was open and so antagonized Syria's nationalist sentiments. Finally, Zaim's reckless intervention in Lebanon's domestic affairs—which ended in the extradition of his Lebanese associate, Antun Saadeh, to the Lebanese authorities and in Saadeh's execution—led to particularly bitter criticism in Syria and thereby contributed directly to Zaim's own downfall.

Sami Hinawi left a fainter mark on Syria's history and politics. He came to power as a friend of the Hashemites, and one of the important reasons for his downfall in December 1949 was his rivals' feeling that he had drawn too close to Iraq, to the point of perhaps establishing an Iraqi–Syrian union. The military group that finally toppled Hinawi was led by Adib Shishakli, who headed a faction of younger, ideologically committed officers. Shishakli came from Hama and was the friend and ally of Akram Hourani, one of the most important politicians of twentieth-century Syria. Hourani and Shishakli were scions of second-rank Hama families. They, like members of their families' earlier generations, fought against the hegemony of Hama's "great families" and at a later stage transferred their struggle and rage to the larger arena of Syrian nationalist politics. Both underwent more than one ideological metamorphosis, and both fought with Rashid Ali against the British in Iraq in 1941 and with Qawqji in Palestine in 1948. As a politician who sent his younger followers to the military academy in Homs and later as minister of defense, Hourani played an important role in the politicization of Syria's military and in the militarization of Syrian politics. In 1953, having fallen out with Shishakli, he joined Michel Aflaq and Salah al-Bitar in the Arab Socialist Ba'ath party.

After staging his coup in December 1949 Shishakli avoided the limelight and preferred to exercise his influence from behind the scenes. But when his indirect rule proved ineffective, he stepped forward and became an outright military dictator. Indirectly and directly Shishakli held power until February 1954. His tenure of power had a significant impact on the institutionalization of the Syrian army's political role and on the radicalization of Syrian politics later in the decade. But Shishakli himself was less radical than his impact on Syrian politics would suggest. All along Shishakli maintained close ties with the U.S. government, and after his fall from power he established contact with Israeli representatives as well.[13]

## Politics in Egypt

Egyptian politics in the late 1940s and early 1950s can be described as a struggle among four principal forces: the king and his court, the Wafd party, other traditional parties, and such radical opposition movements as the Muslim Brotherhood, Young Egypt, and the communists.[14] Later scholarship, as well as press accounts, that portrayed King Farouk as a corrupt hedonist served to conceal the fact that he had actually held considerable power. Indeed, the 1923 constitution gave the king extensive authority that he maximized by exploiting the divisions in his opponents' ranks.

The Wafd party, which had led the nationalist opposition to the British, was in the late 1940s in a state reminiscent of that of the Syrian National Bloc: exhausted, divided, and devoid of legitimacy. Like the Hashemites, the Wafd had been discredited by its collaboration with the British during World War II. The Hashemites were returned to power in Iraq in 1941 by the British, who quashed Rashid Ali's pro-Axis nationalist rebellion. And the Wafd was brought to power in 1942 by the British in the aftermath of the "Abdin incident,'' during which British units surrounded the palace and forced the king to remove the pro-Axis prime minister and to appoint the Wafd's leader, Mustafa Nahhas Pasha, in his place. The king could pit against the Wafd the leaders of the small traditional parties, some of whom had earlier seceded from the Wafd. Several of these political leaders carried impressive personal weight, but unlike the Wafd, even when it was waning, they could not rely on a substantial party organization.

The radical movements—the Muslim Brotherhood, the communists, and Young Egypt—did not abide by the accepted rules of the game and presented a totally different alternative. They did not participate in parliamentary life but brought their growing power to bear through political violence—strikes, demonstrations, and assassinations—which every so often sent shock waves through Egypt and illustrated the extent of the people's discontent with the country's politics. The unrest derived both from the established order's failure to obtain Britain's evacuation and full independence and from its refusal to respond to the pressure to institute social and economic reforms.

One of the chief manifestations of the political system's malfunctioning was the rapid succession of governments:

- Maḥmud Fahmi Nukrashi Pasha was assassinated at the end of 1948.

- He was succeeded by Abdul Hadi (of the Saadist party) who resigned in July 1949.

- Abdul Hadi was replaced by Husein Sirri Pasha (an independent) who held office until January 1950.

- In January King Farouk entrusted the formation of a new government to Mustafa Nahhas Pasha, who served two full years, until January 1952.

- Nahhas was replaced by Ali Maher, who served for three months.

22

- In March 1952 Nagib Hilali Pasha, an independent, became prime minister.

- The next government, headed by Tawfiq Sirri, was formed on July 1 and resigned on July 20.

- On July 22 Hilali formed a new government that lasted for only twenty-four hours.

## Politics in Jordan

In the history of the Jordanian state, December 1948 was a turning point. Although the West Bank was officially annexed in April 1950, it actually had been incorporated in December 1948 after the Jericho Congress, which had been organized by the king to demonstrate the Palestinians' support for Arab Palestine's merger with Hashemite Jordan.[15]

Abdullah had been anxious since 1921 to increase the territory and population under his rule and to obtain control of historically and politically significant territories. But he failed to appreciate the extent of the change that the annexation of a large Palestinian territory was bound to generate. As we shall see, the annexation brought an end to the era during which Jordan had been managed as a personal and family patrimony by the king and his small entourage. Indeed, the Jordanian polity came to include a large educated group, of which many members saw the king as a traitor to the Arab nationalist cause and as personally responsible for their country's misfortune.

During most of the 1948–52 period the Jordanian government was headed by Tawfiq Abu al-Huda, a native of Palestine and a member of a small group of Palestinians who had joined the king's service in the 1920s and had been completely absorbed into the political establishment that had gradually taken shape east of the Jordan River. Abu al-Huda's rival, Samir al-Rifai, was a member of the same group. The group had been fully "Jordanized" before 1948 and was separate from the large mass of Palestinians who were added to Jordan unofficially in 1948 and formally in 1950. Representatives of that larger group were appointed to the government and administration in 1949, and the Palestinian cabinet members who took part in the negotiations with Israel in 1950 came from their ranks.

As the description of the Israeli–Jordanian negotiations between November 1949 and April 1950 will show, Jordan's political and governmental systems did not function well in that period. Some of the difficulties derived from the annexation of the West Bank and its Palestinian population, and some were the result of the controversial and complex policies pursued by the king. In addition, the king's aging and weakening, the bickering among his underlings, and his gradual loss of control accelerated the decline of his regime.

## Arab–Israeli Relations, 1949–1952: A Chronological Framework

The 1948 war did not end with one conclusive act; rather, the distinction between military moves and political developments remained as vague at the war's supposed end as it had been in its earlier phases. During the war the United Nation's mediation apparatus was able to arrange two cease-fires: the first from June 11 to July 11, 1948, and the second beginning on July 18, 1948. Technically the second cease-fire remained in force until the war's end, although in October, fighting was resumed on a large scale. Count Folke Bernadotte, the UN mediator, was assassinated by members of Lehi, the radical Jewish underground movement, on September 17. Before his assassination he had presented two versions of a compromise plan. His first version, which he submitted on June 27, was based on the denial of an independent Jewish state. The second version, put together on the eve of his assassination, accepted the principle of partition but made significant changes in the original UN partition plan. Israel was to have been given western Galilee (allocated originally to the Arab state) but to lose the Negev (which, together with the other parts of Arab Palestine, was assigned by Bernadotte to Jordan) as well as the corridor to (an internationalized) Jerusalem.

The resumption of fighting in October 1948 resulted in Israel's capture of the northern Negev (October 15–22) and most of Galilee (October 28–31). A fresh offensive in the south brought Israel into Egyptian territory in the northern Sinai, in an attempt to cut off the Egyptian forces in the Gaza Strip. The campaign through which Israel took the whole Negev and reached Eilat, on the Red Sea, was conducted in March 1949 after signing the Israeli–Egyptian armistice agreement and on the eve of signing the armistice agreement with Jordan.

During the latter part of 1948 the UN passed several resolutions regarding the war and conflict in Palestine. Most of them called for cease-fires and, after October, for respecting the cease-fire and returning to the lines established before the resumption of fighting. The single most important one, Resolution 194, was passed by the UN General Assembly on December 11, 1948. Its two main clauses established the right of those Palestinian Arab refugees who wished to live in peace with their neighbors to return or to choose between return and reparations and also established the Palestine Conciliation Commission (PCC) in order to assist the acting mediator or to replace him in his peacemaking task.

Before the PCC began its work, the emphasis of the conflict shifted to its bilateral dimension, and the armistice agreements that were negotiated and signed in two phases (from January through March 1949 between Israel and Egypt, Lebanon and Jordan, and from April through July 1949 between Israel and Syria) can be seen as a series of interim agreements that stabilized the bilateral conflicts between Israel and these four states.

The Palestinian and international dimensions of the conflict were represented by the PCC. The commission allowed the acting mediator, the UN's Ralph Bunche, to complete the first round of the armistice talks, but as early as February 1949 it began preparing to seek a permanent and comprehensive solution to the conflict between Israel and the Arab states as well as a solution to the Palestinian refugee problem (implicitly, the commission and most of those concerned had resigned themselves to the idea that a Palestinian Arab state would not be established). The PCC was composed of the representatives of three states—the United States, France, and Turkey—and a technical staff. In February it began a series of consultations in the Middle East, and in March it convened representatives of the Arab states for a preparatory meeting in Beirut. The commission's main effort was at the Lausanne Conference which opened on April 27 and held two rounds of discussions. With the Egyptian, Jordanian, Lebanese, and Israeli delegations, a Palestinian delegation came to Lausanne, headed by Aziz Shehadeh and Nimr al-Hawari, which spoke in the name of the Palestinian refugees.

The United States and Britain monitored the PCC's work as closely as they had Bernadotte's mission the previous year. The guidelines issued in January 1949 by the United States' acting secretary of state, Robert Lovett, to the American representative Mark Ethridge were unequivocal: The solutions to the conflict and the refugee problem should be based on the UN General Assembly's December 11 resolution. Israel's borders should be determined according to the November 1947 partition resolution. They must not be contracted without Israel's consent, but any addition of territory (in western Galilee or in Jaffa) would require compensation elsewhere (in the Negev, for instance). In February 1949 Washington decided that it was essential to move right away with a solution to the refugee problem before Israel settled new immigrants and anything else became established that would militate against a comprehensive solution. From this premise the American position developed, which held that the solution to the problem of the Palestinian refugees should be based on the settlement of about half of them—namely, 350,000— in the Arab world, the repatriation of the other half, and the integration of the rehabilitation effort with a regional development project. Washington's position was clearly much closer to that of the Arabs than to Israel's. Consequently, the American effort to advance the PCC's work was manifested primarily in pressure exerted on Israel.

It was this pressure that induced Israel to sign in Lausanne the protocol of May 12, 1949, while also appending its reservations.

The protocol included a "working paper" and an attached map of the partition lines of 1947. Together they linked the territorial issue with the question of the refugees, in a fashion suggesting Israeli concessions on these two problems. The Arab representatives, however, refused to sign together with the Israelis and so signed a separate copy in another room.

The United States kept up its pressure on Israel, and on May 29 President Harry S Truman sent a letter to the Israeli government stating that the United States might reconsider its attitude toward Israel if Israel refused to alter its policy. That is, the U.S. government suspected that Israel had signed the May 12 protocol only in order to secure its admission to the UN and that having accomplished this, it probably would not now make any real concessions. In more concrete terms, U.S. Ambassador James McDonald in Tel Aviv and the PCC's Mark Ethridge explained to the Israeli negotiators that the United States insisted on Israel's absorption of 200,000 Palestinian refugees.

On June 6 Israel rejected this American demand, but it did respond to Washington's pressure in other ways. As early as April 1949 Prime Minister David Ben-Gurion suggested to Ethridge that Israel be given the Gaza Strip and also its refugee population. In July the Israeli delegation to Lausanne announced Israel's willingness to repatriate 100,000 Palestinian refugees without any connection to the "Gaza Plan." But this offer was considered insufficient by the United States, as well as by the Arab delegations, which on August 15 submitted a counterproposal demanding additional Israeli concessions. The Lausanne Conference was disbanded at the end of August, and the PCC continued its work for another two years. Officially, the Lausanne Conference has never been dissolved.

At the same time as the armistice and the PCC discussions (and sometimes in their midst) possibilities were discussed and efforts were made to reach agreements among Israel, Jordan, Egypt, and Syria that would go beyond the narrow bilateral framework and help resolve the Arab–Israeli conflict, or at least limit it. But these efforts, too, were futile. Lack of progress toward a political settlement of the conflict underlined the other channels along which Arab–Israeli relations were conducted in the following years: boycotts and the lack of direct contact, infiltration and violent conflicts along Israel's borders, friction and disagreement over the implementation of the armistice agreements, fears of a "second round," and the beginnings of a process of mutual demonization.

# 2

## Israel and the
## Arab World, 1948–1949

### *Leaders, Diplomats, Army Officers, and Arabists: The Israeli System at Work*

On April 12, 1949, Israel's prime minister, David Ben-Gurion, held a consultation in preparation for the upcoming Lausanne Conference. It was one in a series of consultations whose importance was signaled by the fact that Ben-Gurion himself chaired the meeting and opened it by outlining his own concept of peace. Moshe Sharett was abroad and did not participate in the meeting. The protocol began by listing the fourteen participants, grouped into four categories: (1) the prime minister, David Horowitz, and Zalman Lifshitz; (2) Yigael Yadin and Moshe Dayan; (3) Walter Eytan, Leo Kohn, Reuven Shiloah, Z. Meron, and Michael Comey; and (4) Eliyahu Sasson, Ya'acov Shimoni, Shmuel Glikson, and Josh Palmon.[1] The arrangement of the list reflected the four institutional actors who formulated and executed Israel's Arab policy: (1) the government at the head of the political pyramid, (2) the Israeli Defense Forces (IDF), (3) the Foreign Ministry and its team of senior diplomats, and (4) the intelligence community and the group of experts on Arab affairs affiliated with it and with the Foreign Ministry.

These lines of division raise two methodological difficulties inherent in the archival sources for this period and also in the academic literature based on them. The first concerns the need to distinguish between a political judgment and decisions and professional assessments. That is, political leaders or politicians may have believed in 1949 that Israel should cultivate an autonomous Palestinian entity in the West Bank, in accordance with their larger concept of an Israeli state and a desirable relationship with the Arab world. An expert on Arab affairs at the Ministry of Foreign Affairs' Middle East Department could reach a similar conclusion from a "professional" or "technical" vantage point. But even though a political leader's statement, in either a closed session or an open political forum, and an analyst's professional opinion could concur, it is important to remember that their origin and significance were quite different.

The second methodological difficulty pertains to the differences in rank between the leaders of the state, on the one hand, and the army officers and government officials, on the other, even when the latter were senior. Thus the minutes of any discussion held in the Israeli government may contain an argument by Shiloah or Sasson in disagreement with Sharett or, more rarely, with Ben-Gurion, but the difference of rank and position between the political and professional levels must always be taken into account. It is true that in the small and intimate establishment of the young Israeli state, such differences were minimized, that the intense experiences of those years created an unusual closeness between the political leaders and their aides, and that the senior officials and army officers were highly "politicized"; indeed, several among them—Abba Eban, Eliyahu Sasson, Yigael Yadin, and Moshe Dayan—later achieved cabinet rank, and yet the distinction between a political decision and a professional view should not be blurred.

## David Ben-Gurion and Moshe Sharett

In 1949 David Ben-Gurion reached the pinnacle of prestige and power as the man who had led the Zionist movement and the Jewish community in Palestine to statehood and who had conducted the military and political campaign that culminated in the victory and formation of a state larger and more viable even than the one envisaged in late 1947 and much of 1948. This position, Ben-Gurion's powerful personality, and his incisive eloquence, however, may create a mistaken impression concerning his ability to make crucial decisions and see them through.

In fact, Ben-Gurion had to fight for his positions in three circles. First, he had to fight within his own party, Mapai, which as a broadly based consensus party comprised a variety of trends, factions, and leaders holding different views on issues of foreign policy and national security, particularly on the Arab question. Furthermore, such leaders as Moshe Sharett and Eliezer Kaplan clung to their own views and also maintained autonomous positions. They accepted Ben-Gurion's leadership and seniority but did not hesitate to voice their disagreement with him. In any event, their support for his positions was never guaranteed but had to be secured.

Second, Ben-Gurion had to fight within the coalition government that he headed. Temporary alliances and factions were formed in the Israeli cabinet over specific issues that cut across party lines. For example, Ben-Gurion carried the cabinet with him against Sharett's proposal to annex the Gaza Strip and its residents. But later in 1949 when Ben-Gurion opposed Sharett's proposal to absorb 100,000 Palestinian refugees (unrelated to the Gaza scheme), he was supported by no more than two cabinet members—Dov Yosef and Rabbi Maymon. Sharett, however, was reluctant to have Ben-Gurion defeated by a show of hands and so settled for the endorsement of a formulation reflecting his own views. In the debate over proclaiming Jerusalem as the nation's capital, Sharett was supported by Eliezer Kaplan, Pinhas Rosenne (Rosenblitt) of the Progressive party, and Rabbi

Levin of the Agudath Israel, but he was defeated by Ben-Gurion and his supporters.[2]

Third, Ben-Gurion had to fight in the larger political arena— the Knesset (parliament) and public opinion—in which he had to contend with the nationalist Herut party and the left-wing Mapam party, both of which were critical (from different points of view) of his Arab policy. Both, for instance, were opposed to Ben-Gurion's virtual acceptance of Abdullah's annexation of the West Bank: the Herut party because it regarded the West Bank as part of the land of Israel and the Mapam party because it was opposed to partition in the first place and also because it viewed Abdullah as a conservative tool of British policy. Ben-Gurion was more sensitive to the Mapam party's criticism, as in the Histadrut (the trade unions' federation) and in the larger political arena his own party, Mapai, and the Mapam party competed for the support and votes of overlapping constituencies.

The disagreements between Ben-Gurion and Sharett raise the question of whether the distinction—made in the current academic literature on Israel's foreign and defense policies—between the Ben-Gurion and Sharett camps is applicable to the period that we are discussing.

Sharett's personal diaries are, indeed, full of references to differences of opinion and style between himself and Ben-Gurion. In the closed lecture he delivered in 1957, Sharett spoke explicitly of "two approaches" in the Israeli national consensus:

One approach holds that the Arabs understand only a language of force. Israel is so small and so isolated, and it may be so weak (based on the criteria of territory, population, and potential) that if it does not double its actual power by a very high factor of demonstrable activity, it will face bleak consequences. The state of Israel must demonstrate every so often that it is strong and able and willing to use force. . . . With regard to peace this approach maintains that it is, in any event, a dubious or very remote issue. If peace comes, it will come only when they [the Arabs] are persuaded that this state cannot be defeated. . . . [T]he problem of peace should therefore not serve as a constraining consideration when the question of a large-scale demonstration of force is contemplated in order to solve an immediate security problem. . . . [T]he fire is there anyway.

What does the other approach say? The issue of peace must not be absent from our consideration, even for one moment. [But] it is not merely a matter of political consideration; in the long term it is a crucial security consideration. [And so] without belittling the importance of the immediate security consideration, we must always include the issue of peace in our comprehensive view of things; we must moderate our reactions.[3]

Sharett's characterization of these approaches clearly reflects the prevailing ideas and sentiments of the years between 1954 and 1956, and so they should not be imposed on the events between 1948 and 1949.

As the first paragraph of his lecture shows, Sharett did not dispute the basic assumptions and concepts behind the mainstream of Israel's policy in those years. Sharett and Ben-Gurion were separated by differences of character and outlook, but they did belong to the same camp. Furthermore, even if Sharett did disagree with Ben-Gurion on several issues, he nevertheless accepted his leadership and did not try to contest it.

Ben-Gurion's diaries, the archival material, and interviews with several of his aides offer a glimpse into his working methods with regard to Israel's relations with the Arab world. He consulted often with both policymakers and experts and was interested in everything they had to tell him. In addition, Ben-Gurion did not seek expert advice on the basis of formal position but, rather, according to his own judgment; for example, he went to Shiloah, Dayan, Sasson, and, on such important technical matters as land and water, Zalman Lifshitz. The details and opinions he collected he first worked into his unusually broad concept of the Israeli state and then applied to practical politics. This process is illustrated in the minutes of the consultation held on April 12, 1949, in preparation for the Lausanne Conference. Ben-Gurion opened with a general statement on the main tasks of the new Israeli state and on the importance of peace as a prerequisite for their implementation. This was followed by a detailed discussion of Israel's strategy in Lausanne, in which, however, Ben-

Gurion did not take an active part. This discussion continued on the afternoon of April 12 and in the following week, but Ben Gurion did not attend. On April 18 in a meeting with Mark Ethridge, the American representative of the PCC, Ben-Gurion raised the idea that the Gaza Strip and its residents be annexed to Israel. But for tactical reasons he preferred that the idea appear to have been an American initiative. How this idea germinated in the prime minister's mind we do not know.[4]

## Israel's Military Establishment

The Israeli Defense Force's leadership, for obvious reasons, played a cardinal role in formulating Israel's Arab policy during the war. The internal correspondence of the Foreign Ministry's Middle Eastern Department reveals the frustration of the seasoned experts on Arab affairs—Eliyahu Sasson, Ezra Danin, and Ya'acov Shimoni—caused by the government's failure to consult with them on the political strategy that, in theory at least, should have guided the military moves. Instead, they watched helplessly while Ben-Gurion and the military, aided by Shiloah, who had a practical monopoly on the political and Arab dimensions of the war, made one decision after another. As they saw it, irreversible facts were thus being established. Thus on September 22, 1948, Ezra Danin wrote to Sasson in Paris:

> You should also know that when the minister of foreign affairs stated his positions in his various speeches, he did not seek our advice and asked us nothing. We do not have many convenient opportunities to speak to him and discuss with him our thoughts in this sphere. With regard to the requirements of the war—the military has not consulted us since April. [Reuven] Shiloah was appointed as the liaison with the [General] Staff, and when we tried to establish contact with the chief of staff or meet with him, we were reprimanded severely.[5]

In September 1948 Sharett demanded that a ''political officer be attached to every front,'' but his demand was ignored. More light on this issue is shed by a memorandum sent by Shimoni to the Foreign Ministry's director-general, Walter Eytan, on November 18, 1948, which dealt with "political problems in Lebanon and the northern border" as well as with "the relationship between the Foreign Ministry and the army's [General] Staff." Shimoni reported to Eytan on two trips he had taken with other Ministry experts to Galilee and the strip in south Lebanon that the IDF had captured and on the political problems they had encountered. Shimoni complained that the recommendations that General Yadin had requested had gone unheeded and suggested by way of an allusion that the pattern might repeat itself with regard to the recommendations for "the sort of a program or the line of thinking regarding our conduct in Mount Hebron and Nablus in the event that [Israel decided to capture them]" that Yadin had requested as well. Shimoni then demanded that Director-General Eytan establish real coordination between the army's General Staff and the Foreign Ministry and accordingly insisted on the implementation of Sharett's demand made in September, because "if this is not done, I have no doubt that we—and 'we' here means not just the Middle East Department but the whole Foreign Ministry—will stay right where we are: Instead of guiding, instructing, and predicting, we will only be dragging along."[6]

The situation changed, however, at the war's end with the beginning of a period of negotiations and other diplomatic activities that were conducted primarily by members of the Foreign Service, although the military continued to play a central role in formulating and implementing national security policies, in the broad sense of that term. This role was based primarily on the nearly unanimous conclusion that Israel would continue to have a security problem, that the political–diplomatic phase inaugurated by the armistice negotiations might prove to be short, and that the Arabs had not resigned themselves to their failure to defeat Israel. From that perspective, the period of negotiations can be seen as an opportunity to regroup in preparation for a second round. As General Yadin observed in April 1949:

Today the position is different—the Arabs have concluded that in order to defeat Israel they need time; a period of time that will enable them to reorganize and restructure their army [armies]. It is in this light that the activities or actions pursued in the neighboring countries should be interpreted. . . . We must find the ways for obstructing the Arab countries. . . . A war may prove to be inevitable, but we must try to avoid it, to prevent it.[7]

Furthermore, the nature of Israel's relationship with the Arab states underscored the importance of military and semimilitary issues. The armistice negotiations were conducted by mixed civilian and military delegations. The questions that remained after the signing of the armistice agreements were handed over to the military, and it was they who led the mixed armistice commissions that became an important channel for the conduct of Arab–Israeli relations.

Two senior army officers who stood out in these negotiations were the acting chief of staff, Yigael Yadin, and Moshe Dayan, who early on acquired a reputation as an army officer who had notable political and diplomatic skills and as such attracted Ben-Gurion's personal attention. Yadin, a very young officer in a very senior position (he was thirty-two years old in 1949), had numerous opportunities to display his grasp of political matters, whereas Dayan, as Jerusalem's military commander and subsequently as the general office commander of the Southern Command, took part in the negotiations with Jordan and dealt with foreign diplomats, quite apart from his position in the military hierarchy.

## Israel's Diplomatic Wing

Over time the position of the Foreign Ministry and its staff in the Israeli system declined. Their failure to reach an Israeli–Arab agreement diminished the importance of political and diplomatic work, which increasingly came to be seen through a security prism. In bureaucratic terms, the defense establishment derived considerable strength from the fact that it was headed by David Ben-Gurion, who served as both prime minister and defense minister, whereas Sharett's leadership was of limited use to the Foreign Ministry in the ever-present conflict over positions and resources. This trend became evident in the early 1950s, as shown in a letter from Sharett to Ben-Gurion on January 22, 1953:

The Foreign Minister to the Prime Minister and the Defense Minister:

I should bring the following issues to your attention:
1. Relations with Jordan. This week a rather harsh statement by the army's spokesman on this matter was published. We also found out that we are about to abrogate an agreement that we had made with the Jordanians or to announce that we regard it as null and void. In these two cases there was no prior consultation between the army and the Foreign Ministry. . . . [A]s for myself, I am opposed to any initiative on our part to abrogate an agreement.
2. The negotiations with Syria. It turns out that these negotiations have been conducted on the basis of considerable territorial concessions on our part without any quid pro quo. As it has been explained to me, the army believes that these concessions are to our advantage if we can obtain free use of the waters in our territory. [But] this assumption raises a number of problems that may not have been thought out properly, namely: What will the impact be on public opinion when we are seen to have given up territory without compensation? Might this not serve as a negative precedent in negotiations for peace with other states? Is our use of the Jordan River water related to [Simha] Blass's [Israel's water expert] plans, and if so, should we regard Bush's plans as approved by the government? None of these activities and the position we had reached in the negotiations with Syria are at all clear, and I would like to avoid surprises. Because you are scheduled to meet tonight with the General Staff, you might want to use this opportunity to clarify this matter, and [then] the two of us could discuss it when we meet in Tiberias on Sunday.[8]

The senior staff of the Foreign Ministry was an impressive group, veterans of the Jewish Agency's political department who had acquired experience and stature through their efforts that had culminated in the establishment of an Israeli state.[9] This group was led by Moshe Sharett, whose standing rested on his party position as well as on his considerable talents—impressive political judgment, a quick grasp of details, and eloquence—which were reinforced by experience. Sharett had a good command of Arabic and a close familiarity with Arab politics. But his stature was diminished by his lack of boldness, excessive attention to detail, formalism, and preoccupation with status and its symbols.

The Foreign Ministry's first director-general was Walter Eytan (Ettinghausen), a native of Germany who had served in British intelligence during World War II. Eytan was a very capable professional diplomat who displayed no particular interest in or affinity for Arab politics. In August 1948 Ya'acov Shimoni, the acting director of the Foreign Ministry's Middle East Department, wrote to Eliyahu Sasson that Eytan was

> very remote from our affairs. He is loaded with work and is not actively interested in what we are doing or in our plans. This week we forced him to set a regular weekly meeting with us because we refused to comply with the present situation, in which he has no idea about our work or plans.[10]

Ranked just under Eytan, Abba Eban and Gideon Rafael[11] stood out with regard to Middle Eastern issues as Sharett's intellectual partners though not his equals. Sharett valued the judgment of his political adviser, Leo Kohn. The ministry's legal adviser, Shabtai Rosenne, in addition to offering legal opinions also took a direct part in the diplomatic negotiations.

Reuven Shiloah, who held the title of adviser for special affairs and the position of director of the Foreign Ministry's Political Department, enjoyed a unique status. Before the formation of the Mossad, Shiloah, as head of the Rashut, stood at the apex of Israel's intelligence community, and his own service, the Political Department, was the main instrument of Israel's political intelligence. It consisted of an operational arm that operated as a full-fledged intelligence service and a research arm that competed with the ministry's Middle East Department in providing political assessments of events in the region. But Shiloah's position was determined less by institutional power than by the unusual access he had to both Ben-Gurion and Sharett. Indeed, during these years Shiloah was the only professional who had the ear and the confidence of both leaders.[12]

Shiloah's colleagues in the Middle East Department resented his bureaucratic victories and complained of the "hypnotic effect" he had on Sharett.[13] But Ben-Gurion's appreciation of Shiloah's performance as a ringmaster of sorts in the arena of Middle Eastern politics was evidenced in 1953 when he conceived the idea that a pro-Israeli coup d'état in Lebanon could transform Israel's position in the region. Shiloah was then stationed in Israel's embassy in Washington, and Ben-Gurion wrote: "It may perhaps be worth our while to bring Reuven [Shiloah] back for this purpose. This is a historic opportunity, and it would be unforgivable to miss it."[14]

Shiloah was a figure characteristic of the transitional period of the 1948 war and the years in which the state of Israel had not been fully formalized and institutionalized. Early in his career he had worked for the Jewish Agency's Political Department and the Intelligence Service of the Haganah (the Jewish community's principal prestate military organization) and maintained a liaison with British intelligence during World War II. In the first years of the Israeli state and government he performed the sundry tasks of confidential adviser, diplomat, head of an intelligence service, and special emissary. Later, when the country had become more stabilized, Shiloah lost his special position and was overshadowed by younger and more junior colleagues.

## Israel's Arab Experts

The absence of a clear distinction among diplomacy, intelligence work, and political analysis also marked the organization of the group of experts on Arab affairs who moved from the Jewish Agency's political department and the Haganah's intelligence service to the fledgling Foreign Ministry. Within the agency's political department an Arab affairs wing had been formed to deal with both the Palestinian Arabs and the neighboring countries. Its staff engaged in research as well as political activity under the stewardship of Eliahu Elath (Epstein) and Eliyahu Sasson. In the late 1940s Elath became a full-time diplomat and subsequently served as Israel's ambassador in Washington and London. Sasson stayed on as the Israeli government's senior expert on Arab affairs and was appointed, accordingly, as the first director of the Foreign Ministry's Middle East Department.[15]

In 1948, however, Sasson became a frustrated man. His deputy in the Middle East Department was Ya'acov Shimoni, the intellectual of the Political Department's Arab wing whose book *The Arabs of Palestine* had been published in 1947 and demonstrated his command of the subject. Ezra Danin, a wealthy farmer from Hadera, who had acquired considerable experience in the Haganah's intelligence service and accompanied Golda Meir to her meeting with Abdullah, was appointed as consultant to the department, but his status was not clear and his relations with Sasson were tense.[16] Shmuel Zeligson (Ziama Divon) and Tuvia Arazi, experienced in both intelligence and political–diplomatic work, joined the department and were entrusted with renewing and maintaining contacts with the Arab world. Yehoshua Pelman (Josh Palmon) also was assigned to Shiloah's Political Department. Shimoni's description of Palmon's work style illustrates the freshness and anarchy of the government service's early days:

> And life keeps bursting forth; namely, Josh keeps bursting forth. Josh is not willing to constrain and limit himself to the issues with which he has been entrusted, [and] when it comes to politics he keeps running forward and does so with relish. Reuven does not justify his conduct but claims that he cannot be stopped.[17]

The staff of the Middle East Department was reinforced by academic and other experts such as David Neustudt (Ayalon), Shlomo Pines, Pesah Shuser (Shinar), and Ya'acov Eyal who were put in charge full time of country or functional "desks." Sasson himself was sent in June 1948 to Paris to oversee the efforts to find opportunities for dialogues with Arab contacts.

Although on paper the organization of the Middle East Department was impressive, in reality it was disappointing. The department and its array of experts were kept on the margins of policies formulated by the political leadership, the military command, and Reuven Shiloah. Not surprisingly, then, Sasson's letters from Paris to Shimoni in Israel during the summer and fall of 1948 reflect his frustration with this situation and with the virtual rejection of the policies he advocated. Having been thus defeated in its efforts to participate in policymaking, the Middle East Department then fought for smaller stakes, for the position as the Foreign Ministry's authoritative interpreter of political developments in the Middle East. Accordingly, in December 1948 Shimoni protested that the director-general had sent to Paris a telegram that had been "elaborated and formulated" by the Political Department and included an analysis of the disturbances that had occurred in Syria. Shimoni argued forcefully that such analysis fell within his department's purview, but Director-General Eytan's response did not go beyond expressing the hope "that in the future all material concerning the Middle East will be shown to you before being dispatched."[18]

Having returned from his mission to Paris, Sasson became active in the political–diplomatic events of 1949. This year and this phase of Sasson's career culminated in the first round of negotiations with Jordan in November and December. By the year's end Sasson had left for Ankara as Israel's first minister to Turkey. It could be argued, justifiably, that it was important to send Sasson to the only diplomatic legation that Israel had in a Middle Eastern capital, and yet to some extent at least, it was a demotion, marking the end of the era that Sasson embodied. From Ankara, and subsequently from Rome and Bern, Sasson continued through his letters and telegrams to offer his knowledge and advice. One of the letters he sent to his son Moshe, a young member of the Middle East Department, encapsulates his philosophy and experience with regard to the cultivation of contacts in the Arab world. His advice was given in response to a query regarding a Jordanian politician who in the past had shunned the Israelis. By 1953, however, he had fallen on hard times and so asked for Israel's financial help:

> I would like to repeat here what I have written to you in the past. . . . [G]o to the proposed meeting . . . but make no demands, and impose no conditions . . . raise no dormant issues, and do not raise the question of the Rhodes Agreement, Mount Scopus, or any other political problem. . . . [H]and out the "financial help," go through a general exchange of views, and return home. Act like a man who

casts his bread upon the water. Do not ask for a quid pro quo, either immediate or long term. He cannot offer us a thing now, but should he be fortunate and regain power, he will remember our kindness and feel awkward toward us and view us not as political dealers but as friends who proved to be loyal in hard times.[19]

## Israel's Arab Policy

Israel's political strategy toward the Arab world in 1948 and 1949 had four phases: the prewar political efforts, the policy that crystallized during the war, the armistice negotiations, and the political and diplomatic activity in the spring and summer of 1949 that focused on the Lausanne Conference.

### Prewar Political Efforts

In 1935 David Ben-Gurion decided that a war with the Palestinian Arabs could not be avoided if the Jewish community persisted in its quest for statehood. From that point on, therefore, Zionist policy under his leadership was conducted along two parallel tracks: preparing for the expected war and continuing to try to reach an agreement or an understanding that would prevent it.[20]

During the 1940s as the Arab states became more committed to the Arab cause in Palestine, the Zionist perspective broadened accordingly. In Israel's preparations for a possible war with the Palestinians, intervention by the Arab states, or at least some of them, had to be taken into account. Consequently, Israel expanded its political efforts to persuade at least some of the Arab states to acquiesce in the establishment of a Jewish state or at least to settle on passive opposition to its formation. The Zionist movement had tried earlier to reach an understanding with Arab nationalist leaders and representatives—of the Hashemite school in particular—on the assumption that it would be easier to reach a compromise with negotiating partners who had greater assets and a broader perspective.

In the latter half of the 1940s the diplomatic effort became even more important and urgent. As the moment of decision drew nearer, it became clearer that neither the Palestinian Arab leadership nor any significant sector of the Palestinian Arab society would accept partition and that in any event the Palestinian Arabs had lost control over their own affairs, in that all the decisions regarding Arab policy in Palestine were being made by the Arab states.

In 1946 the political department of the Jewish Agency succeeded in reaching understandings with three Arab leaders,[21] although two of them lasted only a short time. The understanding reached with Ismail Sidqi, the prime minister of Egypt, became useless when his government fell. Sidqi himself, however, persisted in his opposition to Egypt's involvement in the Palestine question and made an eloquent speech to this end in a closed session held by the Egyptian parliament's upper house on the eve of the country's entry into the 1948 war. Next, the agreement signed between the Jewish Agency and the Lebanese Maronite patriarch never was put into practice and constituted in that respect another link in a long and frustrating chain of attempts to achieve political cooperation between the Jewish community in Palestine and the Israeli state, on the one hand, and the Maronite community, on the other. Finally, the understanding reached with Abdullah, the emir (since 1946, the king) of Transjordan, was an entirely different matter. The relationship between Abdullah and the Jewish community in Palestine had, in the early 1930s, become the dominant axis in a triangle composed of Abdullah, the Jewish community, and the Palestine Arab nationalist movement.[22]

Abdullah, as we have already seen, had never been satisfied with his small Transjordanian patrimony. Although the focus of Abdullah's grand vision was Damascus and Hejaz, the Arab parts of Palestine were an important interim target. Abdullah's ambitions led him into conflict with the mufti of Jerusalem and the other radical Palestinian Arab nationalists and cooperation with the Jewish Agency. In 1937 a British commission of inquiry, the Peel Commission, recommended that Palestine be divided into a Jewish section and an Arab section. When implementation of the partition plan was on the agenda, Abdullah agreed to add the Arab section to his state. From his point of view, such an annexation would finally place him in charge of historically and politically significant territories. And from the British and the Zionists' viewpoint, Abdullah's participation would have endowed a problematic solution with a measure of stability and possibly even legitimacy. In any event, the Peel Commission's recommendations were shelved, but the model of the solution remained an option.

Despite their acceptance of the 1937 scheme, the Jewish leadership and Abdullah treated it with ambivalence both then and later. Sizable segments of the Zionist movement were bitterly opposed to the renunciation of sovereignty over the part of Palestine that partnership with Abdullah would involve. For his part, Abdullah found it difficult to accept the notion of Jewish sovereignty in part of Palestine (because, among other things, he anticipated strong Arab opposition to this concession) and so kept proposing that the Jews agree to autonomy within his state. The Jewish leadership also realized that its cooperation with Abdullah would invite the enmity of the dominant majority of Palestinian Arab nationalists and of Abdullah's rivals in the Arab world. But over time it became increasingly clear that this was the only political–diplomatic option available to them. In 1946 the Jewish leadership reached an understanding with Abdullah whereby he would agree to the formation of a Jewish state in part of Palestine and the Jewish side would agree to Abdullah's taking over the territory designated for the Arab state and, if need be, would facilitate his efforts. But at the same time, the Jewish Agency refused Abdullah's request to help him create a "Greater Syria."

The understanding with Abdullah was reaffirmed in 1947, although it remained an oral agreement and was never put on paper. In addition, a line was not drawn between those territories allocated to the Jewish and Jordanian states, and an agreement was not reached with regard to Jerusalem. During the first half of 1948 the leaders of the emerging Israeli state and their advisers became increasingly worried about the validity and value of their understanding with Abdullah. He had nearly severed contact with his Jewish negotiators, refused to permit contact between the Haganah and the Jordanian Arab Legion—lest they establish cooperation on the ground—and insisted that contact and coordination with the Jewish side be kept as a personal matter, unknown to his own government and especially to the rest of the Arab world. In fact, Abdullah continued all the while to play the part of senior partner in the Arab preparations for a war in Palestine. Although he was determined to keep his agreement with the Jewish Agency, he wanted to do it in his own special way. He would dispatch his army to Palestine as part of an all-Arab campaign but act there according to his understanding with the Jews. In this fashion Abdullah hoped to accomplish his goals without losing his legitimacy as an Arab ruler. And in practice these complex considerations prompted him to play a crucial role in pushing the Arab collective to decide on the May 1948 invasion.

The Jewish leadership concluded in May 1948 that the Jordanian Arab Legion would probably take part in the fighting but, in a final attempt to clarify its relations with Abdullah, dispatched Golda Meirson (Meir) and Ezra Danin to a meeting with him on May 10. The meeting failed and has remained a controversial matter. It may have been a mistake to send a woman, particularly a strong-minded person like Golda Meir, to negotiate with a traditional Arab ruler. The meeting itself might have been conducted differently, but it is doubtful whether Abdullah could have been persuaded to follow a different policy without a fundamental change in the Israeli line. From this perspective it is interesting to examine the subsequent differences of opinion between Ezra Danin and Moshe Dayan. Dayan was among those who argued in later years that it was a mistake to confront Abdullah with a woman. He also included in his biography an anecdote illustrating Abdullah's negative attitude toward Golda Meir which surfaced in his meeting with Sharett and Dayan in January 1949. Danin, whose reputation rested to a considerable degree on his intimate knowledge of Arab society and mores, commented on Dayan's version as published in the Israeli newspaper *Yediot Aharonot* that "in the November [1947] meeting, Abdullah accepted Mrs. Meir's status as the director of the Political Department without any criticism. . . . [T]he fabrication concerning the insult came later and was designed to cover failures and frustration wrought by [the king] himself.''

At the core of Abdullah's May 1948 meeting with Golda Meir was the message that he could not avoid participating in the all-Arab military campaign unless the Jewish community renounced the idea of independent statehood and settled on autonomy under Jordanian sovereignty. Meir explained that Abdullah's proposal was unacceptable and that ''*à la guerre comme à la guerre*,'' or that if Abdullah were going back on his word, "they would meet again after the war and after the establishment of the Jewish state.''[23]

The collapse of Abdullah's understanding with the Jewish Agency cast a long shadow on his relations with the leadership of the young Israeli state. Ben-Gurion came to regard Abdullah as incapable of keeping his word, and his diaries contain several derogatory references to the Jordanian monarch. In January 1949 Ben-Gurion defined him as "a British slave," and in February of the same year he noted that "the man has no value." More graphically, Ben-Gurion wrote in his diary on January 26 (hitting two targets simultaneously) that "the old man reminds me of [the Zionist leader] Sokolov—speaks pleasantly but lacks authority and control.''[24] Abdullah was aware of Ben-Gurion's (and others') feelings, and when direct contact between him and the Israeli representatives was renewed, he treated them repeatedly to his apologetic version of the fashion in which he had entered the war and conducted his part in it.

Indeed, Abdullah's strategy in 1948 was predicated on an attempt to reconcile his participation in the war with his original agreement with the Jewish Agency. The fierce and costly fighting with the Jordanian Arab Legion (in the area of Jerusalem and in Latrun) tended to obscure the fact that the legion operated in those parts of the country that had been allocated in November 1947 to the Arab state or, at least, were not allocated to the Jewish state (Jerusalem). Had Abdullah's army turned during the war's early weeks against the core area of the Jewish state, it would have seriously exacerbated the existential challenge to the Israelis. But it should also be remembered that the Jordanian Arab Legion was a small force and that Abdullah, for his own good reasons, was reluctant to expose it to heavy fighting and losses that could have eroded the mainstay of his regime.

## Wartime Policies

During the first two months of the 1948 war the political and diplomatic muses were silent. But in late July and early August Israel launched a series of initiatives toward the Arab states. Publicly Moshe Sharett issued a call to the Arab states to end the war and make peace. In a more discreet and practical fashion Eliyahu Sasson was dispatched to Paris where he and his men (Ziama Divon and Tuvia Arazi) strove to revive channels of communication with the Arab world, particularly with Egypt and Jordan. In addition to meetings and discussions with Arab politicians and diplomats in Europe (such as Ismail Sidqi and Muhammad Hussein Haykal) and with a variety of middlemen, Sasson addressed several personal letters to prospective Arab negotiators. He thus wrote to Ibrahim Abdul Hadi Pasha, head of Egypt's royal cabinet, stating that Egypt's politicians were prisoners of their own policies and suggesting that only the king was capable of taking the initiative and breaking the deadlock. Sasson also suggested that the king order the establishment of direct contact with Israel. Another letter was sent to Prince Abd al-Majid Haydar, Jordan's minister in London. In it Sasson proposed that Abdullah instruct the military commander in Jerusalem to make contact with his Israeli counterpart.[25]

Several considerations underlay the Israeli initiatives. The first cease-fire and the military achievement of "the ten-day battles" during the first half of July removed the risk to the very existence of the state. Although the military situation on several fronts remained difficult or unstable, generally Israel could start thinking in political terms. The new nation wanted to end the war that had exacted a heavy toll in all respects and to turn to other tasks. It was now worried not so much about the prospect of military defeat but, rather, about a lingering state of indecision and the resulting attrition.

The international context did not favor the Israeli initiative. The United Nations' Count Folke Bernadotte was busy preparing his

THE ROAD NOT TAKEN

second plan, and he saw the Israeli action—and rightly so—as an attempt to bypass him. The United States and Britain adopted in August 1948 a new, united approach to the conflict and the war in Palestine. Britain had drawn closer to the American position, and so the two powers now supported a solution based on full independence and sovereignty for Israel, the annexation of the Arab part of Palestine to Jordan, and the modification of the partition lines so as to create a more compact Israel with western Galilee but without a corridor linking Jordan to the Gaza Strip.[26] From Israel's point of view, this common position represented an improvement in Britain's previous position, but it remained unsatisfactory on two points: Israel was no longer willing to settle on what had been acceptable in May 1948; that is, Israel had then been willing to accept the partition resolution and its ramifications—a small territory, awkward borders, and a large Arab minority. By the summer of 1948, however, the situation had changed: An Arab Palestinian state had not been established; Israel was now in control of territory beyond the partition lines (though not the Negev, which had been assigned to the Jewish state), and the departure (in some cases, expulsion) of the refugees had left Israel with an Arab minority smaller than expected.

The Israeli view was that the new situation was the consequence of the Arab decision to launch the war, and so it was Israel's right to preserve it. The discrepancy between this view and the American and British outlook was clear. Furthermore, as long as the Western powers held on to their position and if Bernadotte presented a similar plan, it would be most unlikely that the Arab states would agree to peace on Israel's terms.

Jordan was the first Arab state to respond to Israel's overtures. In early August, direct contact was made between Sasson and Abdul Majid Haydar in Paris, and a parallel channel of indirect contact was established through the Belgian consul in Jerusalem.[27] Even though the direct channel in Paris was terminated later in August, the Belgian consul remained a constructive link between Abdullah and the Israelis until the reestablishment of lasting direct communication (and negotiations) between the parties. Abdullah's interest in renewing the dialogue and understanding with the Israelis reflected both the impact of their military pressure and the alarming decline of Jordan's political position, as evidenced by the entirely different roles that Bernadotte assigned to that country in his first and second plans. By demoting Jordan in his second plan, Bernadotte was responding to the new military situation as well as to the hardening of the Palestinian and other Arab opposition to Jordan's annexation policy. Thus, in October 1948 the Egyptians formed in Gaza an "all-Palestine government" which, as its name implied, challenged Abdullah's claim that Jordan was Arab Palestine's historic successor. It took the king two months before he was able to strike back, by organizing the "Jericho Conference," a rather impressive Palestinian gathering that supported Jordan's annexation of Arab Palestine.

For its part, the Israeli leadership found it difficult to formulate a coherent policy toward Abdullah. First, the Israelis had yet to make up their own minds with regard to the future of the West Bank and the Gaza Strip, and they were reluctant to make a definite commitment to an Arab partner who was interested mainly in these territories. These reservations were compounded by the Israelis' resentment of Abdullah's conduct in May 1948 and their displeasure with his opening gambit—at that stage he still insisted that Israel give up part of the occupied Arab land and take back some of the refugees. Beyond these immediate considerations, the Israelis had two concerns: Abdullah's intimate association with Britain, which Ben-Gurion and several of his aides regarded as a hostile factor, and the possibility of sweeping changes in inter-Arab relations. As the Israelis saw it, either Iraq's incorporation of Jordan or Jordan's success in forming a Greater Syria would place a powerful neighbor along Israel's long and vulnerable eastern border.

Egypt's response to Sasson's demarche came a few weeks later when a special emissary, Kamel Riyad, was dispatched to Paris to meet and negotiate with Sasson (This episode is described in detail in Chapter 5.) Briefly, in return for agreeing to a separate settlement with Israel, Riyad—whose status and mandate were not clear to the Israelis—demanded far-reaching concessions that the Israeli government was unwilling to make. Along with these diplomatic moves, Israel was considering renewing the fighting in order either to force a decision or at least to improve Israel's position in a future settlement. In contemplating its military options, the Israeli leadership gave priority to an operation in the south directed at the Egyptian forces, so as to secure Israel's access to and control of the Negev. But a decision had not yet been made as to whether a second front should be opened in the north in order to expand the area of Israeli control in Galilee or in the east against the Jordanian Arab Legion in what was known as the Triangle area. These deliberations, furthermore, were not limited to military issues but also concerned the most fundamental questions facing Israel. By capturing the territory that subsequently became known as the West Bank, the Israelis would significantly increase the Palestinian population under their control, destroy the option of settling the Palestinian problem with Abdullah, and generate strong international opposition. But if Israel decided not to seize the area, it would be faced with two alternatives:

First, Israel could agree to Jordan's annexation of the West Bank (or, in the terminology of the time, "the Triangle and the Hebron area") and possibly Gaza, view it as a solution to the Palestinian problem, and thus use the leverage provided by this concession to seek a peace treaty with, at least, Jordan. This option had two main drawbacks, however: It would entail a formal renunciation of sovereignty over the West Bank, which Abdullah's Arab rivals—Egypt and its allies and a significant majority of Palestinian opinion—were bound to oppose and to denounce any such deal between Israel and Jordan.

Second, Israel could agree to the formation of an autonomous Palestinian entity in Arab Palestine which, in official Israeli parlance was called "an independent government of the Palestinian Arabs." This entity would be allied with Israel, and the question of the border line between them would remain open for the time being. In July 1948 Sharett instructed the Middle East Department of his ministry to examine and pursue such an option, but it would be a mistake to conclude on the basis of his consequent guidelines that Sharett supported a "Palestinian option" that differed from the official policy. When Shimoni reported to Sharett in November 1948 that the preliminary steps taken by his department to promote the notion of

Palestinian autonomy had been successful, Sharett's response was distinctly chilly. He explained to Shimoni that from his vantage point, Palestinian autonomy was an essentially tactical move designed to improve Israel's bargaining posture toward both Egypt and Jordan.[28] But besides its tactical considerations, Sharett's position also betrayed his reluctance to extend at that early stage (and indeed during the first half of 1949) formal recognition to Jordan's annexation of the West Bank. One advantage of the idea of Palestinian autonomy, however, was that it left open the issue of sovereignty.

The course of the 1948 war also raised, as a separate issue, the question of Gaza's future. Although the territory was small, it had a sizable population and thus major geopolitical considerations. Continued Egyptian control would perpetuate Egyptian proximity to Israel's center. Jordanian control of Gaza, should Israel opt to support it, would give Jordan an outlet to the Mediterranean but would also raise the question of a passage to the Gaza Strip. Israeli control would bypass these problems but would add a large number of Arabs to Israel's population. In any event, for the time being, the Gaza Strip was still in Egyptian hands.

These were difficult dilemmas, and Israel did not confront them directly. Ben-Gurion, as his diary reveals, was given to violent changes of mood, and he was not above ambiguity, opaqueness, and shifts of policy. Sharett's position was riddled with contradictions. Given the understandable tendency to avoid painful choices, the changes in circumstances and line, and the personal and bureaucratic rivalries of this period, it is difficult to find pattern and consistency in Israel's policy. Instead, it is more, useful to analyze Israel's conduct in terms of a spectrum of views, in whose center are Ben-Gurion's choices.

At one end of this spectrum were those in the military and political establishments who held that for ideological or strategic reasons all of Arab Palestine, or at least part of it, should be captured. Thus, during the consultation convened by Ben-Gurion on December 30, 1948, in preparation for the negotiations with Abdullah, General Yigael Yadin, the IDF's chief of operations and acting chief of staff, was not at all certain that Israel should agree to the annexation of the West Bank by Jordan as the basis of an Israeli–Jordanian settle-ment. His position was that even if such a policy were endorsed,

> that line of the Triangle as it is today is not a border line for the
> state of Israel. . . . [T]he minimum is such that I do not assume that
> we will be able to obtain it through negotiations with Abdullah. . . .
> [T]he state's border should be on the first ridge of the mountains.[29]

On another level several military commanders, such as Yigal Allon, maintained that Israel's military edge over the Arabs at that point was so overwhelming that it could dictate a peace settlement by means of constant military pressure.[30]

The most distinctive opponent of this point of view was Eliyahu Sasson. His letters from Paris to his colleagues Danin and Shimoni, written in September 1948, criticize the policy of seeking a military decision and opposing the return of the Palestinian refugees. Behind Sasson's criticism was his belief that peace with the Arabs could be reached only through compromise and that even if Israel defeated the Arabs, it would not be able to dictate the terms of peace. Danin argued back that Sasson was out of touch with Israel's reality and that he had failed to comprehend the significance of the price paid (in casualties) for the military achievements. Above all, he wrote, "fleeting criticism and noncommittal talk were insufficient and use-less." If Sasson wanted to be effective, he should present a clear and coherent program: "You would have done something tremendous by saying something clear, what you think and what you propose, stage by stage, and what results you hope to accomplish."[31]

Sasson did not prepare a phased plan of action, but in November and December 1948 in his correspondence with Shimoni and in the positions he took on various consultations, he did present a coherent and dissenting outlook. In early November he contended that the war should be ended "as early as possible, even if we have to pay a certain price for it: in territory, in international and private guaran-tees, and in the return of a small portion of the refugees." In his opinion, Israel had to invest "a serious effort—yes, serious—at making peace with the whole Arab world rather than with just one of its states.'' He rejected the notion that ''the mode of dictating terms must be our road to peace with the Arab world or one of its states.''[32] In late December Sasson expressed the opinion that Israel should behave as a state that is living in the Middle East and should act according to the international and political reality of the region. Israel had two choices: living by the sword, defeating its Arab neighbors, and pushing them into the arms of strangers (Britain and the Soviet Union), or integrating into the region while preserving the nation's Western character. ''Logic requires that we follow the second route . . . and it seems to me that the time is right for this.'' In practical terms this choice required supporting the immediate annexation ''of the Arab parts remaining in the country'' to Jordan as well as seeking, ''simultaneously, negotiations with the other Arab states or at least with two or three, with Egypt, Lebanon, and Syria.''[33]

The policy that Ben-Gurion finally chose rested on a compromise: Israel would resume fighting on a large scale in October and would continue until the Negev and Galilee in their entirety were occupied, but it would refrain from capturing the West Bank. Israeli historians are divided over whether Ben-Gurion decided against capturing the West Bank and maneuvered successfully to have his hands tied by his cabinet or whether he genuinely did want that campaign launched but failed to overcome his moderate opponents. The debate continues, but so far the more persuasive case has been made by those who believe that Ben-Gurion did not seek the occupation of the West Bank. The situation in the Gaza Strip was different, however, as it now seems that Ben-Gurion wanted to capture it but was disappointed by the IDF.

It seems, in fact, that Ben-Gurion had agreed to the annexation of part of Arab Palestine to Jordan in 1948 but had refused to do so officially and explicitly. Under the terms that Egypt offered in September and December 1948, Ben-Gurion was not interested in a separate settlement with that country, nor was he interested in too-rapid progress in the ongoing negotiations with Abdullah before Israel completed its hold over the Negev, by reaching Eylat and extending its borders at the center of the country. The notion of an armistice as an interim settlement, which was accepted toward the end of 1948 by both the UN peacemakers and the belligerents, concurred with Ben-Gurion's own thinking.

## 1949: A Transitional Year

The year 1949 as a whole may be regarded as the transition from the 1948 war to the fixed patterns of the Arab–Israeli conflict. In January 1949 the fighting had almost ended, and by December it had become clear that the first full-fledged effort to conclude a peace treaty between Israel and at least one of the Arab states was doomed. During the year four armistice agreements were signed; the United States failed in its attempt to resolve the Arab–Israeli conflict through the PCC and the Lausanne Conference; and talks were held between Israel and Jordan, Egypt, and Syria in the hopes of settling the bilateral conflicts between Israel and its three neighbors. (These talks will be described in detail in succeeding chapters.)

Next we shall consider two topics: the changes that occurred in Israel's concept of peace and settlement with the Arabs in 1949 and the evolution of Israel's relation with Jordan from the end of the fighting until the opening of the negotiations between them in November 1949.

The main elements of Ben-Gurion's thinking on the conflict between Israel and the Arab world and on the prospects of reconciliation and settlement can be found in his diary and in his pronouncements during the latter part of 1948. He was influenced by two entirely different considerations. One was his fear that the humiliation inflicted by Israel on the Arabs and the quantitative disparity between them and Israel would weaken the Arabs' acceptance of their military defeat and would induce them to seek vengence and therefore confront Israel for many years with a severe security problem.[34] But Ben-Gurion was also fully aware of the limits of Israel's power and understood that the domestic and external constraints affecting his country required that the war be brought to an end and that the main tasks on the new state's agenda be addressed. But in what fashion should the war be ended? The term *peace* appeared quite frequently during that period, but it was used loosely and referred at different times and in different contexts to a termination of the war, to an interim settlement, and to a final settlement. During the final months of 1948 a consensus emerged among the belligerents and the peacemakers that a full-fledged peace was not within reach and that it was therefore preferable to seek interim settlements in the form of armistice agreements.

The course of events during the first three months of 1949 confirmed the Israelis' belief that they had made the right choice. Armistice agreements had been signed with three Arab states, and the direct negotiations with Abdullah had shown the Israelis that the cost of a formal peace treaty with Jordan remained prohibitive. The PCC, which began its work in February 1949, was regarded suspiciously by Israel. The Israelis were familiar with the American and British versions of a desirable settlement and so viewed the PCC as an instrument designed to enforce them. Their anxieties were then aggravated by the formula that began to take shape in anticipation of the Lausanne Conference—a meeting in which Israel would face the Arab collective and an international mediating mechanism. The preparations made and discussions held in Israel in the weeks preceding the Lausanne meeting reflected a mood anticipating threats and pressures rather than a welcome breakthrough.

In more positive terms the Israeli leadership's (Ben-Gurion's as well as Sharett's) outlook in the spring of 1949 rested on three main elements. The first was a definition of peace (in the abstract sense) as a vital aim deriving from the central interest of the Israeli state at the time, which, according to Ben-Gurion, was the absorption of the new immigrants. The absorption of the immigrants, in turn, should provide "the three foundations of the state—the gathering in of the diaspora, the settlement of the country, and our security."[35] In order to enable the absorption of the immigrants, therefore, peaceful relations were required with the Arab states that would ease the burden of defense and would guarantee the new immigrants a minimum of security. Peace with the Arabs would also have another beneficial effect: It would reduce foreign involvement in the Middle East. According to this reasoning, Ben-Gurion asserted, there was no point in new territorial conquests, nor should the issue of borders become a central issue "as it is an endless matter . . . no border is absolute." Still, "in order to make peace with the Arabs they should feel that we are powerful. This would induce them to establish peace relations with us. If peace could not be reached with all Arab states, it should be reached with at least some of them."[36]

Second, as he implied, Ben-Gurion's concept of peace was based on preserving the territorial status quo. Two entirely different conclusions were reached from this position. One was the view that Ben-Gurion made public—albeit in less than explicit language—that Israel should not seize the West Bank. On April 4, in a Knesset debate on the armistice agreements, Ben-Gurion defended his position by stating:

> Let us assume that militarily we can occupy all of western Palestine, which I am sure we can; what will happen then? We will become one state. This state would wish to be democratic; elections would take place; and we would become a minority. . . . [W]ell, when the question of nonpartition without a Jewish state or a Jewish state with partition [was posed], we chose a Jewish state in less than the whole country.[37]

Preserving the status quo also meant refusing to recognize formally the annexation of the West Bank to Jordan and any Israeli concessions with regard to the international boundaries of Mandatory Palestine, as well as refusing to give up any part of Mandatory Palestine captured by Israel during the war.

The third element was Israel's willingness to withdraw its demand for formal peace, given the price that this would entail. Ben-Gurion articulated this point in his diary from Eban's perspective: "Abba Eban came; he sees no point in chasing after peace. An armistice is sufficient for us. If we chase after peace—the Arabs will demand a price, borders, or refugees or both. We will wait a few years."[38] Sharett, on his part, reiterated the same idea: "There is an argument to be made for and against. On the one hand, what do we lose by dragging our feet? What should we care? Formal peace with Arab states is not a crucial necessity for us." But on other occasions Sharett spoke differently and presented a more complex view. Thus in a consultation held in his office on July 14, 1949, he said:

> I suggested that we refrain from public declarations and from statements regarding the vital interest we have in peace and our determination to seek it. We have paid our dues. We have repeated it to the point of generating disbelief. The Arabs think that our situation is difficult and desperate and that a measure of stubbornness on their part will lead us to sign any agreement. It is being said that once the armistice agreement with Syria is signed our own lines will be stabilized so that we do not bother further. This version cannot be accepted. . . . It should be assumed that in the longer turn the state of armistice will be the source of many problems. An armistice is stable but not a satisfactory state of affairs.[39]

These abstract principles and ideas, however, had to be translated into a concrete policy that could grapple with the challenges and pressure that in the spring of 1949 focused on the Lausanne Conference. In preparing for the conference and seeking to preempt the pressure he anticipated, Ben-Gurion initiated the idea of Israel's annexing the Gaza Strip and its inhabitants. Under duress, on May 12 Israel signed the Lausanne Protocol, which implied its acceptance of the partition resolution boundary and its willingness to compromise on the question of borders and refugees. Later, Israel agreed to take back a small number of refugees as part of a "family reunification" plan and then to increase the number of these refugees to 100,000. But these moves and concessions failed to satisfy either the Arab collective's or America's demands, although they did help Israel sail through the Lausanne Conference without a lasting crisis in its relations with the United States. Israel also succeeded in being admitted to the United Nations but, needless to say, emerged from this period without a comprehensive agreement with the Arab states.

An alternative strategy for dealing with these pressures could have been an agreement with one Arab state. But during most of this period, Syria was not perceived as a realistic partner for a settlement, and Israel's attempt to open a dialogue with Egypt did not produce any results. As in earlier years, Abdullah appeared to be the only possible partner. In the winter and spring of 1949 he reiterated to his Israeli contacts that he wanted a peace treaty with them. But the doubt and heart searching that had governed the Israeli attitude toward Abdullah in late 1949 had not disappeared. In an analysis he presented in late May 1949, Sharett saw peace with Jordan as offering three advantages: (1) ''neutralizing an important element in the Lausanne Conference and encouraging the other actors to reach a settlement with us, (2) making peace without having to return any refugees, and (3) undermining the American demand for territorial compensation.'' But in return for these advantages, Sharett was aware that by signing a peace agreement with Jordan, Israel would seal the fate of western Palestine.[40]

Moreover, Sharett and his colleagues sensed the growing Jordanian pressure and desire to collect (''exact,'' in Sharett's language) a high price for a peace treaty that from Jordan's point of view would bring only one important advantage—Israel's acceptance of the annexation of the West Bank. The king and his men had harbored a grudge since the armistice negotiations, whose terms Israel had dictated, and they suspected that the Israelis were seeking to win concessions with regard to the practical questions on their own agenda (renewing work in the potash plant in the Dead Sea, activating the power plant in Naharayim, and making various arrangements regarding Jerusalem and the road to the city) without giving the king their endorsement of the West Bank annexation.

It is against this background that Sharett's report on the unusual discussion he conducted with King Abdullah on May 5 in Shuneh should be read:

> The king opened with a general lecture on the need for peace and on the preparation of public opinion for this end. I said that we were certainly interested in peace and that therefore we attach such a great importance to solving the problems that are still open. We were disappointed by the suspension of the work of the special committee that should have completed its inquiry into two questions: Mount Scopus and Latrun. . . . [T]here are additional questions that call for a practical settlement. . . . The king asked whether we merely intended to solve practical questions, or did we think that the question

of peace should be discussed in its entirety and a comprehensive settlement be reached? I said that in our opinion, progress should be made gradually. The armistice agreement had laid the foundation, and so we should now be resolving the outstanding questions, and finally we will build the roof, which is comprehensive peace.

Later during the meeting, the Jordanian prime minister, Tawfiq Abu al-Huda, who was taking part in the meeting, asked Sharett whether "we accept the verdict of the November 29 resolution or whether our intention is, as can be deducted from my statement, to negotiate only on the basis of the existing facts." When Sharett replied that "the November 29 resolution had lost its real validity and that the only practical basis for negotiations is the actual situation," Abu al-Huda responded "with a certain degree of acrimony and not without anger that, if this were [Israel's] position, the Arab world had nothing to talk to us about, and peace will not be established."[41]

An interesting insight into King Abdullah's discussions with the Israelis in the spring of 1948 is brought out in the conversations he had during the same period with one of his confidants, Yusuf Haykal. Haykal was a Palestinian politician who had become the mayor of Jaffa. (Like other Palestinian politicians, having been burned by the rivalry with the mufti, Haykal had drawn close to Abdullah and was subsequently sent to Washington as Jordan's minister.) During the later part of 1948 and the early months of 1949 Haykal stayed close to the king, and he recorded their conversations and published them under the title *Jalasat fi Raghdan* (Meetings at Raghdan Palace). In a meeting between them on April 5, 1949, Abdullah apologized for his willingness to sign an armistice agreement with Israel on disadvantageous terms, and he also hinted that in his opinion, this was not the end of the matter:

We could not have conducted ourselves differently. We made the small sacrifice in order to preserve what had been left. The Egyptians departed from Palestine defeated; the Lebanese constituted a burden on the others; and the Syrians are weak and incapable of entering Palestine. We are left with the Arab Legion, which on its own is incapable of standing up to the Jews. Furthermore, the UN and Britain pressured our government into accepting the Jewish demand. The armistice shaped the military borders, and the Arabs should be prepared to act in unison in order to regain what has been lost. What has happened between the Arabs and the Jews is merely the first act.[42]

The sense that a deadlock had been reached with Jordan gave rise in Israel to thoughts of three possible lines of action. First, the Israelis briefly changed their tack on the question of Greater Syria. As a rule, the Israelis (and before that, the Jewish Agency leaders) opposed Abdullah's "Greater Syria" plan, which they saw as a move orchestrated by the British. But in the immediate aftermath of the coup by Husni Zaim in Syria and on the assumption that it was really instigated by Abdullah, the Israelis toyed with the idea that Abdullah's attention could be diverted away from the West Bank and that his expansionist urge could be channeled to the north. Some of the Israeli experts, headed by Sasson, were bitterly opposed to this idea, but Sharett still tried his hand (as can be seen in his report on the May 5 meeting).[43]

The Israelis also pondered another idea: the cultivation of Palestinian autonomy in the West Bank in order to thwart Abdullah's ambitions. The various versions of this idea run through the papers written and statements made by Sharett, Eytan, and Shimoni between February and August 1949.[44] In March Shimoni still thought that persons such as Musa al-Alami, Awni Abd al-Hadi, and Ahmad Shuqayri might be interested in this idea. By August, though, Israeli expectations had been lowered and now focused on a propaganda approach that Nimr al-Hawari might try in Lausanne with open or covert aid from Israel and Egypt.

These ideas concerning Greater Syria, the cultivation of Palestinian autonomy in cooperation with Egypt, and taking advantage of the complex relationship with regard to Gaza reflected a feeling that Israel had become a participant in the Middle Eastern political game. This feeling apparently derived from Israel's success in exploiting the Egyptian–Jordanian rivalry in 1948 and from the (often misleading) sense of openness that sometimes prevailed in secret talks with Arab leaders and diplomats. During the April 12 consultation, in the middle of the debate on the preponderance of pro-Egyptian, pro-Jordanian, and neutral camps, Shimoni introduced a note of chilly realism:

> Just between us, I am doubtful of our political, practical, and diplomatic ability to intervene in this internecine squabble. . . . I do not believe that we have that kind of power [with regard to the West Bank]. . . . I do not wish to pretend that the annexation of the Arab part to Transjordan depends on our agreement. It would take a certain ability [to convince] Abdullah and the world to think that without our agreement he would not be able to annex any part, but we know that in fact that our agreement is not necessary.[45]

Shimoni, who could in fact phrase his statement in still stronger terms, was right. In internal discussions and in their talks with Arab representatives, the Israelis could revel in the feeling that they could play a role in shaping Arab politics, but in reality they had lost the leverage they had had in the unusual circumstances during the war. In the later part of 1948 and the armistice negotiations of early 1949, because of inter-Arab rivalries over the Palestinian question and with its army poised to inflict damage on its four neighbors, Israel enjoyed a unique ability to affect Arab politics. As a regional power and in the circumstances of protracted conflict with the Arab world, Israel retained some of that influence in the coming years and decades. But by 1949 Israel's ability to affect Arab politics had considerably diminished.

In the Israeli–Jordanian relationship, the Israelis were not the only ones to change their mind. Jordan's position also changed during the course of the Lausanne Conference. On June 22 the heads of the Israeli and Jordanian delegations, Walter Eytan and Fawzi al-Mulki, met to discuss "tentative peace lines." Among other things they spoke of dividing western Palestine between Jordan and Israel, based on the idea that each party could hold on to the territory that it currently held. (Gaza's transfer to Jordan would depend on Egypt's agreement.) Israel would hold on to western Galilee without offering territorial compensation. They also discussed the notion of border rectification "on the basis of mutual interest." In case that peace could be achieved, Israel would agree to talk about a "contribution" in regard to the Palestinian refugees.

Mulki must have felt, however, that he had been overly generous and rushed, on the same day, to make a correction: He was anxious to create a linkage between territory and refugees; namely, "the more territory we give them, the fewer refugees they would insist we take back, and vice versa. We will have to dissuade them of this idea . . . undoubtedly what they most want is peace."[46] But on July 1, Eytan wrote to Sharett regarding the second meeting he had had with Mulki, apparently after the latter had received new instructions from Amman. This message was entirely different: Jordan does want peace, and in order to obtain it, it is willing to invest more effort than any other Arab state is, but "it is very difficult for Jordan to sign a separate peace. The king's popularity and his influence sank after the signing of the armistice agreement, and in Mulki's opinion the king cannot afford to take any more risks." Six months ago "he could act as he pleased; today he is considered a traitor, and he must be overcautious." Jordan, therefore, wants to make peace together with all the Arab states. If this does not happen in Lausanne, Mulki asks that Israel help Jordan "by offering honorable terms." Jordan would try to bring the other Arabs along on the basis of these terms, and if it failed, it would be willing to blaze its own trail to peace in "unity of opinion with the people of Palestine." In any event a comprehensive peace was preferable to Israel, too.

Transjordan would make peace with Israel under all these terms and along with the resolution of December 11, 1949. This, of course, would raise the problem of the refugees to which the formula should be applied that Mulki had already raised concerning the direct relationship between the number of refugees absorbed by Israel and the territory it would like to hold on to beyond the partition boundaries.[47]

Jordan's change of position was based in part on the reasons cited by Mulki as well as on Jordan's continuing disappointment with Israel's attitude. But it seems to have been primarily the result of two developments. One was the integration of a sizable population of Palestinians into Jordan's political system. The other was the course of events in and around the Lausanne Conference during the spring and early summer. If there were good prospects that the United States directly or through the UN would force Israel to make far-reaching concessions, why should Jordan settle for less than that? Moreover, Abdullah and his advisers must have reached the same conclusion as Shimoni had. In time, however, it became clear that Israel's endorsement of the West Bank's annexation was important but not crucial.

In the summer of 1949, King Abdullah once again severed direct contact with Israel. As a result Sasson repeated the technique he had used a year earlier. On August 13, 1949, he wrote to Prince Abd al-Majid Haydar in London and asked to transmit a message to King Abdullah, who was about to arrive for a visit. Things were not moving in Lausanne, and Fawzi al-Mulki had yet to reply to Sasson's suggestion that they meet.[48]

In Israel in the late summer of 1949 a somber mood prevailed, in contrast with the relative complacency of the early spring. The negotiations with Jordan were deadlocked, and the direct contact with the country had been severed. Israel's effort to open a dialogue with Egypt had failed (see Chapter 5), as had the attempt to open a general dialogue with the Arab representatives in Lausanne through the Lebanese delegation. In July, following the signing of the armistice with Syria, the Israeli government decided to examine seriously the possibility of turning Zaim's unorthodox approach into an instrument generating a general settlement (see Chapter 3). The prospect of this move can remain only a matter of historical speculation, however, as Zaim was deposed and killed on August 14. The failure of the Lausanne Conference and the feeling that the United States and Britain were critical of, if not hostile to, Israel's policy added gloom to the picture. This pessimistic mood was reflected by Sasson in an analysis he prepared for Sharett in late September 1949 and in which he described the dominant thinking on the Israeli peace with the Arabs. Sasson, who had traditionally played the role of ceaseless advocate of peace with the Arab world, wrote:

The first view maintains that Israel should be attacked and wiped off the map as soon as possible before it reinforces itself militarily, economically, and internationally. The fact that the Arab states lost the first round of the war in Palestine need not serve as a restraining factor during the attack. That defeat was the result of internal and external factors that had nothing to do with Israel. The second view holds that for the good of the Arab world Israel should be attacked and wiped off the map, but this should not be done for a few more years so that victory can be guaranteed. In the meantime the Arab world should, first, resolve its own squabbles. Second, it should organize its military power. Third, it should find a satisfactory mode for its relations with several Western powers, particularly England. Fourth, it should develop some natural resources in order to restore its economic and social condition. Fifth, it should unite and expand its sphere, but not to include Turkey, Iran, and Pakistan.

The third outlook, which is presumably the most realistic one, argues that the Arab world should (1) seek to reduce as much as possible Israel's territory and Jewish population, in order to prevent either any future territorial expansion at the expense of Israel's neighbors or any economic domination of the eastern markets, or in order to preserve its existence as a weak state dependent on the goodwill of its neighbors and incapable of making its own foreign policy; (2) from now on, for several years we should avoid any cooperation and agreement with and recognition of Israel in order (a) to be able to form an opinion regarding this creature called Israel, its racial [ethnic] tendency, and its political intentions; (b) to keep it for a long time in a state of military tension and instability; and (c) to make a bargain with the West in return for better Arab–Israeli relations. Should it happen in a few years that Israel has passed this test in all respects, survived and became a Middle Eastern state in the full sense of the term, one that has the best interest of the people of the East in mind, then we should draw closer to Israel and come to reconciliation with it.[49]

# 3

# Israel and
# Husni Zaim

Among the various attempts that were made after the 1948 war to reach an Arab–Israeli agreement, the brief quest for a comprehensive Syrian–Israeli accord stands out as an especially intriguing episode. There was nothing in the earlier history of Syrian–Zionist relations to suggest that the head of Syria's government might take the initiative in proposing that Syria and Israel plunge directly into peace negotiations. Discussions had taken place between Syrian political leaders and emissaries of the Jewish Agency in the 1930s and 1940s, but they had failed to produce even a broad agreement. Syria was particularly committed to Arab nationalism and to the Arab cause in Palestine, and so an understanding similar to those reached in 1946 with Abdullah and Ismail Siqdi was impossible in the case of Syria.[1] Unlike the case with Egypt and Jordan, contacts with Israel were not established during the war's final phases, and it was quite difficult to get the Syrian government in the winter and early spring of 1949 to agree to begin armistice negotiations. The abrupt transition from this negative position to the language of peace and comprehensive settlement, therefore, was most dramatic.[2]

Likewise, there is little in the subsequent course of Syrian–Israeli relations that seems to be contingent on this overture. The Syrian–Israeli conflict has been the most bitter of Israel's bilateral conflicts with its Arab neighbors. To those accustomed to the acrimony of nearly four decades, therefore, it is surprising to discover that the notion of reconciliation was on the agenda of the two countries' relationship, albeit briefly and unclearly. Given the isolated nature of the episode there is a natural tendency either to dismiss it or to build it into a tantalizing "missed opportunity." The need for a historian's sober and detached judgment is felt.

An examination of Israel's encounter with Syria's Husni Zaim throws an interesting light on the interplay between the Arab–Israeli conflict and other aspects of Middle Eastern politics. Husni Zaim was the first military dictator in the post–World War II Arab world, and his conduct displayed some of the advantages and disadvantages of dealing with a military regime. Zaim could act swiftly and decisively, or so it seemed, free from the confusion and paralysis of Syria's weak parliamentary governments. But his style was characterized by whim and levity, and his legitimacy and durability were questionable.

Syria's domestic politics in the spring of 1949 and later provided the arena in which inter-Arab and international rivalries were played out. The fluidity produced by the March 30 coup d'état exacerbated the familiar rivalries between the Hashemite and Egyptian–Saudi blocs and, on a different level, between Britain and France. The novel element was the intercession of the United States in an effort to shape the politics of a Middle Eastern country.

There is, finally, an instructive lesson concerning sources. The recent interest in Husni Zaim's relationship with Israel has been to a considerable extent the result of the newly opened diplomatic archives. But as we shall see later, much is still unknown, and most of what we do know comes from the Israeli and American archives. But the core of this story has been available all along, as it was published in 1949 in one of the most underrated sources for the region's history—the contemporary Arab press. Additional details were revealed over the years with the publication of several memoirs.

But it was only the authoritative material released by the opening of the archives and the consequent fresh review of the 1948–49 period that drew attention to this intriguing episode.

## Husni Zaim and Israel: March 30 to August 14, 1949

Husni Zaim, the commander in chief of the Syrian army, staged his coup on March 30, 1949, and ruled Syria until August 14, when a group of army officers led by Sami al-Hinawi deposed and killed him.

On April 5, 1949, armistice negotiations commenced between Syria and Israel, although they had been agreed to in March, before the coup, so that they were one of the new regime's first undertakings and, from an international point of view, a significant act of early recognition. It was the Soviet government that raised this issue with the Israelis: On April 8 the Soviet minister, Pavel Yershov, asked Walter Eytan,

> Why is it that Israel was negotiating with the new Syrian government when no Arab state has recognized it? Have you given sufficient thought to the fact that your willingness to sit with this government constitutes an act of recognition of the Syrian government, so that you appear to be the first to recognize it?[3]

Yershov's criticism reflected his government's belief at that time that Zaim had acted in league with Abdullah and thus was an instrument of British policy in the region.

Syria had not taken part in the Rhodes negotiations, and so its negotiations with Israel were conducted against the background of the three armistice agreements signed earlier in the year with Egypt, Lebanon, and Jordan. The Syrian–Israeli talks were held under UN auspices in the no-man's land near the Israeli village of Mishmar Hayarden. Not surprisingly, the effort to conclude a Syrian–Israeli armistice agreement proved to be the most protracted and difficult of these agreements. The major stumbling bloc was Israel's insistence that Syria, which had ended the war still occupying some territory west of the international boundary with Mandatory Palestine, withdraw its forces to the international border as part of the armistice agreement, and Syria's refusal to accede to this demand.

Several issues were involved in this debate. For the Syrians, ending the war in possession of territory west of the international border would be a considerable achievement, as they would be in a position to claim that they had ended the war with a concrete gain in hand. There also were points of principle: The Syrians had argued against the legitimacy of their border with Palestine, which, they claimed, had been drawn to Syria's disadvantage by two colonial powers. In addition, there was a vague Syrian claim to parts of Galilee and a more explicit argument that Israel had no right to hold on to those parts of Galilee not assigned to it by the UN partition resolution of 1947. More concretely, Syria sought to exploit its advantageous position on the ground, in order to obtain a better hold over two important keys to the region's scarce water resources—the Jordan River and Lake Tiberias.

From the Israeli perspective, the principle of adhering to Palestine's international borders had been established earlier when Israel withdrew from Egyptian and Lebanese territory, and so Israel felt that this principle should also be respected when Israel was at a disadvantage. Israel was as acutely aware as Syria was of the strategic importance of water resources, and so Syria's attempt to acquire new leverage only stiffened Israel's resolve to hold on to the established international frontier. There also were more immediate, as well as contradictory, considerations: on the one hand, a strong urge to end the war, consolidate the existence of the state, and normalize life, and, on the other, a sense that there was no point in making concessions on important issues when Israel enjoyed an overwhelming advantage over a weak Syria practically devoid of Arab support.

The armistice agreement, nonetheless, was finally signed on July 20, 1949. At the time of the negotiations Syria and Israel also were participating in the Lausanne Conference organized by the PCC.[4]

Because there were no bilateral contacts between the Syrian and Israeli delegations in Lausanne, other channels were used throughout the period to exchange messages between Husni Zaim's government and Israel. Through these channels Zaim expressed his willingness to meet with Ben-Gurion, to enter into peace negotiations with Israel, and to settle 250,000 or 300,000 Palestinian refugees in northeastern Syria. This series of informal contacts and exchange of messages between Husni Zaim's regime and Israel unfolded in three phases.

## April to Late May

On April 16, eleven days after the armistice negotiations began, David Ben-Gurion noted in his diary:

> Mordechai (Makleff) and Josh (Palmon) spoke with Zaim's representatives without the UN's participation. The Syrians proposed a separate peace with Israel, cooperation, and a common army. But they want a border change . . . half of Lake Tiberias. . . . I told them to inform the Syrians in clear language that first of all [there would be] the signing of an armistice on the basis of the previous international border, and then [there would be a] discussion of peace and alliance. We will be ready for maximal cooperation.[5]

At the same time, in view of the stalemate in the formal armistice talks, Ben-Gurion was considering military action if the negotiations failed. On April 22 he wrote in his diary: "refusal to meet with Syria and to accept its participation in Lausanne if an armistice agreement is not signed and preparation for expelling the Syrians from the state's territory."[6]

On April 28 Zaim met with James Keeley, the U.S. minister in Damascus. According to Keeley's report, Zaim "had intimated willingness as part general settlement including realistic frontier adjustments, accept quarter million refugees if given substantial development aid in addition to compensation for refugee losses." Later in the same conversation Zaim "reiterated his willingness to resolve the Palestinian problem by pursuing henceforth a policy of give and take, provided that he [Yadin] not be asked to give all while other side takes all.''[7] A more elaborate version of the discussion between Makleff and Palmon and Zaim's representatives was supplied by Yigael Yadin during the consultation on April 19 in preparation for the Lausanne Conference:

> A meeting with the Syrians. They came full of admiration for Zaim. They want to sign immediate peace rather than armistice and to exchange immediately ambassadors, etc. . . . [G]enerally speaking, Zaim wants to fight for control of the Middle East, and he calculated that Israel and Syria together can reach the number of 500,000 soldiers, who, when appearing as a unified bloc, can obtain control of the Middle East. Because they speak of peace, the border line should be adjusted. They want the border line to cross Lake Tiberias and then go down along the Jordan. . . .
>
> I had a meeting with the prime minister, to which I also invited Makleff and Palmon. The prime minister said that if we do not reach an armistice with the Syrians before Lausanne, he doubts whether we would be able to sit with them in Lausanne. With regard to the border, we would agree either to changes in our favor or to an international border, and the Syrians said that they will communicate that to Zaim. I proposed one more thing—a direct meeting between ourselves and Zaim in order to clarify matters—and emphasized that this would not constitute a precedent. The meeting took place yesterday, and we stated our position in no uncertain terms. When we asked them what about Degania, they did not know what to say precisely about its fate. They proposed that the eastern half of Lake Tiberias be given to Syria and that north of the lake the Jordan line be followed. They say this is convenient.[8]

On May 1 Keeley met again with Zaim and reported that he [Zaim] reminded me that several days ago he had expressed his desire for a speedy solution to Palestinian problem and had stated his willingness to accept as part of a comprehensive settlement of the conflict a quarter-million or more Arab refugees for resettlement in Syria, provided that Syria is compensated for its losses and is given adequate financial aid to resettle the refugees. He reiterated his sincere desire for prompt agreement with Israel and his desire to enter direct negotiations with Israel to that end. Zaim went on to say that because Syria, Transjordan, and Egypt are the Arab states most directly concerned with the Palestinian problem, he would meet with Abdullah and Farouk in order to decide on a common basis for their approach to Israel.[9] Although Zaim was eager to give concrete proof of his sincerity—already evidenced by his proffered concessions—he emphasized that "unless Israel also manifested a spirit of compromise, the stalemate would continue, as the Arab states cannot be expected to make all the concessions."

Two days earlier, after the April 29 meeting between the Syrian and Israeli delegations, one of the Syrian delegates, Major Muhammad Nasser, met with Josh Palmon "privately, in order to reach an agreement." According to Ben-Gurion's diary:

> The Syrian proposed that the political boundary be agreed on only in the negotiations for peace and not those for armistice. Josh informed him that he would communicate this to his own government, provided that we agree on a two-month period at the end of which the international border be restored, whether or not peace had been reached. Nasser proposed this after meeting with Zaim. We looked into the possibility of [military] action. . . . [F]or the time being we are putting Bunche and the Americans to work. It was agreed that they meet with Zaim and propose Reuven [Shiloah] and Yigael [Yadin], but Zaim might insist on the prime minister or the foreign minister. Moshe is willing to meet, but not this week.[10]

A few days later the U.S. government and the UN mediator Ralph Bunche—both of whom were mystified by Ben-Gurion's refusal to meet with the leader of an important Arab state who had proposed the meeting—began to exert pressure on the Israeli government. On May 8, Ben-Gurion met with the U.S. ambassador to Israel, James McDonald. The prime minister demanded "pressure on Zaim to evacuate the territories, just as pressure had been exerted on us to evacuate Lebanon's territory. If we sign with Syria, a de facto peace will be reached." For his part, McDonald told Ben-Gurion, as the latter wrote in his diary, that "Zaim and [the U.S.] ambassador in Damascus demand that I meet with Zaim. The State Department did not accept. I said that if Zaim made a prior commitment to evacuate our territory and withdraw to the international border, I shall be ready to meet with him.''[11] When McDonald spoke to Ben-Gurion, he was unaware that the State Department had instructed him by cable to find out whether Ben-Gurion had indeed been informed by his own people of Zaim's willingness to meet with him.[12]

On May 10 Ralph Bunche, worried by the deadlock in the armistice negotiations, approached Ben-Gurion through his (Bunche's) personal representative, the Swedish diplomat Paul Mohn, requesting that he agree to an early meeting with Zaim "to discuss the armistice lines and any other matters relating to the peace between your two countries that you may mutually agree to discuss." Ben-Gurion replied two days later through Shiloah:

> I am quite prepared to meet Colonel Zaim in order to promote peace between the two countries, but I see no purpose in any such meeting as long as the representatives of Syria in the armistice negotiations do not declare unequivocally that their forces will withdraw to their prewar territory.[13]

On May 2 the political adviser of the UN observers' headquarters, the French diplomat Henri Vigier, transmitted a message to Moshe Sharett stating that Colonel Zaim had invited Mr. Ben-Gurion or Mr. Sharett to a meeting. As an internal memorandum of the Israeli Foreign Ministry put it, "Because Mr. Sharett thought that the time, at that stage of the armistice negotiations between Syria and Israel, was not suitable for such a high-level meeting, Vigier suggested that Shiloah and Yadin be dispatched for 'clarification talks'." On May 5 they met with the two representatives of Husni Zaim (whose identity could not be established) for what was defined as a "secret session."

At the end of the meeting they agreed that the Syrian delegation to the armistice talks would bring new proposals to the next day's meeting. This meeting took place on May 6 and was brief and unimportant. Rather, the important discussion that day took place between the Israeli delegation, on the one hand, and between Brigadier General William E. Riley, the American chief of the UN observers, and Vigier, on the other. Vigier was full of complaints about the Israelis: In his opinion Sharett should have represented Israel in the May 5 meeting, and by insisting on the international border rather than the water line, the Israelis missed ''a unique opportunity to come to a long-term agreement with the Syrians.'' The Israelis left with the impression that when Vigier invited Zaim to take part in the discussion, he ''presented it as our initiative, even though a week ago we had emphasized that if we wanted the private talks to break the deadlock, it was necessary that he should present them as his own idea.'' Riley, in turn, made it clear to the Israelis that the U.S. government (and apparently he personally) thought ''that the water line made more sense militarily and politically than did the present international border.'' The Israelis stressed that from their point of view, the water question was a fundamental economic and social matter.[14]

On May 11 Keeley met with Zaim, who complained that the meeting ''on the diplomatic level between Syria and Israel was fruitless and blamed the failure on the Israeli insistence that Syria withdraw to the international border.'' When Keeley asked whether Zaim was still ready for direct negotiations with Ben-Gurion on a comprehensive settlement with Israel, Zaim replied affirmatively, although he was less enthusiastic about it than on earlier occasions. He added that if Ben-Gurion ''were to take the same tough position held by earlier Israeli negotiators,'' little could be expected from such a meeting. But if he were to meet with him ''in a candid spirit of compromise based on give and take,'' mutual advantages could be agreed on swiftly. Zaim stated his general outlook on negotiations between leaders: ''It was natural in negotiations, particularly among juniors, to demand more than was expected and to make minimal concessions, but when candid men with the authority to settle things met, an agreement became feasible if they presented to one another reasonable requests that cannot be rejected.'' Zaim also told Keeley that he sincerely wanted peace with Israel but was ready to fight if Israel tried to take by force whatever he refused to give. As Zaim put it, ''The Syrian army was never defeated during the Palestine war, and Israel would be mistaken if it treated Syria as a vanquished enemy.''[15]

On May 17 the armistice talks were suspended for a whole month. In an apparent attempt to prevent their collapse, General Riley, at the end of that day's meeting, started a conversation with the Israeli delegate Shabtai Rozen, the Foreign Ministry's legal adviser. Using information obtained from "informal" sources in Damascus, Riley briefed Rosenne on Zaim's intentions. This was the first time that Zaim's willingness to settle Palestinian refugees in Syria was communicated to the Israeli government. Rosenne reported:

> According to him [Riley], Husni Zaim wants to resolve the Syrian–Israeli problem in an honorable and peaceful way, in order to devote himself fully to the goals of Syria's revival and advancement. On the other hand, he is afraid that a coup could occur one day in Syria that would restore to power the politicians who would critically scrutinize Zaim's activities, including his negotiations with Israel. He thus is anxious that we help him emerge honorably from his dilemma. For this reason Riley wanted to know how the Israeli government would respond to the following proposal:
>
> In the framework of the Lausanne negotiations Syria would agree to receive and settle within its boundaries 300,000 Arab refugees. Likewise, in the framework of the same conference the problem of frontiers would be resolved, and Riley believes, but is not fully certain, that the Palestine Conciliation Commission would have no choice but to pressure Syria to withdraw to the international frontier as it had existed before the invasion. As a quid pro quo, an armistice agreement between Israel and Syria would be signed now on the basis of the present cease-fire lines and with clear provisions for mutual troop reduction in order to dispel the mutual fear and suspicion that currently exist between the two countries. This agreement would remain valid for a maximum of three months and would contain a clause alluding to Israel's firm insistence on its demand for a Syrian withdrawal to the previous international border.[16]

A brief exchange followed between Rosenne and Riley that resulted in the introduction of minor changes in the draft proposal. Rosenne told Riley that he believed that Ben-Gurion would reject the proposal and gave him his reasons for this conclusion. And indeed Ben-Gurion's reaction was negative, but he determined to delay his final decision until Sharett returned from the United States.

At the UN in New York Abba Eban must have felt Bunche's pressure more directly, for on May 18 he cabled the Foreign Ministry asking for "further clarifications why we unimpressed with prospect Syria absorb 300,000 fact he made proposal through Riley with consequent transmission Washington of readiness accept large-scale resettlement seems to me of great importance."[17] To this Sharett replied on May 25:

> Have informed Vigier am ready to meet Zaim soonest. For your information: intend to try to cut Gordian knot armistice and explore reality his alleged proposal resettle 300,000. Attach tremendous importance latter point, was greatly impressed by it when first learned it Geneva. In talk with Zaim intend to brandish stick Moabit [UN Security Council] must know Bunche's latest firm stand. Believe our position inside UN can only be strengthened by this initiative on my part.

Sharett also made a similar, more detailed statement in a meeting held on the same day with the Foreign Ministry's departmental directors.[18]

## Late May to Early June

Sharett's reply to Eban can also be seen in the context of the effort made in late May and early June by the UN's mediators, headed by Bunche, to break the deadlock in the armistice negotiations, through a high-level Syrian–Israeli meeting. This episode illustrates the UN mediation team's *modus operandi*, as well as additional aspects of Israel's relationship with Husni Zaim's regime.

In his discussions with Israel's representatives, Bunche appeared supportive of their demand for Syria's withdrawal to the international border and as generally more sympathetic than Vigier was, whom the Israelis perceived as leaning toward the Syrians and their position. But both Bunche and Vigier were disappointed in Ben-Gurion's unwillingness to meet with Zaim earlier. Implicit in their disappointment was their feeling that such a meeting could have achieved a breakthrough and prevented the mid-May deadlock. In any event they now tried to arrange a meeting between Sharett and the Syrians. But their effort failed. Zaim refused to see Sharett, whom he regarded as too junior to meet on an equal footing. Sharett did not contest the point but believed that his own willingness to meet Zaim on the latter's own ground was appropriate compensation for the difference in their respective positions in their countries' formal hierarchies. Sharett was also willing, however, to meet with Adel Arslan, Zaim's foreign minister. But on May 30 the Syrians proposed through Vigier a meeting between a delegation headed by Ibrahim Istiwani, deputy secretary-general of the Syrian Foreign Ministry, and an Israeli delegation headed by Sharett. The Israelis understood at that point that Bunche was acting on the assumption that his (Bunche's) compromise proposals were bound to be rejected by the Syrians and that for this reason, he chose not to present them but to organize first a high-level Syrian–Israeli meeting. Ben-Gurion would have preferred that Bunche show his own hand first, but he agreed to wait for the results of Sharett's attempt to meet with Arslan. Indeed, Sharett proposed to the UN staff that he go to Syria and, at their request, suggested also an agenda for the prospective meeting, to include a discussion of the armistice problems and the problems concerning the future peace relations.[19]

On June 8 Vigier brought the Syrian government's negative reply, and so both Husni Zaim and Adel Arslan refused to meet. As for the armistice problems, they were tied to the armistice negotiations, and "the question of future peace relations can be discussed only together with the other Arab states." Sharett felt deceived and humiliated and responded sarcastically: "They probably assumed that we would put on the agenda such topics as medieval Arabic poetry or Bedouin tradition. . . . This impertinent affront by a self-styled Syrian government is decisive proof . . . [that we have witnessed] . . . a series of evasions and deceptions." Implied here was Sharett's contempt for the dubious legitimacy of a military dictatorship.[20] Sharett and his Israeli colleagues were apparently unaware of the debate on these very issues that had taken place between Zaim and his foreign minister.

Zaim was of Kurdish extraction and quite remote from Arab nationalism. He had no ideological commitments and apparently few principles. The members of Zaim's generation who joined and were commissioned in the Troupes Spéciales, France's colonial auxiliary force in the Levant, were men desiring to serve the Mandatory government against the Arab nationalist opposition. It was only later that younger men like Adib Shishakli went to the military academy in order to provide a nucleus for a national and nationalist army.

Adel Arslan came from an entirely different tradition. He was a member of a princely Druze Lebanese family and, like his brother Shakib, had played a prominent role in the politics of pan-Arab nationalism between the two world wars. He was fully committed to the Arab cause in Palestine and was opposed to Zaim's policy toward Israel, on grounds of both principle and tactics. Arslan's position in the spring of 1949 is recorded in both his published diaries and foreign diplomatic dispatches, and both sources reflect the depth of his opposition to direct negotiations with Israel and to the notion of settling Palestinian refugees in Syria.

On May 31 Arslan paid a visit to P.M. Broadmead, Britain's minister in Damascus, and told him in confidence that during the past few days, Vigier had been exerting pressure on Zaim, in Bunche's name, to meet with Sharett. He himself, Arslan said, refused to meet with Sharett, and he had warned Zaim of a trap. At the same time the U.S. minister urged Zaim to accept Bunche's offer. Arslan told Broadmead that if the Israelis had anything to offer, they could do it in the armistice talks or at the Lausanne Conference. In his opinion Israel was motivated by its economic difficulties and by its desire to release those forces currently stationed in the north in order to attack the Old City in Jerusalem. Arslan, who liked to take advantage of the competition among the Western powers, explained to the British minister that the U.S. government was an "agent" of its Israeli counterpart. Broadmead, for his part, characterized Arslan as a "diehard" on the "Jewish question."[21]

Arslan's diary is full of details concerning his opposition to Zaim's Israeli policy. He thus tells that in the Syrian cabinet's meeting on May 25 Zaim announced that Sharett was scheduled to arrive by plane in Quneitra for a meeting with Arslan. Arslan responded by stating that he would not recognize the state of Israel, would not meet its foreign minister, and would not allow any employee of his own Foreign Ministry to meet with him.[22] Shortly thereafter Zaim made some changes in his government. He had himself elected president in a referendum and appointed his confidant, Muhsin Barazi, as both prime minister and foreign minister. Arslan was ousted from the government. These changes were hardly a surprise, however, for when he had staged his coup Zaim needed well-known civilian politicians in order to give his regime a measure of respectability and legitimacy. At the time, Muhsin Barazi was closely identified with the ousted civilian regime. But after three months, this changed: Zaim, whose personal ambitions had become quite grandiose, wanted to be president; Barazi had become his confidant and special emissary; and Arslan had proved to be too difficult and independent. In any case Arslan was lucky that he was not part of the regime when Zaim was toppled on August 14. After Zaim's downfall Arslan settled his score with his former chief by publishing, in the Lebanese press, a derogatory account of this period.[23]

## July Through August

After a month's suspension the Syrian–Israeli armistice negotiations were renewed in mid-June. Bunche's diplomatic ability plus the U.S. government's pressure helped achieve a breakthrough even without a high-level Syrian–Israeli meeting. The compromise was based on the demilitarization of the territory held by Syria west of the international border. The armistice agreement was signed on July 20, but its imminence was sensed earlier that month. On July 9 Ben-Gurion wrote in his diary:

> Zaim stated in a discussion with a Swiss journalist that he wants peace with us. In my opinion we should hold on to this statement. The very fact that Zaim is ready to accept a cease-fire that requires full withdrawal to the border proves that for some reason he wants

good relations with us. Is it because of the conflict with Iraq? Also, the interests of France—Zaim's friend—require peace between Syria and Israel. And should the cease-fire agreement between us and Syria be signed this week, as Makleff believes, it would be desirable for Sasson to go to Damascus to examine the lay of the land.[24]

A similar approach, arguing that upon the signing of the armistice agreement it would be possible to test Syria's willingness to settle in a more serious and relaxed fashion, was evident in the "guidelines to the legations" issued by Moshe Sharett on July 25:

> To the extent that matters depend on our own initiative, the possibility of direct negotiations and separate peace with Egypt should be reexamined, and we should especially concentrate on establishing contact and exploring the possibility of peace with Syria. The changes that took place in the Syrian delegation [to Lausanne] could prove helpful. In negotiations with Syria, any promise or hint of possible promise on our part of a change in the border between Palestine and Syria and along the Jordan and the lakes should be avoided. On the contrary, it should be clear to the other side that under no circumstances can such a change be contemplated. On the other hand, the Syrian delegation should be encouraged to think about a large-scale absorption of refugees that would be combined with Syria's own rehabilitation and the possibility of financial and technical aid by us for the implementation of this scheme.[25]

On August 6 Eliyahu Sasson began acting according to his government's new line toward Syria. From Lausanne he sent a letter to Muhsin Barazi proposing that "direct and informal" talks be opened with Israel. He also suggested three alternative venues—the dispatching of a Syrian emissary to Europe, a meeting on the border, or a trip by himself to Damascus.[26] But this initiative came too late, not merely because Zaim and Barazi were killed eight days later, but also because Zaim had lost any real enthusiasm for a separate settlement with Israel. Zaim had continued to speak to American and French diplomats and to UN mediators about his desire for a settlement with Israel, but he now sounded more reserved and was clearly in no hurry.[27] Hardly less important was the fact that the U.S. government had changed its own attitude. Now that the signing of an armistice agreement had removed the immediate danger of renewed hostilities, the State Department was no longer eager for a Syrian–Israeli summit. Washington now gave priority to the Lausanne Conference. On July 26 the State Department explained to McDonald, in Tel Aviv, that it understood that Ben-Gurion was now interested in meeting Zaim but that the United States preferred the "Lausanne format." A few days earlier the U.S. legation in Damascus had asked Washington what it was that Damascus should do specifically in order to advance a solution to the refugee problem. The answer was: "It will be of considerable value if Zaim would authorize Syrian delegation [to Lausanne] inform PCC officially of its willingness cooperate in facilitating solution of refugee problem by accepting substantial number of refugees for permanent settlement Syria."[28]

The foregoing sequence raises a number of questions: What motivated Zaim to launch his far-reaching initiative vis-à-vis Israel? How could Adel Arslan, a foreign minister with no political power, have stood up to a military dictator like Husni Zaim? Why did Ben-Gurion refuse to meet Zaim, and how did Israel perceive Zaim and his initiative? And how serious and politically viable was Zaim's overture?

Zaim undoubtedly wanted to end the active conflict and confrontation with Israel following the 1948 war. For this he had several good reasons, first and foremost among them his fear of renewed fighting in the face of Israel's overwhelming military superiority. Although Zaim did tell Keeley that he was not worried by the prospect of fighting the IDF, he must have realized that he could not stand up to the Israelis when all the other Arab states had signed armistice agreements and the IDF's full might could be directed against the Syrian army alone. Furthermore, the army was the mainstay of Zaim's regime, and as such its primary task was to protect the regime against domestic rivals and external foes, the Hashemites in particular. During his first weeks in power Zaim was seriously interested in an ambitious program of social and economic reform, and he surely wanted to remove the Israeli issue from the top of his country's national agenda. Moreover, Zaim, was remarkably free from ideological commitments and sensibilities and so was outside the pale of

Arab nationalism. As we noted earlier, members of his age group who joined the French auxiliary troops in the Levant served as an instrument of the Mandatory government against the Arab nationalist opposition. In later years younger men joined the Troupes Spéciales with a nationalist motivation, seeking to form the nucleus of a Syrian national army. Adib al-Shishakli belonged to this group, but not so the older Zaim.

Zaim and his colleagues found themselves in a state of conflict with the patrician leaders of the Arab nationalist movement, who became the country's leaders when independence had been achieved. The latter viewed Zaim not only as a collaborator with the French but also as a social climber. He, in turn, was full of contempt for a privileged group that, as he saw it, had failed in its struggle against the French, had failed to form a stable and effective government, and had been forced to call on the army for protection against the demonstrators who had threatened to topple its regime in the early years of independence. This conflict between the two groups was further embittered by the debate over responsibility for the Palestine debacle.[29]

As a ruler, Zaim was indeed glad to break all the taboos of the Syrian Arab nationalists. He drew close to France, which had just been driven out of Syria and was still viewed by most Syrians as a hostile colonizer. He likewise improved relations with Turkey, which a decade earlier had annexed the province of Alexandretta. And shortly after taking power Zaim ratified the Tapline agreement, providing for the laying of an American oil pipeline from Saudi Arabia to Tripoli through Syrian territory, an agreement that his predecessors had found difficult to enact. Zaim was surrounded by other army officers from a minority background (the French had deliberately recruited into their auxiliary forces a disproportionate number of minorities), and in July he appointed Muhsin Barazi (of Kurdish extraction like himself) as prime minister.[30] Against this background it is evident that from Zaim's personal perspective the conflict with Israel could be terminated with a reasonable compromise.

In early March 1949, on the eve of his coup, Zaim, in his preparatory talks with the U.S. diplomats (the importance of which will be clarified later) stated that he intended to offer Israel more reasonable demands than those presented by the civilian politicians. He was especially adamant about his demand for modification of the border line between Syria and Israel, insisting that it run through Lake Tiberias. Zaim's insistence on this matter is explained in the memoirs of the civilian prime minister ousted by his coup, Khaled al-Azm. Al-Azm admitted that it was his regime that had accepted the principle of armistice negotiations with Israel, but he pointed a barb at Zaim by claiming that his own government had stood firm on the principle of holding on to the positions held by the Syrian army at the end of fighting and shifting the border line to the middle of Lake Tiberias. This is an extended illustration of the mechanism of political overbidding (*muzayada*), about which al-Azm himself complained elsewhere in his memoirs. In this and other cases, Arab politicians sought to raise their political stock by portraying themselves as advocates of a political position more radical and pure than that of their competitors. The practical outcome of these dynamics was a radicalization of the Arab side's position and conduct.[31]

These all were important considerations, but Zaim's reform and economic development plans and his bold initiative vis-à-vis Israel cannot be understood except in the context of a less familiar dimension of his regime—his close relationship with the United States.

## Husni Zaim and the United States

On August 18, 1949, four days after Zaim's downfall and death, the *New York Times*'s correspondent, Albion Ross, filed a story from Damascus entitled "End of Zayim Rule Perils Peace Plan." Probably after having been briefed by a member of the U.S. legation in Damascus, Ross wrote that "the deaths of President Husni Zayim and Premier Mohsen el-Barazi and the apparent restoration of Republican government in Syria have, ironically, wrecked the basis of existing plans for a solution of the Palestine problem and the restoration of peace in the Middle East."[32]

The tension between the dictatorial character of Zaim's regime and his willingness to pursue policies that the United States favored, alluded to in the article's first paragraph, was the thesis of the article. Ross explained that the regime as represented by Prime Minister Barazi was willing to go a long way in settling Palestinian refugees in Syria with American and international support and that Syria was about to take the initiative at the Lausanne Conference and in the Arab League's Political Committee in order to have the other Arab states endorse that plan. In a similar vein, Zaim's regime had been "pushing hard a program of cooperation with Turkey and the formation of some sort of a Middle Eastern defense system based on alliance with the Western powers." But, wrote Ross, Americans and other Westerners were aware and supportive of Barazi's policies, "while in principle they could not approve the circumstance that its rapid realization was based on the existence of a dictatorship." The impression now is that there was little chance that the program could have been carried out effectively and rapidly under a genuinely democratic government.

Whoever thought that Sami al-Hinawi's coup signified a return to a genuine parliamentary regime did not understand the political realities of Syria, but the arguments that Ross used in his story indicate that in addition to his conversation with Muhsin el-Barazi in July,[33] he must have spent time with a member, or members, of the U.S. legation.

Some twenty years later, in 1969, a former Central Intelligence Agency (CIA) agent in the Middle East, Miles Copeland, published *The Game of Nations*[34] in which he described the attempts made by the American intelligence community in the late 1940s and early 1950s to reshape the politics of Egypt and Syria. Copeland, who had served in the American legation in Damascus, explained that the United States was worried that the narrow-mindedness of Syria's traditional ruling elite and its refusal to permit any social, economic, and political reforms were bound to end in a volcanic eruption that would put the radical elements in power and play into the Soviet Union's hands. Having failed in their efforts to generate change in Syrian politics by intervening in the 1947 election, Copeland tells us, a "political action task force" operating out of the U.S. legation in Damascus under Major Stephen Meade, the assistant military attaché, set to work. Meade established contact with Husni Zaim, then the chief of the General Staff of the Syrian army, brought up the idea of a coup, and advised him on the complex preparations for its execution.[35]

As Copeland describes it, there were strong disagreements in the U.S. mission in Damascus over encouraging a military dictatorship, even a temporary one. One young diplomat, Deane Hinton, was vehemently opposed to the idea, whereas Keeley and the State Department came to accept it but "without enthusiasm." Keeley believed that after a brief transitional period of military dictatorship Syria could return to the path of democracy and reform. But the truth of the matter, according to Copeland, was that Zaim had made it clear to the Americans that he was not aiming at an early restoration of democracy. Instead, the four main elements of his program were (1) to put the corrupt politicians in jail, (2) to reorganize the government to be more efficient, (3) to institute much needed social and economic reforms, and (4) to "do something constructive about the Arab–Israel problem."[36]

Although the somewhat pretentious framework into which Copeland fits his story and his condescending and facile tone tended at first to undermine his credibility, the documents now available in the American diplomatic archives at least partially support his version. These documents show that Major Stephen Meade and his superior officer, Colonel Lawrence Mitchell, knew in advance of Zaim's plans and that Major Meade continued to meet with Zaim after the coup and had discussions with him in an atmosphere of intimacy and familiarity not typical of talks between a country's ruler and head of state and an assistant military attaché, albeit of a superpower. In these conversations, issues were raised that were not being discussed between Zaim and Keeley who, in fact, used Meade as a vehicle for transmitting messages to Zaim. He thus asked him to make it clear to Zaim that the United States wanted him to act with moderation toward Lebanon. On another occasion Meade simply asked Zaim for Syria's order of battle.[37]

## Zaim's Conversations with Meade

During the weeks that preceded his coup, Zaim met at least six times with Meade and briefed him in great detail about his plans. He also advised the British military attaché (rather cryptically) of his plans and apparently did the same with the French military attaché.[38] In turn, Meade briefed Mitchell and G2 headquarters about his conversations with Zaim. Meade's comprehensive account of his discussions with Zaim on March 3 and 7 clearly shows that Zaim was willing to go to great length to obtain (direct or indirect) American support for his coup and even more so for his future regime and policies. Given the fact that reliable records of precoup conversations between Arab army officers and Western diplomats are rare, as well as the extraordinary nature of Zaim's statements and their relevance to our subject, it seems worthwhile to examine this document quite carefully.

Zaim began by stressing the secret nature of his statements but asked that they nevertheless be communicated to the U.S. government. He explained that "he wants to see his country militarily allied with the United States" and proceeded to elaborate on the advantages to the United States that such an "alliance" with his regime and the United States' provision of "military aid" to Syria were bound to produce. "A strong and stable government," in his words a "dictatorship," would give the United States "a reliable and permanent authority with whom to deal in Syria." Moreover, the "United States' approval of his plan and subsequent action in accordance therewith would result in Turkey's greater strength, a potential holding force against Russian aggression, and the immediate suppression of the Communist fifth column in Syria."

Zaim then outlined a four-phase plan of action: First, a "seizure of power in Syria that he will ensure." Zaim planned to take advantage of the unrest and disturbances in his country and take over smoothly, preferably in response to the government's own request. He then thought of installing "a selected political figure" as head of state while exercising real power from the Ministry of Defense. Far from being a passive listener to all of this, Meade asked him about his choice for his own replacement as army commander and about the reaction Zaim expected from the gendarmerie's commander. "Concomitant with the execution of the first phase would be a general Communist round-up and internment, together with 'weak' politicians in desert concentration camps for which he has already made plans." At this point Zaim and Meade exchanged information "regarding Communist personalities and their activities," and Mitchell, impressed that Zaim was so well informed, made sure that Zaim would take "the necessary precautions for his personal safety at all times."

"Second and closely following the completion of his first phase Zaim hopes to receive U.S. aid in the form of military material." Zaim listed his priorities and explained the importance of such prospective aid's arriving during his tenure of power (and not earlier).

"The third phase envisages U.S. technical and training missions, particularly in the fields of aviation and armor."

The fourth phase would include the mobilization of the entire country under military supervision, expansion of the army, and the enforcement of social reforms. Citing Kemal Ataturk as his model, Zaim enumerated the reforms he had in mind: breaking the existing "feudal power" of the tribal chiefs and landowners, instituting agrarian reforms, modernizing the medical and judicial systems, and in a more general way, "educating" and "disciplining" the population. Zaim "claimed that there is only one way to start the Syrian people along the road to progress and democracy and that is with the whip, adding emphasis to this statement by striking the desk with his riding crop." Zaim felt that "three to five years will be required to obtain satisfactory results from his program, and following this he plans a gradual lessening of the regimentation of the population over a ten-year period." He contended that "he would be able to develop, with the aforementioned aid and missions, an effective fighting force of 40,000 within one to one and a half years' time." As it turned out, the American military advisers were supposed to replace a group of former German and Austrian army officers who had arrived in Syria after World War II.

Finally, Zaim and Meade discussed Syria's relationship with Israel. Meade had been authorized by the U.S. chief of mission in Damascus to brief Zaim on the state of the Israeli–Lebanese armistice negotiations. Zaim was critical of his own government's approach to Syria's eventual negotiations with Israel. The president and the prime minister, he complained, were going to demand Galilee. His own idea was "to permit the Israelis to keep Galilee, to cede the recently occupied Mishmar Hayarden salient, but to demand that the present frontier be modified to give Syria all territory on the east bank of Lake Tiberias from El-Kursi to Samakh." He would also demand that Lake Tiberias be internationalized: the eastern half to Syria and the western half to Israel. But he felt that such revisions would result in a peaceful future between Syria and Israel.

The U.S. Foreign Service's bureaucratic procedures required that the reporting officer's account be concluded with his own evaluation and comment. Meade's analysis was that "although unscrupulous, bombastic and a complete egoist, it must be admitted that he [Zaim] has a strong personality, unlimited ambition and the backing of the Syrian army. If the ever-present element of fate happens to be in his favor, Zaim may realize his desire to be dictator in Syria."[39] Meade added that Zaim's confidence in him "was at least partially induced through recent efforts by Emir Farid Schehab, Director of Lebanese Sûreté, with whom I have worked for the past two years and who knows Zaim intimately."

Meade and Zaim had another meeting on March 14, and this time Zaim requested specifically that U.S. agents "provoke and abet" internal disturbances "essential for coup d'état" or that U.S. funds be given him for this purpose.[40] There is no evidence that the United States supported Zaim in his coup. It was not really necessary. But Meade's reports clearly indicate that he made no effort to dissuade Zaim but, rather, gave him every reason to believe that the United States was sympathetic to his ideas.

The similarity between the four-phase plan reported by Meade and the four points enumerated by Copeland is readily apparent and enhances the latter's credibility. But it is difficult to accept Copeland's version in full and thus to believe that Meade's encouragement was necessary to prompt Zaim to stage a coup when, since 1946, there had been persistent reports of Zaim's intention to seize power, first in conjunction with Abdullah and later unrelated to the Greater Syria plan.[41] Nor do Zaim's conversations with Meade in early March point in this direction, unless one assumes that Zaim maintained a whole network of parallel contacts and spoke differently with his various contacts.

## Zaim's Other U.S. Contacts

This network of contacts could have included the State Department and its representatives in the Damascus legation, military attachés and members of the intelligence community, and oil executives. The military attaché's dispatches from Damascus in March 1949 clearly point to the centrality of the oil issue in American–Syrian relations at that time and to the effort to mobilize the political system to ratify the Tapline agreement and to neutralize the opposition to it by nationalist opinion. On the basis of the available source material, it is difficult to reconstruct the relationship among the U.S. legation, the American intelligence community, the oil companies, and the Syrian army's officer corps, but a memorandum written later in 1949 by Colonel Mitchell to the U.S. minister, Keeley, offers a glimpse into the unorthodox relationship between Tapline and some of the Syrian officers. On November 1, 1949, Mitchell told Keeley:

> Last evening I called on Lt. Colonel Mohamed Nasser, G3, Syrian Army by prior appointment, to arrange the conduct of official business. . . . Colonel Nasser is my regularly assigned contact for the negotiation of military business. Colonel Nasser was most cordial. The office was filled with other officers, also Mr. Ashley of Tapline, and it was impossible for me to obtain confidential information.[42]

In fact, Zaim ratified the Tapline agreement shortly after seizing power.[43]

The Syrian army officers probably discussed with Tapline's personnel issues of oil and oil pipelines, but it appears that regarding bilateral Syrian–American questions and Arab–Israeli affairs, Zaim dealt with the United States through two parallel channels—Keeley and the State Department on the one hand and the intelligence community on the other. Nonetheless, it is difficult on the basis of the available evidence to establish precisely how the two channels functioned and the degree of coordination between them. And so we also do not know to what extent Zaim's ideas were originally his or whether at least some of them had been planted through the "parallel channel" with or without the State Department's knowledge. More specifically, we do not know whether Zaim's offer to Keeley on April 28, as reported by the latter, to settle 250,000 Palestinian refugees in Syria in return for American aid was the Syrian ruler's idea or whether it had been suggested by his American contacts and was subsequently shifted, in the conversation with Keeley, to a formal level. Copeland asserted that Zaim promised on the eve of his coup to "do something constructive" about the Arab–Israeli problem, which "neutralized any inclination the Department might have had to give us explicit instructions to lay off."[44]

In any case, in Washington's relationship with Zaim, two central themes of the United States' Middle Eastern policy coalesced: the effort to preempt domestic upheavals by encouraging reforms and the effort to settle the Arab-Israeli conflict. Both efforts derived from the underlying fear that instability in the Middle East would play into the Soviet Union's drive to acquire a presence and influence in the region. Washington's endeavors to persuade Syria to accept a political solution to the conflict with Israel and, more concretely, to join in the armistice negotiations had predated Zaim's coup. Thus, in a conversation with Zaim's successor, President Shukri al-Quwatli, and Prime Minister Khaled al-Azm, Keeley acknowledged that "given evidence of Syrian goodwill of which [the] Palestine settlement [was the] first step, it was my personal belief that the United States would increasingly give Syria evidence of its friendship."[45]

From this perspective, Zaim displayed an immense amount of goodwill. Although the principle of opening armistice negotiations with Israel had been established by his predecessors, he not only continued that policy but also proposed to advance the negotiations to a compromise settlement. Furthermore, his willingness to discuss the settlement of 250,000 Palestinian refugees in Syria gave new life to the ''McGhee plan''—the State Department's main effort to resolve the Arab–Israeli conflict in the spring of 1949. The McGhee plan called for about half of the Palestinian refugees to be resettled in the Arab states and for the other half, or at least 200,000, to be taken in by Israel and for this scheme to be part of an impressive regional development project. Then, according to this plan, a political solution would be achieved at the Lausanne Conference.[46] In addition, the massive American aid package that would accompany the resettlement effort in Syria would not merely make it more palatable to public opinion but would also generate economic activities and development schemes and give substance to the model presumably represented by Zaim—an autocratic reformer improving the lot of his country with American support. The two pillars of U.S. policy in the region would thus become mutually supporting and would ensure the policy's success.

The prospect of success on such a large scale aroused among the American diplomats an urgency and an eagerness that are reflected in their own dispatches,[47] as well as in more sober reports by their British colleagues. When the British Foreign Office found out that the Americans had told the Syrians about their intention to raise $200 million for the project (a huge sum of money in 1949), it was remarked in London ''that the State Department and the U.S. Minister in Damascus were exerting heavy pressure on the Syrians with regard to the resettlement of the Palestinian refugees to the point of risking the prospects of their own plan.''[48]

The degree to which Zaim's agreement to cooperate was seen as essential to the State Department's larger plans is evidenced by the telegram from Washington to Keeley on May 13, 1949. Secretary of State Dean Acheson wrote:

> Dept notes with interest marked progress you report re Zaim's attitude resettlement Arab refugees. This is first concrete evidence Syrian willingness take large number refugees and is particular im-

portance since Syria only Arab country except already willing Trans-jordan which can assimilate such number within reasonable limit. If this opportunity can be exploited back of refugee problem can be broken. You should take early opportunity discuss matter further with Zaim giving appropriate emphasis his expression of willingness accept quarter million refugees, which Dept regards as humane and statesmanlike contribution to solution this problem. Express hope Zaim will use his influence with other Arab states adopt similarly constructive attitude towards problem, within limits their absorptive capacity, in order assist PCC in permanent liquidation problem. Emphasize steps USA is taking to persuade Israel make appropriate concessions re repatriation.[49]

In Zaim's mind, in any event, there was a clear linkage between his willingness to resettle the Palestinian refugees and the expectation of vast American aid. But when time went by and nothing happened, Zaim met with Keeley on July 14 and warned him of the dangers inherent in a continued stalemate. He explained that he himself "could not openly take [the] initiative because powerful opposition would attack him for selling out to [the] Jews and their backers." But Zaim pledged his "wholehearted cooperation if the United States would take [the] lead." Later in their conversation, Zaim spoke of "numerous economic development projects which Syria is anxious to implement" and "pleaded for necessary funds and technical assistance promptly."[50] Later, when time was running out, Zaim apparently lost hope of obtaining American financial aid in this fashion and proposed a different kind of linkage. During the farewell visit paid to him by Major Meade, Zaim told his visitor that he was planning to ask the United States for a loan of $100 million to be used strictly for his economic and social program. Meade wrote, "Zaim asked me to have our government make a formal request for air bases in Syria, which request he promised he would grant."[51]

## Husni Zaim and Adel Arslan

As we have already seen, the attempt to promote Syrian–Israeli negotiations in late May and early June had failed. When this issue was raised in the Syrian cabinet's meeting on May 24, Foreign Minister Adel Arslan, after announcing his refusal to meet Sharett, stated categorically that he had ordered all Foreign Ministry staff not to take part in such meetings with Israelis. Arslan left two detailed versions of this episode, in a series of articles published in the Beiruti paper *al-Hayat* in August 1949 and in his diaries cum memoirs.[52] Arslan's version can be compared with reports sent at the time by Western diplomats, and it has been, on the whole, confirmed by their accounts. Arslan, it seems, knew nothing about the ideas and initiatives raised by Zaim's emissaries in their conversations with the Israelis in April or about Zaim's discussions with Keeley in April and early May. All he knew at that time, he wrote, was that Zaim was very eager to reach an agreement with Israel and that he would make considerable concessions to that end. Arslan was particularly perturbed by Zaim's willingness to recognize Israel's borders, even implicitly (and thus to recognize Israel's legitimacy as well). According to his account, Arslan had a direct link to Colonel Fawzi Selu, a member of the Syrian delegation to the armistice talks, and extended support to Selu and to the legal adviser of the Syrian Foreign Ministry, Saleh Tarazi, against Zaim's pressures.

In the cabinet meeting on May 24, when Zaim raised the idea of a meeting between Arslan and Sharett and tried to present it as a fait accompli, Arslan indignantly refused to comply. Zaim then argued that heavy external pressure was being exerted on him and hinted that it was mostly American pressure. Arslan, who did not realize the depths of Zaim's relationship with the United States, arranged to see Keeley and learned from him that the initiative was Zaim's. But he decided not to resign, so as to be able to fight against Zaim's policy from a position of some influence. Accordingly, he asked the Saudi minister to have King Ibn Saud use his influence with the Americans to give up their plans, and he himself sent Vigier a formal letter of rejection designed to serve as a coup de grâce. And indeed, he writes, after the sixth of June, Zaim no longer raised the issue.[53]

Arslan's version of this issue raises the question as to why Zaim failed to act decisively against a reluctant foreign minister. True, he ousted him from his government in July, but in a matter of such importance to him he could have exerted heavy pressure on a minister who enjoyed status and prestige but had no real political constituents in Syria. After all, when Zaim disagreed with Michel 'Aflaq, the leader of the Ba'ath party, he did not hesitate to have him jailed and tortured until 'Aflaq signed an embarrassing statement. This question throws an interesting light on Zaim's regime and on the domestic context in which he conducted his policy toward Israel. Let us now take a brief look at Zaim's career and personality.

## A Brief Biography of Husni Zaim

Husni Zaim was born in 1889 in Aleppo to a family of Kurdish extraction. He went through the Ottoman educational system to become a junior officer in the Ottoman army and was captured by the British during the Ottoman offensive against Egypt in World War I. In 1920, after the French capture of Syria, he attended a French military college and became an officer in the Troupes Spéciales, the French auxiliary force in the Levant, and rose to the rank of colonel. In World War II Zaim chose to fight on the side of the Vichy forces against the British and the French and was sentenced by the victors to ten years in jail.

In 1946 when Syria won its independence from France, Zaim managed to become a senior officer in the Syrian army, and by lobbying among his politician friends he managed to obtain from President Shukri al-Quwatli the posts of director of internal security and commander of the army. He held these posts during the 1948 war and so was able to lead the army that clashed with civilian politicians over responsibility for the debacle. The memoirs of Syrian politicians and various diplomatic dispatches between 1946 and 1949 portray a corrupt officer in the middle of political intrigues cultivating ties with politicians inside and outside Syria. Zaim seemed to stand permanently on the thin line separating the prospect of expulsion from the army from the temptation to seize power.

Zaim seems to have been a person of many contradictions. He

radiated power and leadership but apparently was not very clever. He saw himself as a Syrian version of Ataturk, as a man who would take his country forward, but he was bogged down by his involvements and corruption and his lack of consistency and persistence, and it is not at all clear how he envisaged the country he wanted to lead. Furthermore, while oozing self-confidence he was full of anxiety and insecurity. The foreign diplomats in Damascus who evaluated him on the eve of his coup were clearly not enamored of the man who was to act in league with their governments. Major Stephen Meade depicted him "as a 'banana republic' dictator type," and Deane Hinton thought that he "did not have the competence of a French corporal."

The political establishment that Zaim overthrew in March 1949 was mostly made up of the Syrian Arab nationalist movement's veteran leaders. Between the two world wars, most of them had gathered within the loose framework of the National Bloc, but when Syria became fully independent, the bloc had already disintegrated into several parties and factions. During the 1948 war, Shukri al-Quwatli and Jamil Mardam Bey, two of the bloc's leaders, served as president and prime minister, respectively. But Mardam Bey was forced to resign following the domestic political turmoil in December 1948 and was replaced by Khaled al-Azm, scion of one of Syria's most distinguished families and an independent politician who had not been associated with the National Bloc.

The main opposition to the government from within the ruling establishment came during that period from the People's party—an Aleppo group representing that city's interests, with a fresher, commercially oriented perspective and a pro-Iraqi orientation. Outside the establishment a series of radical ideological parties and movements—the Ba'ath party, the Parti populaire syrien, the communists, the Muslim Brotherhood, and Akram Hourani's party—proclaimed their alternatives to the prevailing order.

As Zaim explained to his American contacts in early March, his original plan was not to assume the premiership but to place at the head of the government a public figure and to exercise power from the Ministry of Defense. His was the first coup in post–World War II Arab politics, and Zaim was very unsure of himself and of the policies he should pursue. His pre-coup conversations with the military attachés of all three Western powers were a manifestation of this lack of confidence. In any event, Zaim was unable to find a respectable public figure to head the government under mutually acceptable conditions.

Zaim did, at first, have the support of the People's party and some of the radical parties and movements, either because they were pleased that he was undermining their nationalist foes or because they were still hoping to promote their own reforms, unionist programs, or personal careers. But all of this was not enough to give the regime a civilian base of support or even a respectable facade. Adel Arslan was not Zaim's first choice for foreign minister, but his role was, anyway, to give the regime (albeit as a minister and not as prime minister) at least some political legitimacy. By June, Zaim had concluded that his regime's political structure was inadequate, and so in July he made two major changes: He had himself elected president by a referendum and entrusted Muhsin al-Barazi (not to be confused with Husni al-Barazi) with the formation of a new government. Husni al-Barazi was a second-tier nationalist politician, from an Arab–Kurdish family in Hama, who had served as a minister in several earlier governments and had been considered close to Quwatli and Mardam Bey. Because of this he was jailed briefly by Zaim in the aftermath of his coup but, in a swift and remarkable about-face, became his confidant and special emissary to the Arab world. Al-Barazi was believed to have great influence over Zaim and even was called by one observer "the evil genius" of Zaim's regime.

As Zaim drew further away from the Hashemites and closer to the Egyptian–Saudi axis, the gap between him and the People's party grew wider. And as the ethos of reform that seemed to have marked his early days in power dissipated, Zaim became, instead of a Syrian Ataturk, an apparently corrupt, megalomaniac, and volatile dictator. Although he lost the support of the radical ideological parties, most crucial was the estrangement of the younger officers led by Adib al-Shishakli, who staged the August 14 countercoup under the direction of Colonel Sami Hinawi.[54]

It is against this backdrop that Adel Arslan was able to stand up to Zaim on an issue that he considered important. Arslan came from a princely Lebanese–Druze family and, like his more famous brother Shakib, embraced Sunni Islam and became a prominent leader of the Arab nationalist movement in the interwar period. For Zaim, Arslan was a civilian and political "fig leaf." Arslan did not have a political base in Syria, but he did have a good public and political reputation and a network of political connections in the Arab world. (When Zaim had a falling-out with the Ba'ath party's leader, he had him jailed and tortured.) Michael 'Aflaq in 1949 was a practically anonymous leader of a new and weak political movement and Zaim assumed that he was free to treat him as he wished, but Arslan enjoyed a considerable degree of immunity. Furthermore, as he himself tells it, Arslan had a direct relationship with Fawzi Selu and apparently with other army officers as well, thus reinforcing his position in the regime. Therefore, although Arslan could not prevent Zaim from pursuing an Israeli policy that he opposed, he could withdraw his cooperation and show him the degree of resistance he should expect from the Arab nationalists.

## Israel and Husni Zaim

Israel's response to Husni Zaim's initiatives was puzzling in 1949, and it still raises questions, albeit different ones. As we saw, the State Department, other American officials, and even Abba Eban could not understand why Ben-Gurion refused to meet with Zaim and at least put to the test his willingness to conclude an agreement with Israel. Sharett, however, had consented to meet Zaim, but he seemed to be taking his time, and when Arslan refused to see Sharett, Sharett's angry response focused, strangely, on matters of status and procedure. Because the Israeli Foreign Ministry was aware of the UN and U.S. criticism of Israel's conduct in this matter, it accordingly prepared a background paper to refute it.

On May 2, 1949, Moshe Sharett presented the Knesset's Foreign and Security Affairs Committee with a survey of Israel's political position:

> As has been published we stated that we will not negotiate with Syria until an armistice has been signed. We decided not to sign an armistice agreement with Syria unless it evacuates the strip of [Mandatory] Palestine's territory that it is presently holding. The territory's importance does not derive from its size, which in fact is negligible. Rather, what is at stake is the water's edge, the shore of Lake Tiberias, the East Bank of the Jordan River, and Mey Marom. We regard this as Syria's expressing its intention to adjust the border, and we are opposed to it for this reason. We want to keep these waters within the state's territory and not to make Syria a partner. . . . Our statement creates a certain pressure on Syria and makes it in advance responsible for the failure of the Lausanne discussions.[55]

Sharett stated also that for Israel, peace was desirable with Egypt and "likewise with Lebanon and possibly with Syria, bearing in mind the reservations concerning the new regime."[56]

Some three weeks later, on May 25, Sharett addressed a forum composed of his ministry's department heads. When he reached the subject of Syria, he commented:

> A difficult problem with regard to which we should clarify our thinking is Syria. We will obviously not agree that any part of [Mandatory] Palestine be given to Syria, as control of the water sources is at stake. There was a proposal by Zaim to meet, but that meeting did not materialize. He thought that the prime minister or at least I would come. We sent distinguished persons, Shiloah and Yadin, but he considered them below his own rank and so sent people without standing, and the meeting did not take place, of course.
>
> In the meantime General Riley, whom we have no reason to distrust, has communicated to us that Zaim is willing to discuss the absorption of 300,000 refugees into Syria. If it is true, it is purely to Zaim's credit. It would mean that he has greater vision than the others do, is more daring, and understands the advantages that may accrue to him from it—the income for the state and the fact that everybody could do well on these monies. . . .

> For us this is something tremendous; it means that he is willing
> to absorb three times the number of refugees who are currently in
> Syria and Lebanon. In any event, if there is a state prepared for
> something of this nature, the [unified Arab] front will be broken. I
> think it is worth our while to meet with Zaim, particularly in order
> to clarify the issue of refugee absorption.[57]

If Sharett really considered Zaim's initiatives "tremendous,"
regarded him as "more daring" than the others, and attributed to
him "greater vision," his policy lagged behind his analysis. In this
case it was not sufficient to observe that "it would be worth our
while to meet with him." The same Israel that conceived the idea
of annexing Gaza in order to cope with the pressures anticipated in
Lausanne could have taken much greater advantage of the opening
provided by Husni Zaim, at least in tactical terms. How, then, can
Israel's policy toward Husni Zaim be explained?

Part of the explanation is to be found in Ben-Gurion's and Sharett's own statements. They gave priority to obtaining an armistice
on the basis of the international frontier and thought, correctly, that
Zaim wanted to adjust the border, particularly in the sensitive area
of Lake Tiberias and the Jordan River. The Israeli leaders knew that
the lake's basin was the key to all of Israel's future national irrigation
schemes and to the development of the Negev and so were not willing
to give up full Israeli control of and sovereignty over the lake. The
Israelis found out from Riley that the United States in fact supported
Zaim's demand for an armistice not based on the international border
line, in recognition of his goodwill, and estimated, again correctly,
that the failure of a prospective meeting with Zaim would be blamed
on Israel. The importance of these considerations to Ben-Gurion's
position in April and May 1949 is revealed by the fact that in July,
when the armistice agreement was about to be signed on the basis
of full Syrian evacuation, Ben-Gurion changed his mind and wanted
a meeting and negotiations with Husni Zaim after all.

The fluid state of Syrian policies at the time, the uncertainty
regarding the stability of the new regime, and the new phenomenon
of military coups and regimes and questions regarding Zaim himself
all contributed to Israel's hesitation. On April 2, immediately after

Zaim's coup, Ben-Gurion told the American consul in Jerusalem that "Israel must always ask itself whether the representatives of an Arab state really represent their country. Farouk is apparently Egypt, but who is Zaim?"[58]

Incensed by the cancellation of Zaim's meeting with him in May, Sharett expressed his disdain for a military dictatorship that he regarded as illegitimate. In his presentation to the department heads in his ministry, Sharett alluded to his suspicion that Zaim expected to profit personally from the forthcoming American aid ("everybody could do well on these monies"). In early April 1949 Israel had information that Zaim was in league with Abdullah and more reliable information that Abdullah was considering taking advantage of the Syrian coup in order to try to seize control in Damascus. Some in Israel argued that it would be to their country's advantage to channel the Jordanian king's ambitions northward. And those who did not agree could assume that a period of change and uncertainty lay ahead for Syria.

## The Reasons for Israel's Hesitation

It can be assumed the Israeli leadership did not take Zaim seriously but viewed him as an ambitious adventurer. Nonetheless, despite the extent of the Israeli archives, I could not find an explicit expression of such a view. Rather, my suspicion that this was the Israeli leadership's view of Zaim is based on two facts.

First, in 1948 Israel's intelligence services maintained at least an indirect contact with Husni Zaim and viewed him as a candidate for staging a coup in Syria aided by Israel and designed to promote Israel's aims. Some writers have argued that there was a direct relationship between Husni Zaim and Israeli intelligence agents. Although this cannot be proved, there is reliable evidence that when the Israeli Foreign Ministry's Middle East Department contemplated in the summer of 1948 a coup in Syria that would take it out of the war, they regarded Zaim as the chief candidate to lead it.

Behind that scheme was the fear that the war might drag on without a definitive terminal point and that Israel might be worn out by the protracted effort. On September 21, 1948, Ezra Danin wrote to Tuvia Arazi in Paris:

> Without knowing exactly what you had initiated regarding a rebellion-revolution in Syria, we have given it a lot of thought here as the only means of ending the war here and opening a way for peace. The assumption was that only if "a respectable show were held" in one of the Arab countries that would attract the attention of the Arabs and divert it away from Israel could we make some progress toward ordinary peace relations. The assumption is that the rebellious government would need our aid and support, would recognize us, and would cooperate with us. . . . Last week we raised this problem for discussion with the foreign minister. We assumed that for the preliminary exploration we may need ten thousand pounds, for the preliminary examination a hundred thousand pounds, and for execution a sum of over five hundred thousand pounds. . . .
>
> We emphasized this estimate of ours because our cause is in a bind: Breaking the cease-fire and continuing the war by one of the parties out of the war will not bring us to either decision or solution; on the other hand, the discussions of peace proceed very slowly and do not promise a near solution visible on our misty horizon.

Sharett responded with a great deal of skepticism. He did not believe in political changes initiated from the outside but, instead, in "self [authentic] action" and did not think that even much less money could be allocated to "explorations and examinations." But he "was not opposed and even suggested that we check what is at stake concretely, listen to what the Druzes or others propose, and discuss it again when we have understood the real intentions." Danin then suggested to Arazi that he "get Josh [Palmon] interested in this proposal so that he too could try to confirm it. After all, he was the last to have explored this area and had even had some success."[59]

Arazi and Palmon operated vis-à-vis Syria through a number of channels. At least some of their activities were conducted through middlemen who promised "to deliver" army officers, politicians, tribes, and minority communities that would carry out the actual operation. That is, not every name mentioned in their correspondence necessarily had a direct contact with the Israelis. In August 1948 Danin managed, after strenuous effort, to meet with Ben-Gurion and told him in detail about the Middle East Department's plans to stage a coup in Syria and to encourage Palestinian autonomy as an alternative to Abdullah's rule. But Ben-Gurion dismissed these ideas and stated that "we will not enter into new adventures."[60] On November 2 Shimoni wrote to Arazi in Paris that

> in the meantime I have received your telegram, informing me that you have not spoken to Moshe (Sharett) about the proposal to invite Husayn Zaim [sic] and Husayn Barazi [sic]. In fact our suggestion that you raise it with Moshe was made in a tone of bitter irony: We have no doubt that Moshe will not agree to invite these men and will not be in a position to allocate the appropriate budget for such an operation. Our intention . . . was to tell you: Because you know that Moshe rejected all our broad and practical plans regarding Syria and the Druzes, how is it that you ask us whether you should invite these two persons to Paris?[61]

The fact that Shimoni spoke in his letter about Husni Zaim and Muhsin Barazi (both given names were given incorrectly), who were of Kurdish descent, reinforces the assumption that this was an attempt to take advantage of a connection established in 1948 between Sasson and Palmon and a group of Kurdish activists in Paris through the Israeli diplomat Maurice Fischer. Fischer had served during World War II with French intelligence in the Levant and had at that time cultivated contacts with various groups, some of which he introduced to Israel's Foreign Ministry and intelligence community. It thus seems that the Kurdish activists told their Israeli contacts in 1948 that they could persuade Husni Zaim to stage a coup in Syria.

In the Israeli correspondence and other records from the spring of 1949 available in the archives, this episode is not mentioned. But it stands to reason that those involved in it in the summer of 1948, who continued to hold senior positions in Israel's Foreign Ministry and intelligence community in 1949, made sure to tell or remind their superiors soon after Zaim's coup that less than a year earlier Syria's new ruler had been a candidate to stage a coup in Syria with Israel's support and financial aid. As we shall see, the Israeli connection was not mentioned in the Foreign Ministry's first evaluations of Zaim's coup and regime. But this may not be significant, because in the Israeli system, as in other foreign offices and intelligence services, there was a clear distinction between operations and evaluations.

The Israeli Foreign Ministry's archive contains an interesting illustration of the ministry's ambivalent attitude toward those Arab politicians who had accepted financial aid from Israel in return for their cooperation. In September 1951 Walter Eytan wrote to Tuvia Arazi, who was then stationed in the Israeli legation in Ankara. Arazi had earlier written to Eytan about a Syrian politician who had taken money from Israel in the late 1940s and had apparently offered his services again. Eytan responded:

> Our general attitude toward the specific question that you raise . . .
> as well as other similar requests transmitted every so often is more
> or less the following: As a general rule we have no great confidence
> in the kind of person who shows up and says that in return for a
> thousand pounds sterling he will stage a coup in an Arab state and
> will put in power a government that will make a settlement with
> Israel. At the same time, we must pursue some Arab policy, and it
> is clear that we must take risks, including financial risks, and spend
> money quite lavishly, even if it is apparent that the prospects of
> success are poor and the money might be lost. It is a matter of cast
> thine bread upon the waters.[62]

Second, after his rise to power and at the same time as his political initiative toward Israel, Zaim and his men also made other moves that must have puzzled the Israelis. We mentioned earlier Yadin's description of the far-reaching and politically unrealistic proposals made by Zaim's officers to their Israeli contacts regarding joint hegemony in the Middle East. But these were not the only proposals they made. According to the authoritative and detailed testimony of Major Itzhak Spector, who was a member of the Israeli delegation to the armistice talks, during one of these meetings, Spector was approached by Colonel Muhammad Nasser[63] who said that with the permission of Husni Zaim he had proposed assassinating Ben-Gurion for "millions." Nasser promised to provide weapons and "everything you may want, including [Syrian] people who will be loyal to you.'' Spector reported this to General Mordechai Makleff, who ordered him to keep silent and said that he himself would report this to Yadin. Following a conversation with Yadin, Makleff ordered Spector to tell Nasser that Yadin too ''was in the business'' and that he belonged to ''our gang.'' Spector delivered the message, and in order to prove to Spector how serious ''the business'' was, Nasser told him that he was ''willing to meet on your territory'' at the Shulamit Hotel in the small town of Rosh Pina with Makleff, Yadin, and Spector. An agreement to meet was reached in principle, and the contact continued for months. One Saturday when Spector was home on leave, Nasser sent Makleff a note saying that ''if you want to meet today, I have final instructions from Husni Zaim.'' Nasser asked that Spector take him over to Israeli territory. But because Spector could not be found, his deputy was sent instead and brought Nasser in an armored car to the military camp in Mahanayim. On the next day Makleff briefed Spector. According to Makleff, Nasser repeated his detailed proposal, and as Makleff told Spector, ''You missed the high point of your life.''[64]

Muhammad Nasser was one of the brigade commanders who took part in Zaim's coup and was considered a key figure in his regime. He survived Zaim's downfall and after Hinawi's coup was appointed head of operations on the Syrian army's General Staff. He has already been mentioned as the Syrian contact of the American military attaché Lawrence Mitchell, in November 1949. In this case there is no doubt that the proposed assassination of Ben-Gurion was reported, albeit indirectly, to Ben-Gurion himself. On April 27 Ben-Gurion noted in his diary that Makleff had told him that the Syrian officer ''proposed to him to expel the government and let the army take power, as in the case with them, to which Makleff responded, you had Quwatli but we have Ben-Gurion.'' The text of the diary entry is somewhat puzzling, in that this sentence was inserted later, but in any case it is certain that at least the gist of the story was brought to Ben-Gurion's attention.[65]

A similar though far less dramatic effect must have been created in the latter half of June 1949, by the visit to Israel of Max Wolf, the emissary of the president of the International Red Cross. On June 24 Wolf met with the American ambassador James McDonald and told him, "as someone unfolding a melodrama," of a statement attributed to Husni Zaim a short time after seizing power that "everything could be settled between Syria and Israel provided that Colonel Zaim's cousin, Ihsan Kamel Maz, be returned to Damascus." According to the Red Cross's information, Maz was captured by the Israelis in May 1948, was wounded, was treated in a hospital in Haifa, and had since disappeared. The Israeli authorities had not responded to the Red Cross's queries in this matter. McDonald passed the story on to General William Riley, who must have raised the question with the Israelis.[66]

It is difficult to gauge the impact of these episodes on Israel's view of Husni Zaim and his regime, but the material available in the Israeli archives enables us to reconstruct several aspects of Israel's perception of the changes occurring in Syria during the spring of 1949.

First, we should stress that throughout Zaim's tenure of power, the Israelis failed to understand his relationship with the United States. They knew that the United States was interested in Syria and had good relations with Husni Zaim but did not perceive the special bond between the U.S. government and the Syrian dictator. As the Israelis saw it, France was the principal external supporter of Syria's new military regime.

In the immediate aftermath of Zaim's coup d'état, Eliyahu Sasson, who was then out of the country, assumed that it had been inspired by Abdullah, to promote his Greater Syrian plan, and that, in line with his general outlook on the region's politics, the changes in Syria were the result of yet another British design. On April 4 Sasson wired Sharett, who was then in New York, that he had had an exchange of telegrams with Eytan regarding the significance of Husni Zaim's coup. Eytan had told Sasson that the "indications that the Syrian coup had been strongly supported by Meir [Abdullah's code name] but not necessarily by the British may be a step on road to greater Syria."

To this and to Eytan's statements that if Bunche recognized the

new regime, Israel would have no other choice but to enter into
armistice negotiations with Syria, Sasson answered:

Any strengthening of the Husni Zaim regime would have the following consequences: (1) It would promote a union of Iraq, Transjordan, Syria, and Lebanon; (2) it would lead Egypt and Lebanon
to sign defense and economic treaties with Britain; and (3) it would
drag out the conflict between Israel and the Arab world and dis-
courage real peace and sincere collaboration.[67]

Sasson's conclusion was undoubtedly reinforced by Walter
Eytan's report on his trip back, early in the morning of March 31,
from Shuneh, where he had met with Abdullah. In the car Abdullah
al-Tal told him that he was about to depart for Damascus to transmit
the king's good wishes to Husni Zaim. As he told it, the king was
to decide within the next two or three days whether to try to implement his plans. Al-Tal raised the possibility of Israel's helping Abdullah in this matter and asked what Israel would do if Abdullah sent
his army north and exposed himself to the danger of an Israeli attack.
Al-Tal was quite specific and explained that Abdullah planned to
move to Damascus while Prince Talal would remain in Amman as
the prince of Transjordan. Furthermore, al-Tal "hinted that our air
force might play a useful part. Nothing would be easier than to paint
our aircraft with the colors and markings of Transjordan." Eytan
and Shiloah replied that "Israel would not interfere."[68]

Ben-Gurion, like Sasson, tended to view Britain's long arm behind many developments in the Middle East and thus noted in his
diary on April 3 that he believed that Zaim's coup had been organized
by Britain:

We are informed from Paris that the coup in Syria is a British product
General [Edward] Spears had arrived in Damascus two weeks ago.
British agents bought the support of the Druze. . . . The revolution
was directed against Shukri Quwatli and Khaled al-'Azm, who had
obstructed the British. . . . Well, in Iraq, Nuri; and in Transjordan,
Abdullah; and in Syria, Spears, and Azem [Zaim]. Bevin rules the
Middle East."[69]

Ben-Gurion traced the information regarding the connections between Husni Zaim, on the one hand, and the British and Abdullah, on the other, to a report from Paris. But the French themselves were not swayed by similar rumors. The first dispatches from the French mission in Damascus after Zaim's coup did reflect France's familiar preoccupation with Britain's quest for influence in Syria but they also portrayed Zaim's coup as the result of the conflict between him and the civilian government rather than as the result of external intervention.

The first account written in the Israeli Foreign Ministry, by Shmuel Ya'ari of the Middle East Department's Syrian desk, was quite perceptive. On March 29 Ya'ari issued a preliminary evaluation stating that "the coup that took place in Syria at the dawn of 29.3 has a distinctive military character like the Bakr–Sidqi revolution in Iraq in the 1930s." Ya'ari determined that Zaim was not connected to the large opposition People's party and that there was no reason to doubt his statement that he was not connected to the "Greater Syria" plan. Rather, Ya'ari saw Zaim's move as a "coup d'état of a purely military nature" and expressed his concern that armistice negotiations with Israel "at least be postponed so as not to hurt the pride of the Syrian army."[70]

Two days later, however, Ya'ari began to doubt his first interpretation and thus concluded, "with all appropriate caution, that a certain connection existed between the authors of the coup in Damascus and those who pull the strings in Amman." In time the Israelis became acquainted with Zaim's regime and the forces affecting it from within and without, as a Political Department paper on "the new Syrian government" written on July 6 shows.[71] Still, Israel failed to understand the complex relationship between Zaim and the military and were completely surprised by the August 14 coup. On that date Ben-Gurion wrote in his diary:

> At 10 o'clock Elkana [Gali, his secretary] came in with a "bombastic" piece of news: Zaim and Barazi had been assassinated by one of Zaim's senior officers. The assassin wants to return the regime to those elected by the people. Elkana added that the oriental [Ori-

entalists] were not prepared for this action, which came by surprise. Zaim should have been prepared, and if he were not, it is not surprising that the thing happened.[72]

It was not the last time in Israel's history that prime ministers lambasted the intelligence community's experts for their failure to predict a dramatic change in the politics of an Arab state.

When Zaim's regime was toppled, the instigators of the coup published a statement that denounced his crimes and justified their actions. The principal themes in this first statement were repeated in greater detail in later statements and revelations: Zaim was accused of deviating from the aims of the original coup and, more specifically, of causing anarchy, wasting the people's money, disparaging the army's honor, exploiting his power for private ends and personal profit, harming the Islamic tradition, conducting unwise and treacherous foreign policy, and granting unwarranted concessions to French interests.

It is curious that the charge of treachery in Zaim's foreign policy was aimed at his relations with France. The ratification of the Tapline agreement was mentioned, but the new regime, which refrained from adopting an anti-American policy, did not accuse its predecessor regarding this issue. It is still more curious that his successors did not castigate Zaim for his relations with Israel, the fact that he had signed an armistice agreement with Israel, and the broad initiatives he had taken toward that country. As we mentioned, Adel Arslan did include Zaim's relations with Israel in the series of revelations he published in Beirut at this time. But his denunciation did not spread. The restraint that Zaim's successors displayed in this matter derived from several factors. First, some of them, led by Fawzi Selu—who was responsible for seizing power and assassinating Zaim and Barazi—had taken an active part in the armistice negotiations with Israel and so hurling accusations in this matter would have been hurting themselves. Nor were Syria's new rulers interested in exacerbating the conflict with Israel, and consequently they did not want to undermine the relations between the two countries during the months preceding the coup. Furthermore, the Syrian public in

1949 was preoccupied with issues other than the conflict with Israel. Accordingly, in his annual report summing up the year's events, the first secretary of Britain's embassy in Damascus wrote that "the problem of Palestine was relegated to the background by Syrian internal affairs during the year. There were the usual storms in the press but after the conclusion of the Armistice agreement in July the public lost interest."[73]

This comment does indeed point to the public's varying preoccupation with the question of Palestine and the conflict with Israel at different times, even in a nation so committed to the Palestinian cause as Syria was. (This issue will be discussed further in Chapter 6.)

The most important question is whether Israel missed a historic opportunity in the spring of 1949 to come to an agreement with Syria and thereby change the course of the Arab–Israeli conflict, or to put it differently, was the Husni Zaim of 1949 an early version of the 1971 Anwar al-Sadat? The question cannot be answered definitively, as it is impossible to establish in retrospect whether or not an opportunity has been missed, and yet historians, political scientists, and students of inter-Arab relations still debate this question. But even if it cannot be answered with any certainty, anyone who passes judgment or expresses an opinion on decisions made by leaders at crucial turning points must deal with this question explicitly or implicitly by stating that a certain decision was warranted or unwarranted. The historian implies that the choice underlying the decision was warranted. In his important text on interrelations Inis Claude offers an elegant formulation of the problem:

A major difficulty in the development of the "science of peace" lies in the fact that we cannot really know when any technique for preventing war works successfully. The evidence of failure is provided by the outbreak of war, but if the technique succeeds in averting hostilities the world may never know and scholars can never demonstrate that it was the effective cause of that negative result. In this as in many other realms disproving is more feasible than confirming.[74]

In any event, the options that confronted the decision makers and the problems with which they had to contend can be analyzed. From this point of view and from the current perspective, it seems that Ben-Gurion's refusal to meet Husni Zaim in April–May 1949 did not destroy the prospect of reaching an agreement that would have transformed Arab–Israeli relations, an assessment based on several considerations.

First, the premises of the two parties were so different and remote from each other that it is difficult to believe that the gap between them ever could have been bridged. Zaim viewed his meeting with Ben-Gurion as the means to an agreement that would eliminate the Syrian–Israeli conflict in one fell swoop. But Zaim also saw an Israeli territorial concession in the area of Lake Tiberias and the Jordan River as enabling him to justify his unorthodox conduct and to present himself as the winner in the 1948 war. But such a concession was unacceptable to Israel, as it would spill over into the conflict over the waters of the Jordan River.

Second, it is difficult to believe that Zaim would have survived in power even if he had reached an agreement with Israel and enjoyed massive American aid. The man who appeared during his first days in power as a popular reformer soon became a corrupt dictator who was consumed with gaining prestige and status but who also had lost the support of his original allies and thus was easily removed by the same military faction that had put him in power. As has been shown, the Israeli leadership had its own reasons for failing to take Zaim seriously.

Third, Zaim's willingness to enter into an agreement with Israel was completely divorced from the prevailing public opinion in Syria and the rest of the Arab world. True, the question of Israel had yet to occupy the position in Syrian public opinion that it came to have later when Arab–Israeli relations grew more bitter and Syria's politics became more radical and ideological, but the Syrian public commitment to pan-Arab nationalism and particularly the Palestine question could not be ignored. As we shall show, Syria might have been able to negotiate with Israel on a practical level but not on a level that touched on values and symbols. Zaim tended to dismiss this dimension of Syrian politics, and this tendency was, indeed, among the factors that led to his downfall. In regard to Israel, Adel Arslan was able to stand up to Zaim precisely because Arslan represented the attitude of most Syrians toward this component of the conflict with Israel. Against this background it seems that a far-reaching agreement between Israel and Husni Zaim in the spring of 1949 would have resembled the Lebanese–Israeli agreement of May 1982 more closely than the Camp David Accords.

# 4

Negotiations for a
Comprehensive Settlement
with Jordan

This chapter considers the negotiations between Jordan and Israel between November 1949 and March 1950 to reach a comprehensive or partial settlement between the two states. This round of negotiations was only one link in a long chain of contacts, discussions, and negotiations that had begun well before November 1949 and continued until Abdullah's assassination in July 1951. But for a number of reasons this particular phase of the Jordanian–Israeli series of negotiations is a well-defined and significant period.

The Jordanian–Israeli negotiations were the first attempt to apply the principles contained in the preamble to the armistice agreements and to conclude at least one Arab–Israeli peace treaty. Unlike the stalemated efforts of the PCC, the emphasis was now on bilateral and direct negotiations. Likewise, the suspension of the Jordanian–Israeli negotiations also marked the conclusion of a period. Although the meetings and discussions with Abdullah and his aides continued until 1951, they acquired an entirely different character. As a rule they focused on more specific issues, and over time the quest for a peaceful settlement was gradually replaced by an effort to arrest the process of deterioration in the two countries' relationship. This change reflected a broader alteration in Arab–Israeli relations as the full-blown Arab–Israeli conflict of the mid-1950's gradually took shape. The obvious interest in studying this first attempt to negotiate peace between Israel and an Arab state after the 1948 war is enhanced by its contemporary implications. To use an anachronistic term, the "Jordanian option," the notion of solving the Palestinian problem through a Jordanian–Jewish (and subsequently Israeli) agreement had surfaced in the 1930s and has remained to date one of the most promising approaches to this issue. The 1949–50 Israeli–Jordanian negotiations were one of the most serious and sustained attempts during the past half-century to implement this idea.

In the winter of 1949–50 the Israeli government was willing to comply with (though not formally endorse) Jordan's annexation of the West Bank and the Gaza Strip (if Egypt were willing to hand it over to Jordan). There still remained the question of whether Hashemite Jordan would and could sign a peace treaty with Israel on the basis of the territorial and demographic status quo and whether such an agreement would lead to the normalization of Israel's relationship with the Arab world. The similarities and differences between this round of negotiations and the various attempts made since 1967 to reach a settlement between Israel and Abdullah's grandson, Hussein, are a subject for instructive comparison and speculation.

The 1949–50 negotiations are documented in three pertinent diplomatic archives (American, British, and Israeli) which recently have been opened for this period (and into the late 1950s). David Ben-Gurion's diaries, the memoirs of Moshe Dayan and other participants, and the contemporary press are important additional sources. For some of the meetings between the Jordanian and Israeli negotiators six different versions are available—the Israeli written record, the oral account given to Ben-Gurion as recorded in his diary, and the British and American reports from Tel Aviv and Amman based on the accounts of their Israeli and Jordanian contacts. The Arab and Arabic sources unfortunately are not as abundant. During the past few years several books and studies dealing in some fashion with this subject have already been published, and others undoubtedly will follow.[1]

After an account of the actual negotiations, we shall try to answer the following questions: Why did the negotiations fail to produce a settlement? Was an agreement within reach, and was an opportunity missed by failing to reach it, and if so, why? What did Jordan and Israel seek to obtain? How did Ben-Gurion and Abdullah communicate their policies through their aides and ministers, and what impact did the domestic politics of the two countries have on the negotiations? What roles did the United States, Britain, and the Arab countries play in the negotiations and their failure? Finally, on the basis of the rich documentation of these negotiations, how deep was the Arab–Israeli conflict in the winter of 1949–50?

## Prelude to Negotiations

The evolution of Abdullah's relationship with the Jewish community in Palestine and then with the Israeli state until the late summer of 1949 was described in Chapter 1. To recapitulate briefly: A political relationship had been established between the Jewish Agency and Abdullah in the 1930s. In 1937 Abdullah considered annexing the Arab part of a partitioned western Palestine, thus facilitating the establishment of a Jewish state in Palestine and resolving—though not to everyone's satisfaction—the Palestine problem. A vague understanding along these lines was reached between Abdullah and the Jewish Agency in 1946 and 1947, but it was too vague and fragile to prevent a war between Israel and Jordan. Paradoxically, Abdullah, the one Arab ruler who sought agreement with Israel, played a cardinal role in pushing the Arab states to join the Arab–Jewish civil war in Palestine.

According to his own lights, Abdullah kept his part of the agreement in 1948, but his Israeli counterparts took a different view of it. Direct contact between Abdullah and the Israelis ceased, in any event, in May 1948 and was resumed some six months later, although contacts with Abdullah's emissaries were renewed in August 1948. In his talks with the Israelis between November 1948 and May 1949 Abdullah stated that he wanted a peace agreement with Israel based on the Israelis' recognition of the West Bank's annexation and other concessions. It is not known precisely what Abdullah had in mind when speaking of peace with Israel. The Israeli leadership was not at that time, however, interested in paying the price of a formal peace with Abdullah and argued that working only through him would have several other significant disadvantages. They therefore thought that for the time being an armistice agreement (whose terms were generally dictated from a position of strength) was preferable as an interim arrangement.

In the early summer of 1949, however, this situation was reversed. Largely because of the impact of the Lausanne Conference and Washington's willingness to exert pressure on Israel, Abdullah could avoid direct contact with Israel, and so it was the Israelis' turn to court him. Against this background the way was being prepared in the fall of 1949 for a fresh and ambitious attempt to reach a comprehensive settlement between Israel and Jordan.

By then the Israeli leadership had changed its view of the relative advantages and disadvantages of peace treaties, as distinct from armistice agreements. First, the Israeli perception of the element of time had changed; that is, they were no longer certain that time was on their side. Haunted by the specter of a "second round" initiated by the Arabs, Israel continued to invest heavily in its security. The economic and social costs of this investment proved to be very high, particularly when it was spending so much of its meager resources on absorbing the huge number of immigrants during these years.

Israel's political perspective had been altered by the events of late spring and early summer, particularly by its clashes with the United States. And new problems were expected: The PCC would continue its efforts, and the problem of Jerusalem was expected to be raised in the United Nations, at which a majority vote for the city's internationalization was anticipated. A peace treaty with an Arab state would greatly reduce, if not eliminate, these international pressures. A different consequence of the stalemate and acrimony of the Lausanne Conference was a change in the American and British approach to the Arab–Israeli negotiations. During the summer the United States and Britain thought they could achieve a comprehensive Arab–Israeli settlement and saw the PCC and the Lausanne Conference as the appropriate framework. Accordingly, they objected to bilateral negotiations between Israel and the Arabs, which in practical terms meant Jordan. But the failure of that policy led the essentially pragmatic policymakers in Washington and London to change their minds and to remove their objection to separate negotiations. This, in turn, reinforced Israel's decision to alter its own approach to the negotiations.

But peace with whom? In theory Israel had two options: Egypt or Jordan (joint or simultaneous negotiations with both were not contemplated). During the war the Israeli cabinet had discussed the merits and drawbacks of the two options, but the discussion was purely academic, as an "Egyptian option" did not really exist and the "Jordanian option" was the only feasible one. Still, the thinking and the discussion had made their mark, and the documents show that the Israeli diplomats and experts had done their homework on this subject.

Ben-Gurion personally was convinced that Egypt was the key to a comprehensive settlement. In a discussion with the American ambassador, James McDonald, in early December 1949 "Ben-Gurion showed keen interest in the talk about peace with Egypt which he described as the key to Middle East peace and far more important than any arrangement we might have with Transjordan."[2]

The fullest exposition of Ben-Gurion's thinking on this subject can be found in the entry in his diary dated February 13, 1951. Reuven Shiloah, the director of the Foreign Ministry's Political Department, came to see him on the eve of a meeting with Abdullah, and Ben-Gurion authorized him to offer concessions in Naharayim (the power station east of the Jordan River) and on the Eilat Road in return for Jordanian concessions regarding Mount Scopus. But having agreed, Ben-Gurion expressed

doubt as to whether a political settlement with Abdullah was now desirable to us: (1) Transjordan is not a stable and natural entity, but one man, who could die at any moment and is totally dependent on England. (2) This political settlement could interfere with and delay an agreement with Egypt. (3) Without peace with Egypt a settlement with Abdullah does not remove the blockade we face with regard to Asia, Africa, and Europe. There is no passage to the east (Iraq will obstruct), the north (Syria will obstruct), or the south (Egypt). (4) Such a settlement would strengthen Britain's position in our environment. (5) Do we have an interest in committing ourselves to these ridiculous borders? (6) A settlement with Egypt would regulate our relations with the Arab and Muslim worlds, open the south as well as the north, and give us important economic relations. (7) Egypt is a natural and stable country, and objectively speaking, there are no conflicts between us. The king alone may not be a permanent and stable element, but the nation and the state will stay. It is not a bellicose people.[3]

This comment was written in regard to a specific conversation with Abdullah and so should be seen as Ben-Gurion's own impression of the issue, in both November 1949 and 1951.

Israel's preferences were also translated into an actual effort to initiate negotiations with Egypt. On November 8, 1949, a letter to that effect, written by Eliyahu Sasson to Colonel Ismail Shirine, King Farouk's brother-in-law, was transmitted through Brigadier General William E. Riley. Shirine was considered close to the king, knowledgeable, and influential, and Sasson felt that a personal bond had been established during the Rhodes negotiations.[4]

But the Israeli initiative was futile. Sasson's letter was not answered; the preference for an "Egyptian option" remained academic; and as in the past, the "Jordanian option" was the only viable one. Indeed, Abdullah was again interested in an agreement, and although he was Israel's second choice he could still become a valuable partner. True, particularly complex issues and problems stood in the way of an Israeli–Jordanian agreement, but should these be overcome, a peace treaty with Jordan would make it easier for the other Arab states to follow suit. Abdullah presented his state as the successor to Arab Palestine, and as Israel knew, he did not insist on the return of Palestinian refugees as part of a settlement. In these respects he could provide a solution to Israel's Palestinian problem.

A settlement with Jordan also would reduce the danger of an Arab-initiated "second round" and alleviate Israel's security problems along a long and awkward frontier. Consequently the social and economic price of the country's defense could be significantly reduced.

There were other economic advantages to an agreement with Jordan, first and foremost being access to the potash plant on the Dead Sea and the power station in Naharayim. And normalization of economic and trade relations with Jordan (including the West Bank) would boost Israel's weak economy. An agreement further-more would help Israel contend with two immediate problems. The issue of Jerusalem was to be discussed at the United Nations under the ever-threatening specter of internationalization, and an Israeli–Jordanian agreement would practically eliminate that threat. On the agenda was also Jordan's expected formal annexation of the West Bank. Israel would have to respond in some way, and as it did not intend to oppose the annexation in practice, it might as well seek to extract some political price for it.

This perspective was shared by the Israeli policymakers with varying degrees of enthusiasm. In his discussion with Washington's and London's representatives in Tel Aviv, Reuven Shiloah projected cautious optimism and seemed willing to gamble on his prestige and position by investing most of his time in the forthcoming negotia-tions. Walter Eytan, the director-general of the Foreign Ministry, seemed to be beside himself as the negotiations were about to begin. On November 24 the acting American ambassador in Tel Aviv, Richard Ford, reported to Washington on his briefing by Eytan in anticipation of the talks with Abdullah. In his concluding comment Ford noted that "Eytan, not normally demonstrative, restrained with difficulty his elation."[5]

Among the Israelis, Ben-Gurion was the coldest and most skep-tical. But, as he had on similar occasions in the past, he did not force his skepticism on his subordinates. As long as the attempt to come to terms with Abdullah did not involve unacceptable risks and costs, Ben-Gurion was willing to let the advocates of this policy pursue it and to exercise his leadership.

The Jordanian side seemed like a mirror image of the Israeli team: At the head of the pyramid was the king, a believer in the idea of a settlement with Israel and in the prospects of these particular negotiations, and under him were his courtiers and ministers, critical or at best reserved and dubious, some of them willing to accommodate the king and others manifesting their opposition or seeking to obstruct the negotiations in more devious ways.

In July 1950 Sir Alec Kirkbride, the British minister in Amman, wrote about Abdullah:

> His drive for a settlement with Israel is also basically selfish and not really due to far-sighted statesmanship. He is obsessed with the idea of recovering his fatherland, the Hejaz, towards which a settlement with Israel is the first step. The next would be the creation of Greater Syria and, then, the final showdown with the Saudis. The fact that there is really no chance of his dream being realized does not diminish the importance of its effects in all his actions and thoughts.[6]

Kirkbride was very close to Abdullah and so was familiar with his ambitions and style, and his opinion therefore is significant. Another dimension of Abdullah's thinking was probably not reflected in his conversations with Kirkbride, however. Abdullah recognized America's growing importance as a Middle Eastern power and appreciated the advantages of dealing with a new Great Power lacking the tradition of a paternalistic and hegemonial involvement in his kingdom's affairs. He believed in Israel's influence in the United States and saw a settlement as a key to improving Jordan's relationship with Washington.

Abdullah and the other Jordanian advocates of an agreement with Israel were also motivated by more immediate considerations. An outlet to the Mediterranean and the normalization of trade relations seemed vital to economic rehabilitation. Like the Israelis he was concerned with his own position in Jerusalem and reasoned that an agreement with Israel would minimize the danger of internationalization. He also thought that a dignified settlement with Israel along the lines he deemed acceptable should improve his standing in the Arab world and go a long way toward removing the stigma that had been attached to his name as a result of the events of 1948 and early 1949. But above all Abdullah was preoccupied with completing the West Bank's annexation. He rejected the United States' advice to continue his de facto control of the territory and to tighten it gradually without the fanfare of a formal annexation act. Instead, the king insisted on elections on both sides of the river and on confirming the unification of the two parts of his kingdom by a parliament representing both. A settlement with Israel that would have the blessings of the United States and Britain and, if impressive enough, could even be accepted by the Arab world, would guarantee a smooth completion of the annexation process, and would give it at least some legitimacy. And even if this scenario failed to materialize and the negotiations led to a more modest arrangement between Jordan and Israel, Abdullah should be able to guarantee at least Israel's tacit compliance with the annexation.

## Negotiations: November 1949–March 1950

The negotiations, which began on November 23, 1949, proceeded through three phases:

- Negotiations for a comprehensive settlement—November–December 1949.
- Negotiations for a settlement over Jerusalem—December 1949–February 1950.
- Negotiations for a nonaggression pact—February–March 1950.

In reality, however, the distinction between the phases was not always so clear-cut. Thus, during the negotiations regarding Jerusalem, elements pertaining to the earlier negotiations regarding a comprehensive settlement reappeared. But the successive phases still were different from one another, with the transitions representing efforts to keep the negotiations alive. When it became apparent that a comprehensive settlement would not be feasible, both parties decided to seek a more limited agreement on Jerusalem. And when they realized that this too would not be possible, Abdullah proposed, and the Israelis agreed to, the idea of a five-year nonaggression pact as an alternative to the negotiations' collapse.

## The Preparatory Phase: November 1949

The opening of the Jordanian–Israeli talks on November 27 was preceded by a series of preparatory meetings and talks whose purpose was to establish what the two parties' initial arguments were and whether on that basis it made sense even to start the negotiations. Moshe Novomeyski and General Riley provided the two principal lines of communications. Novomeyski was the director-general of the potash company and had developed excellent relations with Abdullah during the British Mandate. He reestablished contact with Abdullah at the end of the summer of 1948 and met with him and his minister of court, Samir al-Rifai, in London. Novomeyski requested a meeting in order to discuss the water supply to the new potash plant in Sdom, but Abdullah, who was more interested in negotiations with Israel, shifted the discussion immediately to the question of a comprehensive Jordanian–Israeli settlement. He explained that he would demand broad territorial concessions—Lydda, Ramleh, Beersheba, and Aqaba (by which he was not referring to the Jordanian town of Aqaba but to the neighboring Israeli Eylat).

In November a second meeting took place, this time in Abdullah's winter residence in Shuneh, in the Jordan Valley. The king had by then softened his demands and appeared ready to waive his demand for Jaffa, Lydda, and Ramleh as a concession. His reasoning was that he was not interested in piecemeal arrangements on minor issues but in a ''general settlement in which he regained Arab territory large enough to enable him to ward off the criticism that a separate peace with Israel would receive.'' Abdullah refrained from demanding that Israel give up the southern Negev, thus providing him with both ''an access and a road to the sea'' and the impressive concession that he needed. But his offer to grant Israel free port rights in Aqaba in return for the same rights in Haifa implied an expectation that Israel would give up the southern Negev. Abdullah was more explicit, however, in demanding the return of those Arab neighborhoods that had become part of Israeli Jerusalem.[7]

Abdullah presented similar demands in a meeting held a few days earlier with General Riley, who came to meet him on Israel's behalf. In return for the concessions he demanded from Israel, the king was willing to allow Israel to reactivate the original potash plant and to guarantee access to it through Jerusalem. The king also told Riley that he believed that he could obtain the Gaza Strip from the Egyptians. Riley's meeting with the king was arranged at Riley's request by David Fritzlan, the acting U.S. minister in Amman. The fact that Israel asked Riley to conduct a preparatory talk with Abdullah reveals the limits of Israel's concept of direct negotiations with the Arabs. Israel objected to the Western powers' attempts to impose an Arab–Israeli settlement through the PCC and other UN forums and instead insisted on separate and direct negotiations with the Arab states themselves. But when it reached the threshold of actual peace negotiations, the Israeli government wanted some American involvement. It was less interested in British involvement but realized that it would be impossible to negotiate with Jordan without it. The Israelis knew that Riley would report to his own government, and they themselves briefed their American colleagues on the opening of the negotiations and their progress. The briefings were prompt and precise but, as one might expect, not always complete.

Riley reacted to the king's demands during their meeting and told him that in his opinion they would be rejected by the Israelis. Eight months earlier, he said, a settlement along such lines could have been discussed, but circumstances had changed since then. In his report to the State Department on Riley's talk with Abdullah, Fritzlan wrote that he also did not believe that Abdullah's terms would be acceptable to the Israelis. The king, he felt, genuinely wanted to end the conflict with Israel but sensed the Israelis' eagerness and so tried to obtain from them a better deal.[8] A few days

later the king met Fritzlan, told him about the meeting with Novomeyski (without mentioning his name), enumerated his terms for a
settlement, and expressed his willingness to visit President Harry S
Truman. He also tried to mobilize Washington's support against any
Israeli aggressive designs "in the next few months."[9]

Like the Americans, Kirkbride, too, doubted that Abdullah's
terms would be acceptable to Israel, but he still thought that it made
sense for Samir al-Rifai to meet Israel's representatives and explore
the prospects for a settlement. But unlike the Americans, Kirkbride
felt that his country's protégé should be given advice and guidance.
The difference in their approaches can be detected in Kirkbride's
report to London:

> I feel very doubtful as to whether the Israelis are likely to agree to
> anything like these terms, but it will be useful for Samir to hear
> what they have to say. He will not be in a position to commit the
> Jordan government at this stage. I reminded the king of the unsat-
> isfactory outcome of the last negotiations with the Israelis and coun-
> selled extreme caution. I suggest, however, that we should not
> discourage the resumption of contact and see how things go.[10]

Israel countered the king's opening position with its own terms.
Moshe Sharett was in New York at the time and from there dispatched
a cable to his ministry's director-general listing the terms and issues
that should be included on the agenda:

1. Recognition of sovereignty in the West Bank and transit to
   the [Gaza] Strip should be sold at a high price.

2. Treaty with Britain does not apply to the West Bank.

3. If one of the parties enters into a new merger—the treaty
   will be abrogated. [Sharett had in mind either a Jordanian–
   Syrian or a Jordanian–Iraqi union.]

4. Transit to the Strip—not to the military.

5. Restoration of rights to the Dead Sea, including handing
   over the northwest corner in return—no compensation for
   damages caused.

6. Return of Naharayim, including 6000 dunams.

7. In Jerusalem, linkage to Mount Scopus and the [Wailing] Wall.

8. Latrun.

9. Economic cooperation on our part.

10. Anything you might want to add.[11]

Ben-Gurion wrote in his diary on November 26, on the eve of the first meeting,

Golda [Meir], [Eliyahu] Sasson, [Sahbtai] Rosenne, and Reuven [Shiloah] came at my invitation for a consultation prior to the meeting with Abdullah. Sasson believes that peace with Jordan will open the way for peace with Egypt and Lebanon and possibly with others as well. Until now each state was afraid to be the first.

Following the deliberations I gave the following instructions for the discussion that will take place tomorrow night at Shuneh. We will demand (1) part of the old city from Mount Zion to the Wailing Wall and (2) continuity with Mount Scopus. We will be ready to offer a quid pro quo in the south [of Jerusalem], (3) the whole western sector of the Dead Sea to the end of the potash concession area, (4) the Latrun basin and (5) the annexation of the Naharayim area to Israel in return for territory elsewhere. We will generally agree to border adjustment on the basis of exchange of territory.

We [also] will agree to (1) Egypt's handing over Gaza to Jordan; (2) free passage without sovereignty from Transjordan to Gaza, and (3) a free zone at Haifa port with passage through Israel. We will demand as conditions (1) that no bases in the West [Bank] be given to any power, (2) that the Transjordanian treaty [with Britain] not apply to western Palestine, and (3) that this territory not be annexed to another country in the event of a union between Transjordan and Syria or Iraq.[12]

The phrase "this territory" in Ben-Gurion's diary referred to the West Bank. It is both curious and significant that he did not commit to paper his consent to Jordan's annexation of part of western Palestine.

# Negotiations for a
# Comprehensive Settlement

At the center of the negotiations' first phase was the attempt to reach a comprehensive Jordanian–Israeli agreement based on Jordan's willingness to sign a peace treaty with Israel in return for an Israeli concession affording Jordan access to the Mediterranean under terms acceptable to Israel. During this phase the meetings were held in Shuneh, with Samir al-Rifai acting as Jordan's principal representative. Israel was represented by Reuven Shiloah and Eliyahu Sasson. Sasson had already been appointed as Israel's minister to Turkey and upon his departure in December was replaced by Moshe Dayan as the second Israeli representative.

Besides the main issues of Israel's territorial concession and Jordan's access to the Mediterranean, most of the other issues that Sharett raised—the question of Jerusalem, Israel's opposition to the application of the British–Jordanian treaty to the West Bank, Latrun, the potash plant on the Dead Sea, and the power station in Naharayim—were discussed only briefly, owing to the Jordanians' objection to broadening the scope of the negotiations before reaching an agreement on the key issues. They argued that from their perspective it was a sine qua non and that if an understanding could not be reached in this matter, discussion of the other issues would be a waste of time. This position was also guided by the fear, repeatedly reinforced by British advice, that Israel's tactics would be to skirt the main issue and avoid the concessions that Jordan desired, by seeking to shift the negotiations to a series of agreements on minor issues, particularly those desirable to Israel.

Jordan's demand for a territorial concession was made by Samir al-Rifai in the first meeting. He preceded it with an analysis of Israel's basic problem from the viewpoint of an Israeli statesman. According to Shiloah's account, Rifai explained:

> The tasks with which we [the Israelis] are encumbered are enormous, and despite all this help [from the United States] we will not be

able to go on being surrounded by a hostile [Arab] world that had never liked us and whose hatred has been exacerbated by failure in war. The Arab world is speaking of settling the score with us. It is weak today but could become strong tomorrow. We, immigration notwithstanding, will always remain a minority. Israel's vital interest is, therefore, to have peace. Despite Arab statements, Jordan recognizes us as a reality and an existing fact.[13]

Al-Rifai repeated the familiar argument that in order to make peace with Israel, the king needed a dignified settlement. He presented the waiving of the demand for Lydda, Ramleh, and Jaffa and Jordan's willingness not to turn to the UN with the demand to impose the partition boundaries as concessions. But then he argued:

On the other hand, access to the sea is vital and necessary for Transjordan. And in order not to make things difficult, they [the Jordanians] do not mean Haifa but Gaza, but for this they need territorial linkage to Gaza, namely, the whole of the Negev. The territory is not settled, and for us it is merely a question of prestige. But from a farsighted vision of peace and considering the fact that the Negev is a desert that we occupy only in the military sense without any economic interest, they ask that we rise above the limited interests and agree to the proposed arrangement. If we need an outlet to the Red Sea, they are willing to give us a free port in Aqaba in return for a free zone in Haifa. Furthermore, except for Transjordan the whole Arab world is seeking revenge, and it is to our advantage not to have a common border with Egypt but to have Transjordan serve as a barrier between us. The whole Arab world views the disruption of territorial continuity by our wedge in the Negev as a grave injury . . . though Samir himself views Egypt as belonging more to Africa. The elimination of the wedge would be an achievement with which the king could face the Arab public. If we reach an agreement in this matter, no other problems will constitute obstacles to peace . . . the Negev is the fundamental issue. When Novomeyski came to speak about potash, they told him that a settlement should not be reached in a piecemeal fashion, penny by penny, but that the main problem should be solved and the rest would fall into place.

The Israeli negotiators were quick to reject the demand that Israel give up the Negev. But they were ready to have Jordan take Gaza and stated that "a way should be found to give Transjordan access to Gaza without affecting our territorial control."

In the first report written upon their return to Israel, Shiloah and Sasson contended that the Negev issue was closely related to the policies of Britain and Egypt. They assumed (as did Ben-Gurion and other Israelis) that the Jordanian claim to the Negev was inspired by the British. They could well understand Abdullah's quest for an impressive territorial achievement but did not see why Jordan should be so interested in the Negev, let alone in having a common border with Egypt. They were fully aware of the hostility and rivalry between the two states and courts and had in fact exploited it during and immediately after the war. At the same time the Israelis knew that Britain wanted the southern Negev for its own strategic purposes— a secure land bridge between the Suez Canal and the Persian Gulf— and suspected that it was the British who urged the Jordanians to demand the Negev for themselves.

The Israelis knew also that Egypt had an interest of its own. In 1948, at the war's outset, when they faced no real obstacle, the Egyptians made no effort to capture the southern Negev. But ever since the first contact with Israel was established in September 1948, the Egyptians had been consistent in demanding the southern Negev. From their talks with the Egyptian diplomat Abd al-Mun'im Mustafa earlier in 1949, the Israelis learned about Egypt's desire to have a buffer separating it from Israel. They also knew that the Egyptians had had a hard time deciding whether they wanted Jordanian control of (and a British presence in) the Negev but assumed that Egyptian–Jordanian negotiations on the subject had taken place and that Egypt's willingness to hand Gaza over to Jordan was made conditional on Jordan's ability to obtain the Negev from Israel, thereby ensuring the creation of an effective barrier. But in fact this was not what Mustafa had said to the Israelis and indeed was not the case. But Israel insisted that it, and not Jordan, negotiate the future of Gaza with Egypt. The issue came up several times in December and re-vealed an interesting difference of perspectives. The British and the Jordanians suspected Israel of seeking to sow dissension between Egypt and Jordan. Shiloah explained to McDonald that "the Israeli government attached the greatest importance to avoiding any injury to Egypt, which they viewed as a most important neighbor, even though they were tied to Jordan by the greatest interest. The Israelis believe that by reaching an agreement with Egypt, the danger of 'a second round' could be eliminated."[14]

The debate over the Negev was resumed in the second meeting held on December 1. Rifai then withdrew (temporarily, as it turned out) his original demand and asked for a corridor granting to Jordan free and secure passage to the port that it would obtain on the Mediterranean coast. This concession was played down in the account given by Rifai to Kirkbride but was emphasized in the Israelis' written account of the meeting and in Shiloah's oral report to Ben-Gurion the next day. The question of the Negev was raised again in several subsequent meetings, but from that point on, the bargaining focused on questions concerning the corridor—its route and terminal point, its width, and the sovereignty over it. The debate had ups and downs, including an apparent breakthrough, until it finally became clear in mid-January that the negotiations were deadlocked.

On the question of sovereignty, the Israelis began by rejecting any infringement of sovereignty and offered the Jordanians no more than transit rights. Then on December 8 the Israelis offered Rifai a compromise: jurisdiction (but not sovereignty) over the corridor based on a precedent established by the United States and Panama. The offer was rejected, and when the Israelis realized that the rope could not be stretched any further in this matter, they announced in the December 13 meeting that Israel would be willing to give Jordan sovereignty over a corridor. The Israeli concession was qualified by three reservations: (1) Israel would be given free passage at three points along the corridor; (2) the establishment of a military infrastructure and the maintenance of military units in the corridor would not be allowed; and (3) the Anglo-Jordanian treaty would not apply to the corridor.

During the same meeting (December 13) the debate continued over the corridor's terminal point. Israel began by insisting that the corridor end in Gaza. But the Jordanians saw this as both an evasion and an attempt to create a conflict between them and the Egyptians, and they knew that it was not at all certain that they could obtain Gaza from the Egyptians. They therefore demanded the town of Majdal (Ashkelon). Israel rejected the demand and offered a coastal strip just north of the Gaza Strip. Shortly thereafter, when Egypt and Israel reached an agreement on the partition of the no-man's land along the coast north of Gaza, the Israelis decided (on December 23) to hand over to Jordan their half of the territory. In this way the principle, so important to Ben-Gurion, that Israel not unilaterally concede its territory could, to some extent, be upheld.

The Israeli concession on the question of sovereignty and the fact that, for the first time, Abdullah took part in the negotiations enabled the parties on December 13 to have a substantive discussion on other issues and to formulate points of agreement for an eventual Jordanian–Israeli treaty. Entitled ''Political Questions and Territorial Changes'' the document reads as follows:

> Both parties agree formally to negotiate the territorial settlement on the following principles:
>
> 1. Israel recognizes that the obtainment of a sea outlet on the Mediterranean is a vital interest of Jordan.
> 2. Israel agrees to cede to Jordan a corridor beginning from Hebron to Beit Jibrin and thence to a point on the Gaza coast, provided that the said corridor shall be an integral part of the territory of Jordan and under its full sovereignty and provided that the alignment and width of the said corridor shall be agreed upon by the two parties.
> 3. By the term the Gaza coast, Jordan means the coastal strip situated between the town of Majdal and the frontier line of the Gaza area held at present by the Egyptian government. By the same term, Israel means the Gaza area itself, which is held by Egypt. Therefore, the two parties will refer to their higher authorities for agreement on the final interpretation of the said term.
> 4. Jordan agrees to the fixing of ''passage points'' on the Jordan corridor referred to in paragraph 2 to facilitate Israel's communications, provided that the number and localities of such points shall be agreed upon later.
> 5. Israel stipulates that no military bases and centers shall be set up over the said Jordan corridor.

6. Israel stipulates that provisions of the Anglo-Jordan treaty shall not apply to the said corridor.[15]

Some analysts have suggested that this document constituted a breakthrough that brought the negotiations within view of success. Indeed, one historian of the period, critical of the Israeli leadership, argues that there is sufficient evidence to accuse Ben-Gurion and Dayan of missing—not to say destroying—an opportunity to reach an agreement with Abdullah at this stage.[16] But a close examination of the evidence shows that a breakthrough did not really occur on December 13, 1949. Samir al-Rifai expressed his reservations at this meeting, persisted in demanding the southern Negev, and contended that the corridor's terminal point must be in Majdal, as there was no certainty that Egypt would hand over Gaza to Jordan. Abdullah, in turn, withdrew soon thereafter Jordan's territorial concession in the Dead Sea area.[17] The Israeli negotiators did not return elated or with a sense of achievement, and Ben-Gurion's diary testifies to the same effect.[18] Likewise, the briefings dispatched by the Foreign Ministry to Harry Levine, Israel's chargé d'affaires in Australia, and Mordechai Eliash, Israel's minister in London, suggest that Israel did not feel that it had made an actual concession on the question of sovereignty. The language used in the briefings is "the furthest we were prepared to consider." The same briefings also reveal how alarmed the Israelis were by Abdullah's demand for a corridor that was "kilometers" wide and by his allusion to his intention to settle Palestinian refugees in it.[19]

The crucial issue of the corridor's width was addressed in the unsuccessful meeting held on December 23. The Israelis opened by proposing as a terminal point a three-kilometer coastal strip north of Gaza and half of the no-man's land, but only if the agreement with Egypt in this matter materialized. They also suggested that the corridor be somewhere between fifty and a hundred meters wide. Rifai, with Abdullah's support, rejected the offer. In the ensuing debate, Sasson—completely out of character—made a tactical error by observing that Jordan was not the key to peace with the Arab world. The implication was that this being the case, extensive concessions to Jordan were not warranted. Not surprisingly, Abdullah was insulted, and the incident, through not crucial in itself, added a sense of drama to the stalemate into which the negotiations had slipped.[20] Another meeting was not called for nearly a month. In an attempt to break the deadlock, the Jordanians suggested a meeting between Ben-Gurion and Rifai. Consistent in his reluctance to participate in the negotiations, Ben-Gurion refused, and so the Israelis proposed that the meeting be held with Sharett. Although Sharett was acceptable to the Jordanians, for some reason the meeting did not take place. And a letter sent by Shiloah to Rifai expressing Israel's willingness to continue the negotiations but reiterating its opposition to a "kilometers-wide" corridor predictably failed to salvage the negotiations, thus marking the end of their first phase.

## Negotiations over Jerusalem

Toward the end of January 1950 Israel initiated the resumption of the negotiations and suggested that they focus on an agreement regarding Jerusalem. The Israelis' move was motivated by their concern with the anticipated discussion of the Jerusalem issue at the UN and by a feeling that the stalemate in the negotiations might be overcome by agreement on a more limited issue.

The new phase was inaugurated on January 23 in Shuneh. The Israeli side was represented by Shiloah and Dayan, and Jordan was represented by Samir al-Rifai and Fawzi al-Mulqi, the minister of defense. Mulqi's participation was significant in that it marked the acknowledgment of the negotiations by Jordan's Council of Ministers. The council, headed by Tawfiq Abu al-Huda, had been aware earlier that talks were being held with Israel but preferred to pretend that it was not. Although Rifai's title was minister of court, he was not a member of the Council of Ministers, so that during the first phase of the negotiations it could be said that at least in a formal sense the king and his men were negotiating with the Israelis but that the government was not.

It was generally assumed that if an agreement were reached, Abu al-Huda would resign and al-Rifai would form a new government and sign it. If the negotiations ended in failure, the problem would not arise. Abu al-Huda himself denied in mid-January that his government was engaging in negotiations with Israel. Technically he was right, but the American chargé d'affaires, David Fritzlan, understood the statement's significance in the psychological context of Arab–Israeli relations and regretted the cumulative effect of such statements in reinforcing in the public's mind the feeling that contact with Israel was illegitimate. Fritzlan commented: "Though Tawfiq's denial technically correct, it left completely false impression and it will be difficult in face of it to prepare state of mind of people for any eventual settlement with Israel."[21]

On January 24 when the negotiations assumed a more limited character, the Council of Ministers could be brought in. The argument could also be made that the question of Jordanian–Israeli arrangements in Jerusalem were being discussed within the framework of Article 8 of the armistice agreements. The Arab consensus had determined in 1949 that the armistice agreements were legitimate and that Abu al-Huda's government could authorize the minister of defense to participate in the negotiations on its behalf. Furthermore, in the meeting held on January 30, Khulusi Khayri, one of the Palestinian members of Abu al-Huda's cabinet, was added to the Jordanian delegation. Both Abu al-Huda and Rifai had been born in Ottoman Palestine, but they had settled in Jordan, had joined the king's service, and so were considered Jordanian. Khayri was a 1948 Jordanian-Palestinian. His participation in the negotiations reflected at least a partial recognition of the transformation of the Jordanian polity by the virtual annexation of the West Bank. Abdullah understood also that an arrangement with Israel and the concessions it was bound to involve could gain greater legitimacy if it became known that a Palestinian representative had played a part in its negotiation. But Khayri's participation also complicated the negotiations by disrupting the relative harmony that had characterized the earlier meetings, a result of the tradition of cooperation between Abdullah's representatives and their Israeli counterparts and a sense of shared interests. But this measure of disharmony could prove to be a worthwhile investment should an agreement be reached.[22]

During this phase of the negotiations, four meetings were held, on January 24 and 30 and February 3 and 17. The February 3 meeting took place in the Israeli part of Jerusalem, at the home of Avraham Biran, a senior government official. Although the negotiations focused on the question of Jerusalem, the effort to reach a comprehensive settlement was not totally abandoned. Whether directly or through the Americans and the British, Jordan and Israel continued to discuss the corridor. Israel expressed its willingness to broaden the proposed corridor by a few hundred meters, and Jordan agreed to reduce its own demand to two kilometers, but the gap could not be closed.

With regard to Jerusalem, Israel had two main proposals. The first urged a "radical solution" (which may have been a bargaining position) to divide the city neatly into a northern part to be under Israeli control and a southern part under Jordanian rule. It was rejected by the Jordanians right away. A more limited proposal centered on Israel's demand for the Wailing Wall, the Jewish quarter, and Mount Scopus—including access to all three. Israel also suggested minor border adjustments in other parts of the city. To the main Jordanian demand for the return of the Arab neighborhoods of Jerusalem that had been occupied by Israel, the Israelis responded with an offer for a significant quid for a significant quo. In other words, in return for the three areas that Jordan demanded, Israel was willing to hand over equivalent territory. And because Israel held more Arab territory, it offered financial compensation in order to redress the balance.[23]

But as the negotiations proceeded, it became apparent that Abu al-Huda's government was opposed to any territorial concession to Israel in Jerusalem. Indeed, Abu al-Huda made a point of passing a resolution to that effect in the Council of Ministers.[24] Moreover, his initiative exposed the king's powerlessness vis-à-vis his prime minister. Both men realized that the prime minister could tender his resignation as the principled defender of a proud, patriotic position in conflict with a king who would once again be cast in the role of seeking an agreement with Israel at the expense of the Arab nation's and, more specifically, the Palestinians' interests. Such a vociferous resignation would have placed the king in an awkward position on the eve of the planned elections and the ensuing annexation. Furthermore, in conversation with foreigners, Abdullah made no secret of the fact that even al-Rifai could not be fully trusted. He knew the rules of the game in his court as well as any minister or courtier did. He knew that Samir wanted the premiership and suspected that in order to obtain it, he would pretend to be willing to accommodate the king, only to forget his promises once the position was his.[25]

Having concluded that he could not force his prime minister's hand, Abdullah changed his mind and, as the experienced Kirkbride remarked, was "endeavoring to convince everybody (including himself) that he was never prepared to agree to Israel obtaining any territory inside the city walls."[26] Israel had entered the negotiations on the assumption that it was dealing with an autocratic king who was not free from domestic constraints but was capable of managing the political system that he headed. In time the Israelis discovered, as did the king and the Western powers, that by annexing the West Bank the king gained territory and other political assets but lost much of his control.

When the negotiations over Jerusalem ran aground as well, it was decided to hold one more meeting in order to decide whether it was worthwhile to continue them. This meeting was held in Shuneh on February 17 between the king and Rifai, on the one hand, and Shiloah and Dayan, on the other. Al-Rifai made it clear that an agreement could not be reached on Jerusalem. He personally could well understand Israel's "minimum demands" with regard to Jerusalem, but his country's present government "was composed of people who are incapable of understanding this demand and who under no circumstances could sign an agreement containing this concession by Jordan." He was quite candid and open in explaining to the Israelis what the considerations were that precluded Abu al-

Huda's replacement. Later in the meeting yet another attempt was made to find a compromise formula for a comprehensive settlement. The Jordanians presented their demand for Majdal, the coastal strip between it and the Gaza Strip, and a two-kilometer-wide corridor as a sine qua non. But this was unacceptable to the Israelis, and so the negotiations seemed to have come to an end.

But Abdullah was determined to prevent the negotiations' total collapse and at that point came up with an entirely new approach. As he put it, in the prevailing atmosphere it was impossible to make the concessions necessary for an agreement, and so a transitional period was needed for the atmosphere to change. In order to create the necessary conditions the king suggested that a nonaggression pact be signed for five years that would include the following:

- The present border line, as agreed upon in the armistice agreement, would be maintained.
- Special committees, composed of the two parties' representatives, would be entrusted with studying the possibility of a comprehensive settlement, including the question of Jerusalem.
- Jordan and Israel would give the UN guarantees that they would respect the holy places and would avoid armed conflict in these areas.
- The question of special compensation for the property of Jerusalem's residents would be studied. If Israel could find a way to give up various neighborhoods, the road to the great task [namely, peace] would be facilitated.
- Negotiations over the renewal of trade relations between the two countries for the duration of the treaty and over the creation of a free port for Jordan in Haifa would continue.
- Permission would be given to every Arab to cross the border into Israel or to send an attorney in order to settle his property, by selling it or in any other fashion.

Abdullah added two other sentences that kept alive the offer to trade neighborhoods in Jerusalem and his demand for a territorial concession and an outlet to the Mediterranen. Shiloah and Dayan responded by stating that such a radical change in the course of the negotiations would require consultation with their superiors. It was agreed that once the new direction of the negotiations was approved by the Israeli cabinet, the king would present his proposal to his own government.

One of the most interesting developments in this meeting was al-Rifai's evasiveness when the king wanted him to write down the text of his proposal so that it could be brought before the Israeli government. Thus it was Shiloah who put the king's words on paper. Al-Rifai had, of course, agreed to take part in the negotiations with the Israelis, but he would not leave a record in his own handwriting of his willingness to serve as the instrument for transmitting the text of a proposed agreement between Jordan and Israel.

## Negotiations for a Nonaggression Pact

The proposal brought forth by Abdullah on February 17 was a political masterpiece. It included advantages for both Jordan (Israel's recognition of Jordan's control in the West Bank and east Jerusalem) and Israel (a political agreement with an Arab state and termination of the economic boycott by that state). Its other clauses were aimed at pleasing the UN (with regard to Jerusalem) and the Palestinians in Jordan (by giving them the possibility of regaining at least part of their property). The main problems on the agenda were to be postponed to an ill-defined future.

The Israeli government was impressed and surprised by the rabbit that Abdullah pulled from his hat. But in fact Abdullah had sent signals in this direction two weeks earlier. On February 3, the king's confidant Abd al-Ghani al-Karmi met with the young Israeli diplomat Moshe Sasson (Eliyahu's son) and presented to him a "personal idea" of signing a peace treaty "emptied of its contents" and drafted in a way that would enable Abdullah to overcome the obstacles facing him. A quick glance at the text of the ideas raised by al-Karmi on February 3 reveals that they were an earlier version of the proposal raised by the king two weeks later. In other words, by early February if not earlier the king had consulted with his confidants about salvaging the negotiations with Israel.[27]

The Israeli cabinet discussed the king's proposal on February 22. Ben-Gurion was among those who found in it disadvantages to Israel (such as recognition of the West Bank's annexation to Jordan), but he thought that they were outweighed by the advantages it offered and so supported the cabinet's decision to approve the draft agreement and to instruct Israel's representatives to reach a final agreement on its basis.[28]

The minutes of the Israeli cabinet's discussions are still classified, but at least part of the protocol of the consultation held on February 20 is now open to researchers. In this consultation Sharett reflected on possibly distinguishing between the Israeli–Jordanian border (in the Negev, for instance) and "our borders with the territories held by Transjordan." He argued that "we have always wanted to sell our recognition of the Triangle's annexation at the highest possible price. It follows that so far we want the king to know that we have yet to recognize the annexation of the Triangle." To this Shiloah responded:

> As for our recognition of the Triangle, we should once and for all shed the illusion that we could obtain a price for it. . . . What matters to the king is peace and nothing else, certainly not recognition of the annexation. Samir al-Rifai spoke most decisively in this matter, leaving no doubts.

The Israeli government knew full well that the agreement in question had no real content and that, instead, its significance was primarily symbolic. The principle of nonaggression had already been inserted into the text of the armistice agreements, and so what advantages could be gained by signing a treaty reaffirming a principle that had already been established? The answer to that question was that in the specific circumstances of the Arab–Israeli conflict, symbols and values were particularly important. As Sharett explained in a briefing to Israeli editors on March 9:

> With regard to the element of nonaggression in the proposed agreement, it does not, of course, represent an innovation from a legal and factual point of view in comparison with the armistice agreement, as the armistice agreement can also be described as a nonaggression pact, whereas this treaty should be made for a certain period of time. But life is not a matter of factual logic or legal logic. Things have a psychological logic, a psychological effect, and this issue of nonaggression should have its effect on this particular period when swords are brandished and talk is heard of a second round. . . . He [Abdullah] sees fit to reinforce it with an additional treaty. . . . He does it without relying on UN mediation . . . and the other party does it without any connection to the position of other states. . . .
> . . . The formulation of a common position toward the UN with regard to the holy places is particularly important. The breaking of the Arab boycott and the renewal of economic relations were particularly important. This was bound to provoke a sharp reaction in the Arab world and was ultimately bound to reinforce the elements working for peace in the Arab world, as against those promoting siege and hostility and kindling the fires of a future war.[29]

But the Israeli government's willingness was not enough to satisfy the Jordanians. The first difficulty concerned the very attempt to arrange the next Israeli–Jordanian meeting. For some reason Samir al-Rifai tried to prevent the meeting, and so he had to be circumvented in order to organize the meeting, which finally took place in Shuneh on February 24. When the meeting began, the Israelis deliberately exposed the sabotage attempt by Rifai, who, they reported, sat there "white and pale as an exposed man." Along with the king and Rifai, Jordan was represented by Fawzi al-Mulqi and Amman's city commissioner, Jamal Bey Tuqan. After the two delegations put the finishing touches on the text of the agreement, the king literally forced Rifai and Mulqi to initial it, with Shiloah and Dayan signing on the other side. They all decided to meet again on February 28, with both sides bringing their drafts in order to sign a final agreement.[30]

On February 26 the Jordanian Council of Ministers discussed the draft. It approved the agreement in principle as a revision of and an annex to the Rhodes armistice agreement. It also introduced a number of modifications so as to preempt any complaint that Jordan had signed a separate peace with Israel. Thus the five-year framework and the reference to the principle of renewing trade relations were omitted. But being aware of the importance attached by Israel to the principles underlying the issue of trade normalization, the Council of Ministers authorized Fawzi al-Mulqi to communicate to the Israelis that the agreement constituted ''a big step toward a formal peace treaty and is destined to give rise to developments that will be formally endorsed by that peace treaty.''[31]

But the meeting held in Shuneh two days later, on February 28, was not successful. Jordan was represented by Fawzi al-Mulqi and Jamal Tuqan, and the king and Samir al-Rifai participated in part of the meeting. Afterward, the Jordanians complained to the Americans and British that the draft presented for discussion elaborated on the clauses desirable to Israel but failed to do so with regard to those desirable to Jordan. The Jordanian prime minister, Abu al-Huda, was ''green with anger'' when making his complaint and was quoted by Kirkbride as saying that there was no point ''in making business with tricksters like the Jews.'' Kirkbride invested great effort in persuading him that this was the way of all negotiations, that everyone began by trying to obtain the best terms for himself. Abu al-Huda finally calmed down and took back his threat to convene the Council of Ministers and pass a resolution terminating the negotiations.[32]

The Israeli reports paint an entirely different picture. Israel's representatives were given a modified version of the original draft reflecting the dominant trends in the Jordanian Council of Ministers— the text was based on the armistice agreement and the five-year framework, and the clause concerning a renewal of trade relations was omitted. These changes were rejected by Shiloah and Dayan, who stated that they had no intention of ''signing a new edition of the armistice agreement, let alone an inferior one.'' Fawzi al-Mulqi sought to defend the Jordanian position, and an acrimonious debate ensued. During the debate the king even went so far as to reprimand his ministers in the presence of the Israelis. According to the account given by Shiloah to the Israelis, the king claimed that he had not seen the Jordanian draft and that he was incensed. His own plan was the result of much cogitation, and he was determined to hold on to it. According to Shiloah, the criticism leveled by the king at his ministers was so sharp as to be "somewhat embarrassing." The king finished by stating that if need be, he would have a new government formed.[33]

Indeed, within a few days Abdullah provoked a governmental crisis. On March 2 he tried to force his Council of Ministers to accept the principle of renewing trade relations with Israel. The strong reaction of the three Palestinian ministers—Ruhi al-Hadi, Musa Nasser, and Khulusi Khayri—and his own position on this issue led Tawfiq Abu al-Huda to tender his resignation, which the king immediately accepted.

This had not been Abu al-Huda's original intention, however. He had planned to hold on to his position until April, after the parliamentary elections, when he would become president of the Senate and pull the government strings through his protégé Said al-Mufti, the minister of the interior, who had been designated by Abu al-Huda as his successor. But the king forced Abu al-Huda to abandon his original plan and to resign in early March.

The king asked Said al-Mufti to form a new government, but he declined and so the task was assigned to Rifai. It appeared briefly that al-Rifai would be able to form a government along lines similar to those of Abu al-Huda's, but it soon became known that Abu al-Huda's resignation was prompted by the king's pressure to make concessions to Israel. Moreover, the Egyptian and Syrian press launched an anti-Jordanian campaign that exacerbated the dilemma facing any politician who was willing to cooperate with the king. The outgoing ministers refused to join al-Rifai's government, and it became clear that Rifai could form a government composed of only second- and third-tier politicians unless the king promised to give up the principle of resuming trade with Israel. It is an interesting comment on Abdullah's relationship with his own coterie that— according to Kirkbride—he did make such a promise to al-Rifai, but the latter told Kirkbride that the king was determined to break it.

Kirkbride himself was forced to play a role in Jordanian politics more active and conspicuous than he was used to, when the king, Abu al-Huda, and al-Rifai all asked for his advice. Kirkbride advised the king to concede, to enable Abu al-Huda to resume the premiership, and to make the successful conduct of the parliamentary elections his priority. He also reminded him of the Arab League's session about to open in Cairo on March 25. As a concluding comment on this episode, Kirkbride wrote:

> The refusal of the "Palestinian" members of the council to be pushed by the king is an interesting phenomenon of which further examples may be expected after the elections are completed and the new parliament meets. In fact it would appear that the times during which the king could act as a benevolent autocrat without giving rise to serious opposition by his subjects are drawing to an end. The process of change is likely to be somewhat painful for the monarch.[34]

Whether under the influence of Kirkbride's advice or because he had reached the same conclusion himself, the king decided to concede, and Abu al-Huda withdrew his resignation. On March 7, Abdullah, Fawzi al-Mulqi, and Said al-Mufti held a brief meeting with Shiloah and Dayan. Mulqi read the text of a "note verbale" he had brought along. In essence, according to Shiloah's report to the U.S. ambassador, the message was that Jordan's government accepted the king's plan as a basis for settlement. But because of the rumors and lies circulating in Jordan, it was decided not to continue negotiations but ask for their adjournment. Hope was expressed that negotations would be resumed at the earliest date possible and conducted in the same spirit toward achieving the same goals as in previous meetings. Abdullah added that he would rather continue the negotiations, but because his government had yet to accept his plan, he had agreed to postpone them.[35]

Along with these events, there were two other important developments: a brief propaganda war between Jordan and the king's critics in other Arab states and an attempt by Israel to mobilize American and British support for Abdullah so as to enable him to continue the negotiations.

The strongest criticism of Abdullah's policies was voiced by Egypt's and Syria's press and their radio stations. The Egyptian government refrained from taking any action, but Syria's prime minister, Khaled al-Azm, in a press conference held on March 6, threatened to close his country's border with Jordan if the latter decided to resume trade with Israel.

For a brief period of a few days Jordan deviated from the norms of the Arab world, when its media engaged in an explicit (though not always precise) defense of the king's policy of seeking a settlement with Israel. Thus a commentator on Radio Ramallah stated on March 8 that "the Jordanian government's efforts are the only way for finding a solution to the problem of the refugees and for guaranteeing every man's right to return to his home even in the areas held by the Jews." The commentator asked rhetorically: "In what way other than an agreed settlement according to the armistice guidelines can the return of the refugees be guaranteed?" He then contended that Jordan held the largest part of Palestine and the largest number of refugees and that it was its right to improve the terms of the armistice. Indeed, this was not a separate peace, and it entailed no territorial concessions.

The editorial of the Jordanian daily *Falastin* on March 8 called on the public to keep calm: The people's will is also the will of its rulers. And what did the public want? A just and reasonable compromise, honorable peace, a restoration of its property and land, and an outlet to the sea under Arab sovereignty. "The people, briefly, want a final solution, the responsibility for which should be shouldered by those states that first pushed it into the swamp and subsequently failed to extend help." This was well put but did not last long. The analyst in the Israeli Foreign Ministry who commented on the Jordanian propaganda remarked that a few days after Abu al-Huda's return to the prime minister's post, the Jordanian line was moderated. It was now argued rather lamely that the issue at stake was a modification of the Rhodes agreement in the Arabs' favor.[36]

The principal effort to persuade the United States to flex its muscles in support of the negotiations was made by Sharett on March 6. He stated to Ambassador McDonald that "the crisis in Amman is more than a focal test of strength between king and opposition; it is clash between negative and affirmative forces. Now Amman is the crossroads of the Middle East. Any decision there will affect whole course of history for next few years.'' Sharett therefore asked that the "United States encourage the king by official but secret assurance of U.S. moral and economic support.'' He likewise asked that the United States guarantee Jordan's supply of sugar and rice if Egypt and Syria should impose sanctions. McDonald wanted to know whether Israel was making a similar overture to Britain, and Sharett's reply was, "I am considering it.''[37]

Later that day McDonald took the unusual step of sending a telegram addressed to both the president and the secretary of state. He began by stating that "for the first time in many months I ask your personal consideration'' and requested that a message of support be sent to Abdullah and that "friendly advice'' be given simultaneously to Cairo to show understanding with regard to the Jordanian monarch. On the next day McDonald reinforced his plea by quoting the British minister, Alexander Knox Helm, whom, he said, he consulted regularly. In their conversation on March 16 Helm told him that the "maintainence of strong Israel at peace with Arab neighbors is essential to UK and U.S. vital interests. Present Arab policy refusal to make peace with Israel is futile and dangerous to UK and U.S.'' McDonald described Helm as "able and objective with no Palestine background to confuse his judgment'' and reported that Helm had transmitted a similar recommendation to London.[38]

But both the State Department (represented by Raymond Hare, the acting assistant secretary for the Middle East, South Asia, and Africa) and the minister in Amman, Gerald Drew, opposed the line advocated by McDonald. Hare argued in a memorandum that "motivated by his own personal interest, King Abdullah has gone as far as he could in attempting to reach an understanding with Israel. . . . [T]he message from the president to the king would in our opinion not help the king vis-à-vis his government.'' Hare thought that the president's message to the king on December 30 would be sufficient and drafted a telegram to the minister in Amman instructing him to encourage the king discreetly to continue the negotiations (without a new message from the president). Nor did Hare see any point in turning to the Egyptian government, as, he pointed out, "we have received no information that Egypt is actively intervening concerning the Jordan–Israel conversations beyond the usual radio and press criticism of Abdullah." Hare's recommendation (supported by that of Drew) was adopted.[39]

## Collapse of the Israeli–Jordanian Negotiations: March–April 1950

Even after having resolved the governmental crisis and suspended the negotiations with Israel, Abdullah still faced important challenges: the Arab League's session in Cairo and the expected anti-Jordanian offensive, and the elections of April 11 and, in their wake, the formal annexation of the West Bank. Abdullah may not have admitted it (even to himself), but it seems that (with Kirkbride's encouragement) he chose a line that offered the Palestinians in Jordan and his critics in the Arab world a compromise of sorts—a tacit acceptance of the West Bank's annexation in return for an indefinite suspension of the negotiations with Israel.

The Arab League's twelfth session began stormily. Egypt supported the mufti's invitation to the session as "Palestine's representative" and stated that Egypt would oppose the act of annexation. Abdullah, in turn, announced that Jordan would boycott the session and threatened to withdraw his legation from Cairo. He finally, however, accepted his government's position and sent a delegation to the league's session. Then on April 1 Jordan joined the league's other members in endorsing a resolution stating with regard to the negotiations with Israel that all members of the Arab League were forbidden to enter negotiations with Israel or to sign any agreement with Israel. The resolution stipulated further that any state that violated this norm would automatically be expelled from the league according to Article 18 of the league's convention.[40]

The elections of April 11 proceeded smoothly on both sides of the Jordan River. Even though some of the king's opponents on the West Bank were elected, both the conduct of the elections and their results were considered a success for the king. The two houses of parliament were called into session on April 24, and through an adroit maneuver the king succeeded in producing a unanimous decision on uniting the two banks.

Israel responded with a formal protest that was delivered to Abd al-Ghani al-Karmi by Moshe Sasson at the latter's home in Jerusalem. The text of the Israeli cabinet's decision as transmitted to Jordan stated, in part, that "the government of Israel does not recognize the annexation, and the question of the Arab areas west of the Jordan remains open," but an informal message was simultaneously transmitted to the king asking for an urgent meeting and mentioning that Israel's protest should be treated as a formal matter.[41]

A meeting was therefore hastily arranged for April 27. The circumstances were new and seemed to point to the changing nature of the Jordanian–Israeli relationship. The meeting was held in Amman at the home of Muhammad Ḍubati, the manager of the king's properties, who was well known to the Israelis as "one of the king's loyal confidants." Abdullah took unusual precautions, disguising himself and being accompanied only by al-Karmi, who served as the interpreter. Israel was represented, as usual, by Shiloah and Dayan.

The king began by congratulating himself on his latest achievements. He radiated self-confidence and optimism and emphasized his "firm stand regarding the agreement with us." He asked the Israelis to ignore the false rumors that he had gone back on his word. The Israelis responded by stating that the annexation was "a unilateral act that cannot bind us. Our attitude to the annexation will largely depend on the agreement reached between us and the Jordanian government." They then asked for a clearer statement regarding the pace and content of the negotiations. Shiloah and Dayan repeated to the king the alarming information that had reached Israel regarding the attitudes prevailing in his government toward negotiations with Israel. The king again denied the rumors. He reiterated his opinion that no refugee should be allowed to return to Israel and solemnly announced his final decision to withdraw from the Arab League. Abdullah then referred to Sir Alec Kirkbride's and the British government's support of his position. As he told the Israelis, Sir Alec had been to see him that morning and had encouraged him on behalf of his government to continue the negotiations to a successful conclusion. At the same time Kirkbride advised him "to prepare the ground with his own government so that when the negotiations were resumed, they could be completed swiftly and without interruption." The king was indeed busy trying to regroup his forces and was therefore not in a position to set a precise date for resuming the negotiations. He thought that some ten days would be needed, but he could not be more specific.[42]

But when the king had met with the American minister the day before, his message to him had been quite different. He had stated that any idea that Jordan's negotiations with Israel were to be resumed shortly was overly optimistic and premature, that the storm raging in the Arab world against the resolution of April 24 must be settled first.[43]

As the written account of the April 27 meeting shows, Shiloah and Dayan were suspicious that the king was trying to lead them in circles, a suspicion that can be verified through the second tier of the Israeli–Jordanian network of contacts, when Moshe Sasson met Abd al-Ghani al-Karmi on May 1. A few days earlier Karmi had promised to bring along a new version of the "note verbale" in which the king would enumerate the measures he was about to take in order to persuade his government to go along with him in pursuing the negotiations. But Karmi brought an entirely different note, using ambiguous language and including old demands such as an Israeli withdrawal from "Aqaba." Sasson reacted sharply and the face-saving device that salvaged the meeting was the decision that Karmi would read the note to Sasson personally and not as a message to be transmitted to his government.[44]

It is interesting that in the report he sent to his father in Ankara regarding the May 1 meeting, Moshe Sasson wrote that "I may invite the 'doctor' to a meeting and possibly hear from him something clearer and more authoritative."[45] The "doctor" was the (rather transparent) code name given to Dr. Shawkat Aziz al-Sati, Abdullah's personal physician and adviser who was entrusted with the most delicate missions to the Israelis, including the transmission of personal letters written in Turkish from Abdullah to Ben-Gurion. If Karmi were a "second tier" of the contacts—beyond the formal negotiations conducted with the king himself—Sati can be seen as the "third tier" of this unusual relationship. Sati was, indeed, invited to a meeting with Shiloah and brought with him a letter, written in Turkish, from Abdullah to Ben-Gurion, in which he reassured the Israeli prime minister that he was standing firm against all attacks.[46] Turkish was the only language that Abdullah and Ben-Gurion shared, and their correspondence in the former imperial language of the region that both had acquired in very different circumstances before 1914 added an archaic flavor to a relationship that extended into the 1950s.

During most of this period it was Abd al-Karmi who had served as the main channel between Israel and Jordan. Karmi had been a journalist in Mandatory Palestine. He had married a Jewish woman, and the bitter animosity between him and the mufti led him to carry on a dialogue with the Jewish side. In 1948 he had a brief flirt with communism and even visited the Soviet Union. Disappointed with both, he joined Abdullah's court and became one of his close aides. Immediately after Abdullah's assassination, he was sent to Spain as Jordan's ambassador. Soon after, he lost that position and ended up in London, where he barely made a living working for the BBC's Arab service.

By late April and certainly by early May, even the most optimistic Israeli should have been persuaded that the negotiations that had been interrupted on March 7 were not likely to be renewed at any time soon. But something else, more profound, had occurred in the Israeli–Jordanian relationship. The concluding paragraphs in the Israeli account of the April 27 meeting read as follows:

> At the meeting's end Moshe Dayan raised the question of the deteriorating security situation in the south and the rising number of clashes between us and Jordanians who came across the border to

graze their herds and harvest fields within our territory. As the officer responsible for the southern command, Dayan must on occasion react for security reasons. He is anxious that as the harvest season approaches, the clashes may multiply, and who knows whether the mufti's men would not exploit it to their advantage. Dayan suggested that the king appoint an authorized person to negotiate with him and reach an on-the-spot agreement on all these points.

The king responded that as long as Moshe Dayan was in charge of security in the south, he was confident that his intentions would be peaceful. He understands that as a military man he must from time to time act briskly and willingly accepted the proposal to appoint an authorized representative to negotiate with Dayan. He promised to give all possible support to Dayan's suggestion and would inform us in a few days of his representative's name.[47]

Contacts and discussions with Abdullah continued after April 1950, but as the exchange with Dayan revealed, their focus shifted from the quest for a settlement to an attempt to arrest the process of deterioration in what had become the Arab–Israeli conflict.

## The Forces at Work

In mid-April 1950 before the failure of the Jordanian–Israeli negotiations had become apparent, Moshe Sasson wrote to his father:

As for Transjordan it seems that two distinct concepts have been confused here, a confusion between *will* and *ability*. In my mind Abdullah's candid will to go through with the agreement should not be doubted. But his ability to implement what he wants should be doubted. And in the term *ability* we include domestic capability from the Jordanian "public" sense, external capability from an inter-Arab point of view, and external capability from the British and American point of view.[48]

Sasson's statement provides a convenient point of departure for analyzing the failure of the Israeli–Jordanian negotiations, in that it enumerates the principal actors that had shaped the negotiating process—except for Israel, a subject rarely scrutinized by the Israeli Foreign Office. Sasson also addressed an issue with which the Israeli experts were preoccupied in 1950 and in later years. Some of them disagreed with Sasson and argued that Abdullah had deliberately misled the Israelis. Thus in 1955 Gideon Rafael reminded Moshe Sharett that on April 19, 1950, Shiloah arrived at Sharett's home with a message brought by the "doctor" that the king would announce the annexation of the West Bank on April 25. According to his own testimony, Rafael had argued that "the negotiations that Abdullah had conducted with us were aimed only at silencing our opposition to the annexation in view of the prospect of achieving peace." Rafael thus recommended that Abdullah be notified that "we will not put up with his action if the treaty that he had already initialed is not signed."[49]

Indeed, several elements of this story seem to support this version: the Jordanian effort to obtain, while negotiating with Israel, the extension of the British–Jordanian treaty to the West Bank; the king's persistent endeavors to keep the negotiations alive until the eve of the annexation; and at least one pronouncement by Samir al-Rifai in June 1950. Rifai told a foreign visitor that he opposed a renewal of negotiations with Israel through the PCC. He maintained that Jordan's position in June was better than it had been during the secret negotiations with Israel because of (1) the annexation of Arab Palestine to Jordan, (2) the application of the 1946 treaty to Arab Palestine, and (3) the guarantees to the borders and the Three Powers' declaration (of May 1950).[50] The fact that Abdullah ceased in early March 1950 to tell the truth to the Israelis also seems to support Rafael's version.

And yet Rafael's version is not a satisfactory explanation of Abdullah's complex conduct of the negotiations with Israel. It is clear that after the governmental crisis of early March 1950, he concluded that the negotiations could not be continued, that he had to choose between continuing the negotiations and implementing tasks he considered more important. Furthermore, at that point the stability of Abdullah's regime and perhaps even the survival of his state in its new incarnation seemed to be in jeopardy. There is no denying that one of the considerations that had guided Abdullah throughout the negotiations was his concern with neutralizing Israel's possible opposition to annexation, but he undoubtedly and sincerely did want a settlement with Israel.

As Abdullah became more personally identified with the notion of a settlement with Israel, the question of the negotiations and their failure became increasingly a test of the king's prestige and position. A successful conclusion would be the king's personal achievement, but failure would be sure to be exploited by his domestic and external foes. It was also quite clear that Abdullah was preoccupied with his image in American and Israeli eyes. It was important to him to be seen as a reliable and effective partner. Several aspects of Abdullah's character—a topic for rumination by both friends and critics—offer equally important clues to his conduct. He was impulsive and impatient, and his eagerness to accomplish his purpose and to reach a settlement caused him more than once to overplay his hand. He could also be utterly pragmatic and change his mind while persuading himself that he was being persistent, thereby ignoring the maze of contradictions into which he had in fact maneuvered himself.

The Jordanian–Israeli negotiations were also shaped by two developments that had affected Jordan in the late 1940s and early 1950s: Abdullah's personal decline and the transformation of the Jordanian political system by the de facto and subsequently formal annexation of the West Bank. Abdullah, ironically named "the old man" in Ben-Gurion's diary, was not in fact so old—he turned seventy in the winter of 1949–50. But the years had taken their toll, and on certain days he struck his visitors as an old, sick, and tired man who had lost his energy, vitality, and ability to rule his kingdom. His mood shifted from euphoric to morose. On one such day, about a year later, Abdullah complained to the American diplomat, Hamilton Fisher: "I am an old man . . . I know that my power is limited; I know that I am hated by my own son. . . . I also know that my own people distrust me because of my peace efforts."[51]

This distrust became all the greater when the West Bank's population was added to the Jordanian political system. Jordanian politics could no longer be comfortably conducted within an intimate circle according to the rules of a game controlled by the king. That is, the West Bankers' participation required an expansion of the circle and a change in the rules of the game. Although the April 11 elections did not transform Jordan's government into a Westminster-style constitutional monarchy, they also were not elections that could be carried out purely on the basis of force and manipulation. In order to win at least a measure of consent and legitimacy, the political system had to accommodate the better-educated and more highly mobilized population of the West Bank. Needless to say, that population had definite views on a settlement with Israel.

Behind the Palestinian population were the Palestinian politicians, some of whom were irreconcilable foes of Abdullah and his state and so had to be treated as such. But even those defined as moderate Palestinians, like the Palestinian ministers in Abu al-Huda's government, had perspectives and views different from those of Abdullah and felt that they had to respond to the expectations of the public they were supposed to represent. But Abdullah's difficulties with the Palestinian politicians were more than just ordinary political disagreements. To him they represented a novel type of an educated urban politician with whose demeanor and language the king was not familiar and certainly not comfortable.

All this might have been understood before the negotiations, but Abdullah himself—as well as the British, the Americans, and the Israelis who watched from a greater distance—realized the full implications of this "Palestinian phenomenon" only as the negotiations unfolded. Furthermore, Abdullah's loss of control also became apparent in his relationship with the traditional Jordanian politicians, his veteran group of lieutenants—Tawfiq Abu al-Huda, Samir al-Rifai, Fawzi al-Mulqi, and Said al-Mufti.

From the source material there emerges the picture of a Byzantine court in which the courtiers fought for positions of power and influence, their status and their relations with the king in a permanent state of flux. It is clear that Samir al-Rifai strove during that period to obtain the prime ministership while Abu al-Huda protected his chair and tried to preserve his influence through Said al-Mufti in the aftermath of the elections. It is likewise clear that the course of the negotiations became inextricably linked to this power struggle. At the outset of the negotiations Rifai was entrusted with their conduct, and it was widely known that if the negotiations succeeded he would be made prime minister in order to formalize and implement the agreement. Abu al-Huda was opposed to the negotiations for reasons of principle but also because they were destined to promote his rival, and so he openly sought to obstruct them. Later, when Abu al-Huda's government joined the negotiations, Rifai, too, assumed an obstructionist role.

To Abu al-Huda's credit, he was quite open in displaying his opposition to negotiations with Israel along the lines set by Abdullah. As he stated over and over to Kirkbride: "He did not feel able, personally, to be a party to a settlement with Israel. He admitted that his objections were mainly sentimental and not connected with the necessity or desirability of such a settlement."[52]

Presumably Rifai was expected to support Abdullah's pragmatic line, free from emotional and ideological inhibitions with regard to Israel. But as we have seen, he also refused to sign the December 13 draft, and Abdullah had to force him to initial (with Fawzi al-Mulqi) the February 17 draft. Later Rifai also assumed an Arab nationalist position toward Israel: A report in June 1950, that the Israeli Foreign Office defined as "authoritative," depicted Rifai as having lost faith in a settlement with Israel and

> as one who often speaks the language of Abdullah al-Rimawi [a leader of the Ba'ath party in Jordan] and looks forward to a second round [with Israel]. He believes in the second round and its prospects of success. When told that Israel was making its own preparations, he responded by saying: If not this generation, then the next one. Thirty-five million Arabs are bound to overcome one million Jews.[53]

## The Arab System

As an actor affecting the negotiations with Israel, the Arab system played an important role in three contexts: as a normative system determining the rules of the game and its limits, granting and denying their legitimacy; as an important arena of Jordan's foreign policy; and as a group of states from which Abdullah could seek partners and supporters or find critics and rivals.

Abdullah was both a senior and a rebellious member of the Arab system. His and Jordan's position in the system dropped in the absence of allies and as a consequence of the decline of the Hashemite version of Arab nationalism. This was a conservative version predicated on the historic role of the House of Hashem and its contribution to modern Arab history, the Arab Revolt of World War I in particular. By the late 1940s the Hashemites' position had clearly been eroded vis-à-vis the Saudis, whose Arabism was considered more authentic, in regard to the power of the Egyptian state and in regard to the radical trends in Arab nationalist thinking. The Arab radicals viewed the Hashemites in general and Abdullah in particular as outdated, subservient to the British, and disloyal to the Arab cause in Palestine.

Given this state of affairs Abdullah toyed from time to time with the idea of a radical break with conventions by withdrawing from the Arab League and pursuing his own path. But he understood very well that he could ill afford to do this, particularly after the annexation of the West Bank. The majority of his subjects saw the Arab League, its shortcomings notwithstanding, as the political embodiment of Arab nationalism. Secession from the Arab League thus would deal a grave blow to the legitimacy of the House of Hashem. Abdullah found himself therefore grumbling in discontent but playing according to the Arab system's rules of the game prevailing during the latter half of the 1940s. On the question of Palestine these rules meant no deviation from the consensus that derived primarily from the radical positions. In 1949–50, radical regimes had yet to emerge in the Arab world, but in Syria and, to a lesser extent, in Egypt, radical perspectives were already affecting the government's conduct. Syria stood slightly to the right of the mufti, himself in the periphery of Arab politics, as the representative of the resolute and principled Arab position on the question of Palestine.

The actual impact of this configuration was magnified by the fact that in the ranks of the Arab League Abdullah had several rivals and not a single real ally. With Saudi Arabia he had a bitter dynastic rivalry. With Egypt it was an interstate rivalry aggravated by the personal animosity between Abdullah and a number of Egyptian leaders. Syria also felt menaced by the king's expansionist design. And Hashemite Iraq demonstrated that intradynastic competition could be just as bitter, though less open, as interdynastic rivalry was. At the height of Abdullah's confrontation with Egypt and Syria in early March, all that the Iraqi regent Abd al-Illah could offer him was a piece of advice: "In order to accomplish our holy aims, we must always follow the noblest course that we learned from our grandfather Hussein . . . which means that we must seek guidance and advice according to the serious opinions of the men of sincerity in our kingdom." In less ornate language this amounted to a recommendation to Abdullah to let his underlings do the work and to avoid the political cost of personal involvement in controversial negotiations.[54]

During the first three months of the negotiations the Arab system remained in the background. Egypt was aware of the negotiations and familiar with their broad lines, but as a rule the details of the negotiations were kept confidential. In this period the Arab system affected the negotiations mainly by defining the limits of Abdullah's maneuverability. Abdullah thought that in order to satisfy the Arab consensus he had to obtain from Israel an important territorial concession. And this was a crucial point, for such a concession was unacceptable to Israel, and so the negotiations for a comprehensive settlement were doomed. But because Abdullah was the interpreter of the limitations imposed on him and given the absence of formal and precise definitions, the deadlock could be circumvented, at least temporarily, and the negotiations could continue. In March, however, things were different: The negotiations became public; an open debate was conducted in Jordan and a crisis broke out; information leaked out of Israel; the Arab League's session and the Jordanian elections drew nearer; and the Arab system took a definite stand and concrete measures. To these Abdullah had to respond.[55]

One way of overcoming the limitations imposed by the Arab system was to obtain Egyptian support for the negotiations and the eventual agreement. Egypt did possess the power to legislate different rules of the game with regard to Israel, particularly if it did so in cooperation with Jordan. This indeed was the principal reason for the preference given by Ben-Gurion to negotiations with Egypt. But as we shall see later, Egypt was not, during this period, a real candidate for negotiations with Israel or for tripartite negotiations involving Jordan as well. True, at an earlier stage the Israelis believed that Egypt wanted to have the Negev given to Jordan or to a Palestinian state and to serve, together with the Gaza Strip, as a barrier separating Egypt from Israel. But this had been only a marginal theme even then and remained marginal during the 1940–50 Israeli–Jordanian negotiations. Furthermore, in 1949 at least, it was accompanied by a reluctance to have Jordanian control and a British presence in the Negev. Although Egypt was anxious to remove Israel from the Red Sea coast, it was far less anxious to obtain the Negev for Jordan.

It is difficult to speak of a definitive Egyptian stand on these matters in 1950, as domestic rivalries and a change of government produced diversity in the Egyptian position.[56] A fundamental position could be formulated only in negative terms. Egypt in 1950 had no profound commitment to the Arab cause in Palestine and saw no point in defying the norms prevailing in the Arab League, in which Egypt enjoyed a hegemonial position. It did not want another war with Israel but was equally not anxious to make peace with that nation and did not think that such a peace would produce important advantages for Egypt. The one advantage that Egypt sought—a land bridge to the eastern Arab world—was a concession that Israel was clearly determined not to make. During the Jordanian–Israeli negotiations Egypt was concerned first that Jordan might conclude an agreement with Israel that did not provide for an Israeli withdrawal from the Red Sea. The Egyptians felt that such an agreement would consolidate Israel's presence on the Red Sea and deal a final blow to the land-bridge idea.[57]

In the early stages of the negotiations, the British considered having Egypt join them or, failing that, creating the mechanism for a Jordanian–Egyptian coordination. Britain faced a familiar dilemma.

Its interests were spread among several states in the region, and the clash of interests between two or more of these states complicated its policy. Having weighed the pros and cons of the issue, the Foreign Office decided in late December that if the Egyptian government attached importance to any specific issue that might arise in future Jordanian–Israeli negotiations, it should be taken up directly with the Jordanian government.[58]

# Britain

The official and semiofficial French scholarship of the twentieth-century Middle East and Zionist and early Israeli historiography have a common view of British policy in the region. Like the French, the leaders of the Jewish community in Palestine had a complex relationship, a mixture of partnership and rivalry with Britain, and they regarded Arab nationalism as a hostile force. Like them they tended to perceive most events in the region as instigated by Britain, an omnipresent and omnipotent power and the creator and manipulator of the Arab nationalist movement.

A telling manifestation of this outlook can be found in the Israeli interpretation, which blamed the failure of the Israeli–Jordanian negotiations on Britain's negative influence and more specifically on Kirkbride's opposition. Thus Moshe Dayan, one of the three Israeli negotiators, wrote in his autobiography that "when we came to the king to continue the negotiations, he told us that his British friend, Sir Alec Kirkbride, was opposed to Jordan's making peace with Israel as long as the other Arab states–and particularly Egypt—refrained from doing so."[59] But one did not have to be Israeli to favor this version. It was in fact reinforced by another British diplomat, Sir Alexander Knox Helm, the former minister in Tel Aviv. In February 1955, on leave in Britain from his post in Sudan, he told the Israeli ambassador, Eliahu Elath, that during the Israeli–Jordanian negotiations, he had been strongly in favour of it. Mainly responsible for putting the brakes had been Alec Kirkbride. Not that Kirkbride had been opposed in principle, but he had thought it would be better for Abdullah to complete the annexation of the West Bank of the Jordan ... and to get the parliamentary elections out of the way, before proceeding toward any agreement with Israel. In fact, however, these things not only failed to improve the chances of a settlement, they actually diminished them.[60]

The British Foreign Office was aware of the version current in Israel and of its negative impact on the British–Israeli relationship. In May 1950 the head of the Foreign Office's Middle Eastern Department, Sir Geoffrey Furlonge, told an Israeli diplomat that he was forced to conclude that since assuming his post, all his efforts to improve Britain's relations with Israel had been to no avail. "He felt a special bitterness in view of the deliberate distortion of British policy in certain Israel quarters, as, for example, by the accusation that [the British government] is hindering Abdullah's endeavors to reach a settlement with Israel. This is simply not true."[61]

The availability now of the relevant diplomatic archives has helped refute this version.[62] It is true that earlier in 1949, Britain, like the United States, had been opposed to a separate Jordanian–Israeli agreement. It also is true that Britain and its representatives were so careful in voicing their opinions with regard to the negotiations to Abdullah and his aides that the distinction between cautious encouragement and reservation might sometimes have been blurred. Moreover, there is no denying that during the domestic political crisis of early March, Kirkbride encouraged Abdullah to suspend the negotiations and attend first to the stability of his regime and to his relations with the Arab world. But earlier Kirkbride had supported the negotiations and encouraged Abdullah and his subordinates— cautiously, however—to proceed with them.[63]

But important and interesting as this issue may be, the study of British policy toward the 1949–50 negotiations should not be reduced to an analysis of whether Britain encouraged or discouraged them. The documents that have become available reveal the complexity of Britain's policy, even in the twilight of its hegemony in the region, its relationship with the United States as the latter was gradually replacing the former, its complex attitude toward the Israeli state, and the style and mode of operation of Britain's last great proconsul in the region—Sir Alec Kirkbride.

Britain's guarded support for the negotiations during their early phase was summed up in a memorandum prepared in the Foreign Office for the War Office:

> We ourselves are in no way involved in these negotiations. We have in the past advised against separate negotiations, but have now decided that we need do nothing to discourage them. We have merely instructed our representative in Amman to say to King Abdullah, if he gets the opportunity, that we presume that if any agreement results it will be put to the Conciliation Commission for their endorsement.[64]

The change in Britain's position largely reflects its acceptance of a new reality—the consolidation of Israel as a state in the region and part of the Middle Eastern political landscape, and the failure of Britain's effort to impose a solution through the PCC. Like the United States, Britain wanted an Arab–Israeli settlement as part of a broader quest for stability in the region. A Jordanian–Israeli agreement contributing to an Arab–Israeli settlement would be welcome. But support for the settlement was moderated by anxiety lest the negotiations adversely affect other vital British interests in the region, such as Britain's strategic deployment; its interests in Egypt, the Gulf, and Aden; and its concern for the stability of the Hashemite regime in Jordan.

Britain's interest in the Negev in 1940–50 derived primarily from considerations concerning the region's defense in the event of a conventional war with the Soviet Union. The Negev was seen as providing a secure land connection between "Egypt and the Ramallah line or any line or position in Palestine or the Levant which we may wish to defend in war."[65] As a power with a comprehensive view of the Arab world, Britain was also interested in territorial contiguity between Egypt and the eastern Arab world. In the light of subsequent events Britain's insistence on this point does not appear wise or farsighted, but in 1949–50 the configuration was very different.

The British knew also that for its own reasons, Egypt's fragmented political establishment was interested in the southern tip of the Negev. They were correct in assuming that a Jordanian–Israeli agreement leaving Eylat in Israeli hands would pit Egypt against Jordan as well as against Britain, Abdullah's patron. This, from a British point of view, was yet another reason to encourage Jordan to insist on the southern Negev or to consider Egyptian participation, at least indirectly, in the negotiations.

As the Hashemite regime's traditional patron, Britain was understandably concerned about the negotiations' potential impact on the regime's stability. Familiar with Abdullah's political style, the events of early 1949 still fresh in their memory, the British were anxious that Abdullah might be tempted to make concessions that his own subjects and the rest of the Arab world would find unacceptable.

The sources currently available offer no documentation of an explicit British request from or advice to the Jordanians to insist on an Israeli territorial concession in the southern Negev, nor is one likely to be found in the archives. But indirect evidence indicates that the Jordanians presented this demand, and prominently, in deference to the British. Thus Sir William Strang from the Foreign Office in London—in a letter to Sir Ronald Campbell, the British ambassador in Cairo, updating him on the early rounds of the Jordanian–Israeli negotiations—wrote that the Jordanians had not coordinated their line with the British beforehand but had presented those positions desirable to them: "In fact we did not give the Jordanians any briefing about these talks though the attitude which they are taking fits in very well with our strategic ideas."[66] Indeed, after decades of influence and close cooperation, particularly under the stewardship of Kirkbride, direct pressure or formal coordination were not usually required.

Nor did Kirkbride believe that London had to be briefed in detail on how the influence was exerted. Allusion sufficed. Thus in mid-December Kirkbride reported to London that al-Rifai had proposed to the Israelis on December 8 to grant Jordan access to the Mediterranean and a common border with an Arab state in the north, near the Lebanese border, rather than in the south. The proposal was not submitted seriously but, rather, was an attempt by al-Rifai to persuade the Israelis that the demand for the Negev was a genuine Jordanian requirement and not an idea forced on them by the British. Kirkbride told his alarmed colleagues in London that the "desirability of a common frontier between Egypt and Jordan is fully appreciated by all concerned here." In other words, Kirkbride was explaining that the message had been transmitted and absorbed.[67]

To the Americans, the Jordanians sounded a different tune. When briefing Fritzlan, the American chargé d'affaires, Samir al-Rifai stated that the crucial issue was Jordanian access to the Mediterranean. His country's demand for the Negev, he said, was "formal."[68]

As we have already seen, it suited the British to emphasize that the southern Negev was an issue that Egypt, too, viewed as vital. Britain's diplomats deliberated among themselves whether it would be fair to brief Egypt on the opening and subsequent course of the Jordanian–Israeli negotiations. They soon discovered that the Egyptians were aware of the negotiations and indeed were worried by the prospect of Jordan's signing an agreement leaving Eylat in Israeli hands. The British therefore decided that Egypt would better be left out of the negotiations and settled on communicating to the Jordanians the need to take into account Egypt's interests and sensibilities.

The Israelis, in any case, saw the Jordanian demand for the southern Negev as the result of British pressure or inspiration. The importance they attached to this issue is evidenced by the fact that it led Ben-Gurion to one of his more direct interventions in the negotiations. At the end of November he met with the British minister, Alexander Knox Helm. Although Shiloah had told Knox Helm that the first meeting with the Jordanians on November 27 was of "a preliminary nature," Ben-Gurion asserted that it was his impression that agreement could be reached on all the points submitted by the Jordanian representatives except the one concerning the Negev. He presumed that the Negev demand had been put forward at the behest of the British government, "as Jordan itself had no interest in the Negev."[69]

In December the issue of the southern Negev as the stumbling block to an agreement lost its saliency, but the issue of the application of the British–Jordanian treaty to the West Bank was still on the agenda. Israel's opposition reflected its mistrust of Britain's intentions and the residue of the recent conflict and acrimony between Britain and the Jewish community in Palestine and Israel. Walter Eytan, the director-general of the Israeli Foreign Ministry, said as much to the British minister on December 13. Eytan admitted that the question of the treaty's application to the West Bank had no practical importance and that Israel's opposition derived from purely domestic reasons, but whatever the reasons, Israel was vehemently opposed to the application, whereas Jordan's representatives intimated that for them it was not vital.[70] From this Eytan concluded that a peace between Jordan and Israel depended on Britain. This was not quite true and certainly was an overstatement, and the British must have seen it as such. In any event, they decided to please Jordan by recognizing the annexation and applying the treaty when the time came and to calm Israel by refraining from establishing British bases west of the Jordan River.

But Israel's mistrust of the British was not the result of pure paranoia. Among such senior British diplomats in Cairo as the ambassador, Campbell, and the head of the Middle East Office, Sir John Troutbeck, an anti-Israeli frame of mind was evident. Thus on December 15 Campbell wrote from Cairo (in coordination with Troutbeck):

> Whatever may be thought or said about difficulty, or even impossibility, of our ever getting the Jews from the Akaba Coast without the use of force and persuading them to accept a southern frontier for Israel that would be acceptable to the Egyptians, the only substantial hope now as so often in the past, of securing political results would be in the agreement and joint action in the shape of strongest possible pressure by Britain and America.[71]

Such views and attitudes remained a significant component of Britain's policy toward Israel until the latter part of the 1950s, but they did not play an important role during the 1949–50 negotiations. The minister in Tel Aviv, Kirkbride in Amman, and the pertinent officials in London recognized the limits of their influence on Israel. Indeed, Britain's ability to affect the negotiations directly was confined to its capacity to exert influence on Jordan. In order to pressure Israel, therefore, the British had to enlist the United States.

The United States and Britain pursued similar policies toward the Jordanian–Israeli negotiations. Information was exchanged and positions were coordinated on a regular basis, by the legations in Amman and Tel Aviv as well as in Washington and London. Both the United States and Britain supported the negotiations, monitored them sympathetically, lent their subtle support, but thought that massive intervention would be counterproductive. In early March they both determined that there was no point in continuing the talks and decided that it would be better for them to be suspended. But as we shall soon see, Washington's discreet support for the negotiations was far more determined than that of London. In fact a comparison of the U.S. and British positions and of the respective messages the two countries communicated to Jordan would clearly reveal that Britain's support was so subtle and cautious as to make it almost meaningless.

## Kirkbride and Abdullah

On the British side it was primarily Sir Alec Kirkbride who monitored the negotiations and occasionally sought to adjust their course. In the winter of 1949–50, Sir Alec was in his eleventh year as Britain's representative in Amman, but he had known Abdullah since 1921. It was Kirkbride who, as a young British officer and a veteran of T. E. Lawrence's campaign, had met Abdullah in Transjordan on the latter's trek from the Hejaz to Damascus. Abdullah stayed in the territory that became his state, and Kirkbride returned on the eve of World War II as the British resident. Then when Jordan was granted formal independence, Kirkbride became Britain's first minister in Amman.[72]

Between the two men there developed an unusual relationship. Kirkbride liked Abdullah and held him in high esteem. He saw him as a humane, wise, and humorous man, comparatively easy to work with and, on the whole, an asset from the British Empire's point of view. Abdullah regarded Kirkbride with affection and esteem, but curiously it was Abdullah, the older of the two (by fifteen years) who treated his British friend with circumspection. This reflected the fact that Abdullah also viewed Kirkbride as an embodiment of Britain's imperial might. Abdullah would usually first try out his ideas on Kirkbride and withdraw them when he sensed opposition or reservations. But when the matter was particularly important to him, Abdullah did not hesitate to act behind Kirkbride's back. It seems that when he did so, Abdullah trusted that he could still rely on Kirkbride's support. Indeed, on several occasions, this was true. The most intriguing example of Kirkbride's ability to find a compromise (successful on that occasion) between his imperial responsibility and his personal relationship with Abdullah happened during World War II when Kirkbride discovered that Abdullah had established contact with the Germans. He did not report this immediately to London but chose to let the issue die. No real harm was caused to British interests, and Abdullah continued to be a useful and, on the whole, reliable client.[73]

Sir Alec was an astute observer and practitioner of politics. He knew full well that the Britain of 1940–50 was a waning power, that the Jordanian political system had been transformed, and that his influence must be applied with a very gentle touch. This did not mean, of course, that Kirkbride did not have considerable influence on Jordanian politics in 1949–50. His own reports reflect his effectiveness ("My own opinion, that Samir is gradually coming to share"). As we saw, the king and his prime minister solicited his advice and asked him to mediate between them. Kirkbride's influence was used most of the time in support of the negotiations. He was clearly apprehensive—in December he alerted his superiors to his displeasure with the negotiations—and he kept warning Abdullah throughout the period against crossing red lines and straying into mine fields. In February he tried to persuade Tawfiq Abu al-Huda not to obstruct the effort to reach a nonaggression pact, but in early March he decided that the negotiations were better terminated, and then, according to Knox Helm's description, he "put his foot on the brakes."

The best description of Kirkbride's influence on Jordanian politics was provided by Kirkbride himself, in a letter to Furlonge:

> Before leaving the personal note, I want to speak of the belief, so widely current in neighbouring countries that I am able to make the Jordanian do anything that I wish. This is not the case at all. I do not deny that I can wield considerable personal influence but, the fact that this influence has been retained for many years and survived the change of regime, is due to my care not to abuse its use and because King Abdullah and his ministers believe that I would not personally advise them to a thing unless I believed that it was in the best interests of the country. If I ever destroy that belief, I will be left with the official influence which can normally be expected of one of His Majesty's representatives in the Middle East plus some allowance for Great Britain's special position in Jordan.[74]

## The United States

On February 27, 1950, the acting secretary of state gave the National Security Council a report on the application of an earlier report entitled "United States Policy Toward Israel and the Arab States."[75] The latter had been formally designated on October 17, 1949, as officially expressing U.S. government policy in this sphere. The follow-up report commented that despite the State Department's protests, Israel had failed to comply with the recommendation that it accept the principle of repatriating the greatest number of refugees possible and immediately begin the actual repatriation of refugees "on a reasonable scale." The report likewise complained about the Israeli policy of encouraging Jewish immigrants to come to Israel and of settling them on and in houses belonging to the Arab refugees. The report also pointed out that the Arabs had rejected as insufficient Israel's offer to absorb 100,000 Palestinian refugees. It noted that the Arab states had turned down the recommendation to settle the bulk of the refugees in their territories but that they were coming to recognize that the return of most of the refugees to their homes was "physically impossible." The authors noted with satisfaction that

> a favorable development has occurred in connection with subparagrah (h) of paragraph 16, which states in part that the United States should assist the Israelis and the Arabs to achieve a final settlement of the territorial question in Palestine. Encouraged to do so by the United States government, Israel and Jordan have entered into direct negotiations toward a final settlement of the problems outstanding between them. Although progress in these talks has been slow, the fact that they are being held at all is encouraging.

On a more pessimistic and realistic note they observed that "the possibility of the full implementation of the territorial solution recommended in this subparagraph is becoming increasingly unlikely as the passage of time enables the parties in control of part of Palestine to consolidate their position."

This document is useful in clarifying the framework of Washington's policy toward the Israeli–Jordanian negotiations. The basic components of the U.S. policy toward the Arab–Israeli conflict had not changed from earlier in 1949. The United States still wanted the conflict to be resolved by a compromise that, unfortunately, was not acceptable to either side. The only change in the U.S. policy as it was reformulated in October 1949 was the removal of opposition to bilateral negotiations, to the point of the United States' decision to facilitate them. But the change was tactical. Direct negotiations between Israel and an Arab state were one element in a complex puzzle; they were to be supported but must be seen in that limited perspective.

Within this framework the U.S. government was willing to extend its good offices. Hence the encouraging letter to Abdullah in December 1949 and the offer to help Israel involve Egypt in direct negotiations. But the United States rejected all efforts by both sides to gain their respective position or to draw the United States into a massive intervention in the negotiations, according to the minutes of two conversations held in January 1950 between the assistant secretary of state, George McGhee, and the outgoing Jordanian minister, Yusuf Haykal. On January 11 Haykal called on McGhee for a routine farewell meeting, and in their conversation McGhee noted that the corridor under Jordanian sovereignty that Jordan had demanded had no real value, that it was indefensible in case of war and unnecessary in peacetime.[76]

Haykal had not prepared for a substantive discussion, and so he returned on January 24 armed with a briefing and instructions by his government.[77] He offered McGhee a review of the negotiations, beginning with Abdullah's meeting with Novomeyski. Among other things he argued that

> Jordan, in making a request for a substantial section of the Negev in order to ensure solid access to the Mediterranean, had been guided by President Truman's message of last spring to King Abdullah, in which the president explained the U.S. policy: If Israel wanted to retain territory beyond that granted to it by the 1947 partition resolution, it should make appropriate territorial compensation.

To this McGhee replied:

> The territorial policy that the minister had referred to had been, and still was, the general policy of the United States concerning a territorial settlement in Palestine. He emphasized, however, that this policy was a general one and did not refer to specific pieces of territory or to the specific nations to which territory might be allotted. . . . The question of exactly what was involved in an Israeli–Jordanian settlement was a problem that would have to be solved by Israel and Jordan alone, without interference from outside parties.

But McGhee clearly intimated that he felt that if Jordan were really interested in a settlement, the demands it had presented were unreasonable:

> He personally did not consider a corridor to be a very feasible proposition, but if Jordan desired a whole section of the Negev, he could understand the difficulty which Jordan and Israel were having

in arriving [at an] agreement on this particular point. He wondered whether Jordan had given full consideration to the economic burden for establishing a seaport.

Thus subtly and elegantly, McGhee communicated to the Jordanians what he thought of their principal demand in the negotiations. But he also made it clear to them—as the Americans pointed out to the Israelis on other occasions—that the United States would not be drawn into a heavier involvement in the negotiations.

The framework established for the U.S. policy toward the Arab–Israeli conflict in October 1949 also helps explain Washington's refusal in March 1950 to take action in order to resuscitate the Israeli–Jordanian negotiations, as well as its refusal, six weeks later, to join Britain in extending formal recognition to Jordan's annexation of the West Bank. There were in the principles and practices of the U.S. policy toward Israel and its neighbors elements that the Israelis regarded as hostile, such as the reference quoted earlier to Jewish immigration, as opposed to Arab refugees. The Israeli outlook on this particular issue was rather different. The Israelis could not understand Washington's policy on the question of Jerusalem. There were, indeed, American diplomats of the school that later came to be dubbed ''Arabist'' who displayed a fundamental hostility to Israel. But the senior diplomat at the State Department, McGhee, did not belong to that school. The ambassador in Tel Aviv also was very friendly (so friendly that British minister Knox Helm, in one of his dispatches to London, referred to ''the problem with McDonald.'' Jefferson Caffrey in Cairo and Gerald Drew and David Fritzlan in Amman dealt with Arab–Israeli affairs in a businesslike fashion. In this respect the U.S. minister in Damascus, Keeley, whose personality and style were described in Chapter 3, was an exception.

In the context of the Jordanian–Israeli negotiations, Keeley's political preferences surfaced when he was asked to take action with regard to Syria's threat to close its border with Jordan, in view of the possibility that trade relations might be established between Jordan and Israel. In a telegram dated March 14,[78] Keeley responded to the directive:

Assume "Damascus for action" at end of DepTel does not mean Department desires Legation to endeavor to dissuade Syria. To attempt to do so could have only adverse results, as Syria unsympathetic to what it considers our greater concern for Israel's economic plight than for threat to Syria sovereign existence inherent to Israel's declared destiny.

Keeley was alluding to Syria's fears of Israel's "expansionist nature" and made no attempt to express his own disagreement with that view. To this, Acting Secretary of State James E. Webb responded:

Dept's interest in estab. normal relations between Israel and Jordan and between Israel and other Arab states, motivated by desire see present instability N.E. with its resultant adverse effects upon strength and unity of area, disappear. Syrian notion that this attitude based on U.S. concern over Israel's economic situation of course utterly unfounded and you should make every effort disabuse Syrians of this idea.

Dept. disturbed by Syrian government's interference in Jordanian–Israeli conversations by such means as PriMin.'s statement reclosing Syrian frontier with Jordan if Jordan–Israel agreement reached. Dept. realizes task most difficult and Legation's position difficult, but desires Legation endeavor discreetly persuade Syrian Gov't cease interference and take no retaliatory action if agreement actually reached.[79]

But as we know, a Jordanian–Israeli agreement was not reached: The Israeli–Jordanian negotiations collapsed in the spring of 1950, and the focus of the effort to reach an Israeli–Arab agreement shifted toward Egypt.

# 5

The Israeli–Egyptian
Relationship

During the 1920s and 1930s there was a gradual and steady change in the Egyptian political system that led Egypt from a position of general indifference toward the Palestine question to increasing interest in it, to identification with the Arab side in the conflict, and then to a deep involvement in it. This complex process was shaped by the interplay among several forces at work that continued to affect both the efforts to settle Egypt's bilateral conflict with Israel and the developments that exacerbated it.

The primary factor that governed Egypt's position on the Palestine conflict was the quest for regional hegemony, manifested on different levels by the Egyptian state and royal house. From this quest derived the rivalry with the Hashemites, the alliance with the Saudis, and the understanding that if Egypt wanted to lead the Arab world, it had to take the lead in what had clearly become the most important issue for all pan-Arab activists. It seemed equally important to deny the Hashemite rivals the advantages that any territorial or political achievement in Palestine was likely to yield.

But Egypt's regional policy must not be construed in only political terms. The gradual adoption of a pan-Arab orientation also was important. By the late 1930s Islam and Arabism came to acquire a central position in Egypt's self-view, at the expense of the secular, territorial concepts of its identity. As a consequence, Egypt's commitment to the Arab cause in Palestine became the norm, and the freedom of maneuver available to Egyptian governments in formulating policies toward the Palestine question became steadily narrower.

The complexity of the Egyptian position on Palestine reflected the pluralism of its political system. Thus the royal court's quest for Arab and Islamic leadership derived also from its desire to obtain political assets for the king to use to compete with his principal domestic rival, the Wafd party. At the same time, the Wafd's leaders, as well as their Constitutionalist and other competitors, engaged in political overbidding on an issue that evidently interested a large segment of Egyptian society. In an entirely different fashion and in line with their efforts at mass mobilization under the banner of Islam, the Muslim Brotherhood conducted its own policy in Palestine to the point of sending its own volunteer units to take part in the 1948 war.

A linkage was thus quite naturally created between Egypt's Palestine policy and the issue that until 1954 stood at the top of the country's national agenda—the question of full independence and Egypt's relationship with Britain. The state of its relationship with Britain had a clear bearing on Egypt's outlook on the Palestine question and, since 1948, on its perception of the Negev, which became a crucial issue in the Egyptian–Israeli conflict. With regard to the Negev, Egypt's position was not characterized by unanimity or persistence. Rather, the Egyptians were ambivalent about the possibility that Britain, through Jordan, would establish military bases in the Negev. The Egyptians could see the advantage of creating an alternative to the British bases in the Suez Canal zone, thereby expediting the evacuation of their territory. But some Egyptians felt that the Negev was too close and that the transfer of Britain's forces there would not provide the comfort and confidence that Egypt desired.

The relative importance of the geopolitical dimension of the

Egyptian–Israel conflict changed over time. In the 1950s and 1960s, these geopolitical considerations took shape as a conflict between the two strongest and most assertive states in the region, one seeking regional hegemony and the other feeling threatened by such hegemony. Egypt saw Israel as a buffer obstructing its access to the eastern Arab world, and Israel viewed Egypt's closure of the Suez Canal and the occasional blockade of the Tiran Straits as designed to cut the Israeli state down to size and limit its geographic horizons. But in the 1940s, the situation became more ambiguous. The Jewish and Zionist leadership had anticipated their Egyptian counterparts' recognizing the geopolitical importance of a physical presence on the Red Sea coast. Several Egyptian politicians believed that the presence of a Jewish state or entity on their border was undesirable, but they did not craft this belief into a strategic doctrine. In fact, discomfort with Israel's potential presence on Egypt's border could be translated into more than one policy. That is, Egypt could join the all-Arab effort to prevent the establishment of the Jewish state, but it could also assume that it was an inevitable development and that Egypt's best interests required that the relationship between the two states be settled in advance and that a potentially dangerous conflict be averted.[1]

The most persistent advocate of this policy line was Ismail Sidqi Pasha, a conservative independent politician who in the early 1930s, with the king's backing against the Wafd, served as an autocratic prime minister. He then regained that position following World War II. As prime minister in 1946 he reached an understanding with Eliyahu Sasson but lost power before the understanding could be converted into a full-fledged agreement. On the eve of the May 15, 1948, invasion of Israel, the upper house of the Egyptian parliament held a closed session to discuss the question of war with Israel. The minutes of this meeting, published by Anwar al-Sadat's regime in the mid-1970s, are intriguing. Among the series of speakers who articulated the gamut of Egyptian opinion, Ismail Sidqi stands out in his attempt to present a cool-headed analysis of Egypt's national interests, as opposed to the ideological and emotional arguments made by the advocates of war.

Sidqi built his case by putting fourteen rhetorical questions to the prime minister: "Does the prime minister not think that Egypt's supreme interest calls for the establishment of stable peace, given that it has yet to overcome its domestic problems? Is Egypt ready, militarily and politically, to conduct a long and expensive war?" Sidqi argued further that it could not be said that

Egypt has a principal share in the Palestine conflict, in comparison with the Arab states bordering Palestine or those Arab states in which the prevailing conditions, the language, and other ties with Palestine create a particularly close bond and a particular interest in solving the problem they have with Palestine. Egypt is considered distant even if it is counted among the Arab states. [And in response to a question addressed to him, he added] . . . Yes, we do have a common border with Palestine, but we are separated by a large desert.[2]

In any event, the discussion in the Egyptian upper house was purely academic. The king, motivated mainly by considerations of his Arab policy and his rivalry with Abdullah, decided on his own to join the all-Arab invasion and so ordered his army to attack. The 1948 war between Egypt and Israel, its course and outcome, provides an excellent illustration of how the internal dynamics of a conflict can become an independent factor. Egypt's military defeat deepened the conflict, which until 1948 had been quite superficial. This sense of failure and humiliation was reinforced by a fear of vulnerability along a border with a new state whose nature—Jewish? Zionist? Socialist?—the Egyptians had yet to determine. The Negev acquired a new importance in Egyptian eyes. During the war's early stages, when the southern Negev could have been taken over easily, Egypt, concentrating on its competition with Abdullah, engaged its troops on other fronts. But toward the end of 1948 when contacts with Israel were established in order to end the war, Egypt put forward a strong demand for the Negev or at least its southern part.

The war resulted also in a much deeper Egyptian involvement in the Palestinian issue. Egypt ended the war in control of part of Palestine (the Gaza Strip) and some 300,000 Palestinians. Another consequence of the war was the exacerbation of Egypt's rivalry with Jordan. The measures taken by the two rivals left a residue of hostility and mistrust. The possibility, which occasionally surfaced, that Abdullah would annex parts of Palestine, including the Negev, so that Egypt would face a strong and hostile Arab neighbor on the Sinai border, alarmed the Egyptian leadership. In more immediate terms, in late 1948 and early 1949 they felt a need to end the war with a visible concrete achievement so as to reduce the political costs of the military defeat.[3]

## Wartime Diplomacy and the Armistice

As we mentioned, Egypt made two brief attempts in late 1948 to conclude a separate agreement with Israel. The first attempt took place in September 1948 when, in response to Eliyahu Sasson's overtures, a special emissary of the Egyptian court, Kamel Riyad, arrived in Paris. On September 21 he established contact with Sasson. Riyad—whose code name in the Israeli documents was "the assistant"—told Sasson that he had been sent directly by the court, that the Egyptian legation in Paris had been instructed to assist him and to place its diplomatic mail service at his disposal, but that its staff was not aware of the nature of his mission.[4]

The talks with Riyad presented the Israelis with a two-pronged difficulty: They had to establish that he was a genuine and authoritative emissary and then to respond to his demands. In his discussion with Sasson, Riyad brought up some of the issues that reappeared also in subsequent discussions with other Egyptian representatives— Egypt's fear of Israel and its expansionist intentions, its perception of Israel as a propagator of communist ideas, and Riyad's superiors' hostility to Abdullah and the British. Riyad thought that the time was ripe for a separate Egyptian–Israeli agreement and so asked Sasson for a concrete proposal that would serve as the basis for negotiations. After consulting with his Paris colleagues Sasson drew up a draft proposal for an Egyptian–Israeli agreement, based on the guidelines that Sharett had sent earlier for negotiations with the Arab states (except Jordan, for which special instructions were presumably to be issued). One of the more interesting ideas raised by Sasson in his draft was the transformation of the Arab League into an Eastern League (of which Israel too could, in theory, be a part). It is ironic that the Israeli experts who could not see a clear way out of the war with the Arab states would entertain, and put to paper, such far-reaching notions of Israeli–Arab cooperation. The actual course of the negotiations, however, once they began in earnest, disabused them of any such ideas.

On September 30 Riyad again met with Sasson and told him that the deputy head of the Egyptian royal court had instructed him to consult with several members of the Egyptian delegation in Cairo. This gave Riyad's mission the overt and official character that a week earlier he had so clearly tried to avoid. Still, he stressed that Sasson's discussions with him should not be viewed as ''entry into formal talks or negotiations. Everything so far is no more than clarification.''[5] He also stated that ''the Egyptians were seriously thinking of annexing the Arab part of southern Palestine.'' In order to compensate ''the rest of Arab Palestine'' for the loss of part of Gaza (which was to be annexed to Egypt), the Egyptians wanted to give it an outlet to the sea by way of a corridor to Haifa. Egypt, Riyad asserted, had no claims on Jerusalem, but it could not acquiesce in Jewish control of the holy places. He justified Egypt's claim to southern Palestine with two arguments: Egypt needed a forward position in the event of an armed conflict with Israel, and it was opposed to permitting the area to be annexed to Jordan and to become a British military base.

By early October Sharett had arrived in Paris, and he took part in formulating a careful and evasive reply to Riyad's opening position. Sharett and Sasson were fully aware of the problems raised in Riyad's demands. Furthermore, they still did not know whom he represented and how credible he was. Sharett passed on their decision to Ben-Gurion, who rejected the demand that Palestine's southern coastal strip be annexed to Egypt.

But this did not end the dialogue with Riyad that Israel's increasingly effective military pressure clearly served to sustain. On November 2, 1948, Sasson reported to Sharett that Riyad had told him that King Farouk had responded positively to a fresh proposal made by Sasson. Sasson believed that Farouk would agree to sign a full armistice in return for such terms as Israel's acceptance of Egypt's annexation "of the southern part of Arab Palestine as well as that desert part of the Negev that the Israelis had defined in the past as negotiable." Then, in return for all this, Egypt would be willing to promise not "to budge" in the event of war between Israel and any other Arab state, as well as to find a way of recognizing Israel de facto.[6]

On November 4 Sharett briefed Israel's temporary government on these proposals (Ben-Gurion was sick and did not attend the meeting). The foreign minister told his colleagues that until recently he had had reservations about the emissary and his mission but that once Riyad suggested a meeting with the head of the Egyptian delegation (to the UN General Assembly in Paris), he became convinced that the Egyptian prime minister, Maḥmud Fahmi Nukrashi, had agreed to the mission, or at least had not opposed it.

Sharett explained that the Egyptian proposal presented two main difficulties: (1) its insistence on Israel's evacuation of all the territories it had captured in the south that had not been assigned to the Jewish state in November 1947 and (2) its demand that Israel agree that the coastal strip from Ashdod to Rafah as well as a strip along the international border southeast from Rafah be attached to Egypt. Sharett suggested that in its reply to Egypt, Israel should distinguish between southern Palestine's northern and eastern and its western and southern boundaries. The former would be the subject of negotiations between Israel and "the future Arab state." But Israel was willing to discuss its own border with Egypt. At this point Sharett made another distinction, between the coastal strip—regarding which he shared Ben-Gurion's view—and the border strip separating the Sinai from the Israeli Negev. With regard to the latter Sharett would make a concession in return for Egypt's endorsement of the international border "to the coast of Aqaba and inclusive of it."

After discussing it, the cabinet approved Sharett's position and determined that "our representatives will meet officially with representatives of the Egyptian government and will present them with our comments with a view to continue the negotiations and not to terminate them."[7] Sharett referred to this issue in a detailed briefing he sent to Golda Meir in Moscow. After bringing her up-to-date on the essentials of the negotiations, he added: "It is not clear which element plays the decisive role in Egypt's policy, whether it is the opposition to us or to a British base in the Negev. The answer to this question will determine Egypt's preference—a compromise with us or with England and Transjordan."

The considerations that guided Ben-Gurion and Sharett can be found in Ben-Gurion's diary and in Sharett's report to the cabinet. Ben-Gurion instructed Sasson to object to the annexation of any part of Palestine, particularly Gaza and the coastal strip, because he was opposed to an Egyptian physical presence in Palestine, let alone so close to Israel's center. A leader whose forces had difficulty checking an Egyptian column thirty miles south of Tel Aviv just a few months earlier was obviously aware of the strategic significance of such proximity. But Ben-Gurion had at least two other reasons. Egypt's conditions were stiff (even when regarded as opening terms), and Ben-Gurion could safely assume that given the military balance of forces between Israel and Egypt, Israel had every chance of ending the war with a clear-cut victory. This would also mean establishing Israeli control over the whole Negev. Indeed, Egypt's feeling that this was the case must have contributed to its decision to send Riyad.

In any event, the Egyptians found Israel's position unsatisfactory and so the negotiations were stopped. But then additional Israeli military exploits led to a second Egyptian overture. In early December Mahmud Fawzi, Egypt's representative at the UN, transmitted through Ralph Bunche, the acting mediator, an offer for a separate settlement based on Israel's conceding the Negev south of the Majdal–Beit–Jubrin–Dead Sea line to Egypt. Israel rejected the offer as it did another idea, to open immediately armistice negotiations on the basis of the November 16 UN resolution (which called for Israel's withdrawal from recently occupied territories). Egypt was clearly alarmed by the prospect of defeat and was anxious to end the war, but it still hoped to exact a high price. Ben-Gurion thought otherwise, however, and was able to open the armistice negotiations without any preconditions.

The Egyptian–Israeli negotiations were made easier by the fact that both parties were interested in a similar outcome. Egypt did not want peace but, rather, an end to the war and a removal of the prospect of defeat. The Israeli leadership, as we have already seen, had decided that the price of peace under the terms acceptable to the Arabs was prohibitive and would settle temporarily for armistice agreements. At the same time, two Egyptian demands—for the Nitzana area (which Egypt viewed as vital to the defense of Sinai) and the appointment of an Egyptian military governor in Beersheba (for prestige reasons)—were regarded by Israel as harsh and unwarranted. But when Ben-Gurion realized that without some concession in Nitzana an agreement would not be forthcoming, he agreed to demilitarize the Nitzana area.

In addition to the armistice agreement, the Egyptian–Israeli negotiations in Rhodes had two by-products. One was the personal relationship between the Israeli group and the two chief Egyptian negotiators—Colonel Ismail Shirine, the king's brother-in-law, and Abdul Mun'im Mustafa, a professional diplomat who had most recently served as the director of the Arab League's political department. Mustafa left with the Israelis a list of questions, the answer to which were to provide the basis for a new round of talks and the establishment of a dialogue between the two countries. But this failed to happen and Israel's subsequent attempts to take advantage of Shirine's closeness to the king, in order to revive the negotiations with Egypt, were to no avail. Abdul Mun'im Mustafa, however, did remain the chief contact person with Israel for a full year after the conclusion of the Rhodes negotiations.

Hardly less important were the insights into the other party's position that were gained by at least some of the participants during the formal and informal talks in Rhodes. Thus when the question of Gaza came up during the April 12, 1949, consultation in Israel, Sasson remarked that "the Egyptians in Rhodes said to us that if we had not held the territory we would have gladly opted out of the whole business, but because it is in our hands, we must shoulder the burden.''[8] Such openness was a result of the intimacy created in such settings as Rhodes and Camp David, and when the necessary conditions for peace negotiations exist, such intimacy can contribute to their success. But in 1949 such conditions did not exist between Egypt and Israel, and thus the Rhodes talks became a terminal point rather than an interim stage.

# From Rhodes to Lausanne: Spring–Summer 1949

The next phase in Egyptian–Israeli relations can be named the "Lausanne phase," as it was shaped primarily by the Lausanne Conference and the American effort to bring about a comprehensive Arab–Israeli settlement through the PCC. Or it could also be named "the Abdul Mun'im Mustafa phase," as this senior diplomat became Israel's almost-exclusive contact.

The first post-Rhodes meeting with Abdul Mun'im Mustafa was held on April 19 with Tuvia Arazi. The atmosphere still radiated the optimism and familiarity of the Rhodes talks, and the meeting was conducted on the assumption that relations between Egypt and Israel were at a stage of transition toward a more comprehensive agreement that would bring normalization and possibly even political cooperation. In his report Arazi reminded his superiors that "it was said that we will consult with them before opening political discussions with the king [namely, Abdullah] and that we will look for ways of coordinating our line with theirs.''[9] In that spirit Arazi and Mustafa discussed the situation in Syria (after Husni Zaim's coup), the Syrian–Israeli armistice negotiations (which had begun a few days earlier), Abdullah's Greater Syria plan, and the prospects for Egyptian–Israeli economic cooperation.

Arazi's conversation with Abdul Mun'im Mustafa, as reported

by the Israeli diplomat, could be read as reflecting a relationship between two states on the road to partnership and cooperation in Middle Eastern politics. But in reality, entirely different trends were unfolding. The Lausanne Conference was about to be convened; the Arab states were meeting for a preparatory session in Beirut; and Egypt was seeking to play its traditional role as the leader of the Arab collective and so adopted a policy congruent with the Arab consensus. The day before Arazi's report was dispatched, Ben-Gurion, in a meeting with Mark Ethridge, the U.S. representative to the PCC, had brought up the idea of annexing Gaza and its residents to Israel. Ben-Gurion, as we mentioned earlier, had raised this idea in anticipation of the United States' pressure on Israel, but his initiative had had obvious repercussions on Israel's relations with Egypt.

With the opening of the Lausanne discussions the Israelis sensed the change in Egypt's position. Abdul Mun'im Mustafa led the Arab line and avoided direct contact with Sasson and the other Israelis. If the Israelis had hoped that the Rhodes pattern would be repeated in Lausanne—that they could reach a separate understanding with the Egyptians or the Jordanians and then apply it formally to the plenary sessions—they were disappointed. Consequently, Sasson tried another familiar technique: turning to a high authority. On May 16, 1949, he wrote a letter to Ismail Shirine, complaining that Abdul Mun'im Mustafa was avoiding him and asked that he be instructed to respond to his overtures.[10] It was possibly as a result of this letter that Mustafa finally agreed to a separate meeting with Sasson, which took place on June 2 in the small town of Lotrey near Lausanne. Mustafa's position was summed up by Sasson as follows:

- At this stage the Arab states are not ready to sign peace agreements with Israel.

- Any agreement reached in Lausanne will have to be brought by the PCC before the UN in September for discussion and approval. If approved, it would become valid without any party's signature.

- After that, Israel could open negotiations with every Arab state separately, on the establishment of economic and diplomatic relations.

• The Arab states are firmly determined to oppose any borders for the state of Israel exceeding in quality and size the November 1947 boundaries. Should Israel demand, for instance, western Galilee, it would have to offer territorial compensation elsewhere.

• Egypt will not give up the Gaza Strip and will, furthermore, insist on receiving the southern Negev along a line running from Majdal to the Dead Sea; in other words, the Bernadotte plan. Mustafa claimed that the Americans were aware of this point and had promised their support.

• Egypt strongly rejects the Ethridge plan (namely, Ben-Gurion's initiative) with regard to Gaza and the refugees.

• The insistence of the Arab governments on the return of all refugees is merely tactical.[11]

Two weeks later, on June 16, the director-general of the Israeli Foreign Ministry, Walter Eytan, joined Sasson for his next meeting with Abdul Mun'im Mustafa. This discussion had a sharper focus: the Egyptian demand that Israel give up the Negev. According to the telegram sent by Eytan to Sharett, Mustafa insisted on Israel's withdrawal to the Majdal–Dead Sea line. He tried to buttress his position by arguing that the British, French, and American military experts consulted by Egypt had confirmed the importance of this line. The two Israeli representatives proposed what was defined in the Israeli government's parlance as "the territorial arrangement that had been discussed with Ben-Gurion." Although Mustafa rejected these ideas, he promised to pass them on to his government. Another meeting was agreed upon, but Eytan's conclusion was that "it is crucial that we settle and fortify the Negev in the swiftest and most effective manner."

At this time the United States changed its own line, at least temporarily. Having concluded that progress in the Lausanne talks was not very likely but that a breakthrough with regard to Gaza was feasible, the State Department offered its good offices to Egypt and shifted its pressure from Tel Aviv to Cairo. But this was to no avail; the Egyptians rebuffed Washington's pressure. Yet another meeting between Sasson and Mustafa took place in a comparatively relaxed atmosphere. They discussed Husni Zaim and the PCC's work. "It was agreed," Sasson reported, "that we should meet often and avoid [hostile] publications and mutual recriminations." They also agreed that Shiloah would join their next meeting.[12] Sharett commented on Sasson's letter by noting: "Very interesting. I suppose we should stop the attacks in the radio." But he was mainly interested in applying the positive atmosphere reflected in Sasson's report to the Lausanne Conference's plenary discussions. Accordingly, Sharett issued the following directive:

> To refrain from investing all efforts in the quest for separate negotiations [with Egypt] but to invest them also with a view to affecting Egypt's position in the negotiations conducted under the PCC's aegis. We should, in the first place, limit ourselves to and pressure others to settle on a contribution of 100,000 [repatriated refugees]. At this stage the issue of Gaza's annexation must not be raised at our initiative lest we be presented with conditions. It is better to wait and see whether they raise the question, in which case we would be in a position to present conditions. You ought to consider whether it would be to our advantage to say just the following—that we would offer Jordan passage only if Gaza is in our hands but that we would not mind if for the time being it remains in their hands.[13]

But Sharett's observations and ideas remained an academic matter. The Lausanne talks remained deadlocked, and the Americans' attempt to salvage them through direct Israeli–Egyptian negotiations on Gaza was not successful. In July the deliberations were temporarily suspended, and the Israelis, like the other participants, took advantage of the pause to discuss their future strategy. During a consultation convened by Sharett, Sasson brought the fresh information and insights he had acquired during the previous weeks, to argue that there was no point in seeking a separate settlement with Egypt. He explained that Egypt's position might change only when the United States informed the Egyptians that it was unwilling to support their line. Even more interesting than this observation was Sasson's interpretation of Egypt's position on the basis of his talks with Mustafa. In order to make it more dramatic, Sasson presented the statement as if it had been made by the Egyptian diplomat himself:

We, the Egyptians, were unsuccessful in our war. You defeated us. We then signed an armistice agreement that stipulates that any [border] line adjustment must be made with mutual consent. And why do we need complete peace now? Peace would merely give you an opportunity for economic improvement and reinforcement. It would have been an entirely different matter had you invaded Cairo and dictated peace terms to us there. But now we do not need peace; quite to the contrary, we are interested in a situation of no peace in order to prevent you from digging in and reinforcing yourselves. . . . [The] fate of the refugees is not Egypt's business . . . but you are the ones who need peace, so you should come and tell us what you have to offer us . . . what price you are willing to offer.[14]

Mustafa and the Israelis talked yet again at the Lausanne Conference. Privacy was provided by meeting in a small town—La Pierret, near Lausanne. The meeting lasted for seven hours, and both sides spoke with unusual frankness. It was agreed in advance that the purpose of the meeting would be ''to establish directly what each party's demands were and whether a mutually acceptable arrangement between us and the Egyptians were possible'' and to discuss ways of continuing the direct talks, should the PCC decide to terminate its work in Lausanne.[15]

Abdul Mun'im Mustafa opened by suggesting that they all be candid and that the Israelis speak first. Three issues were put on the agenda: borders, refugees, and economic cooperation. Mustafa agreed to the premises suggested by Shiloah and Sasson: that he participate in the meeting as a representative of Egypt and not of the whole Arab world and that the meeting deal exclusively with Israeli–Egyptian relations. The substantive part of the meeting was begun by Shiloah, who responded to the arguments raised by Mustafa during his previous meeting with Sasson. He explained the Negev's importance to Israel and tried to show that the Egyptian claim to the

Negev—either on grounds of security or in order to obtain territorial contiguity with the eastern Arab world—had no basis in reality. Rather, the best way to guarantee Egypt's security, said Shiloah, was through "a military agreement between Egypt and Israel." Then in response to the advice given to Egypt by foreign military experts, Shiloah proposed that the two armies talk about this directly. But Mustafa disagreed, and the ensuing debate lasted through most of the meeting. Sasson's feeling was that instead of narrowing the gap between the two parties, the exchange only widened it. He and Shiloah shared the impression that a change for the worse had taken place in Egypt's position during the past few days, and they attributed this to the American diplomat Stuart W. Rockwell, who—they gathered from their contact—had implied that Egypt could obtain from Israel at least part of the Negev.

Like other meetings between these Egyptian and Israeli representatives, the August 19 meeting produced disappointing results but an intriguing summary. Mustafa spoke openly, and his statements offer unusual insights into Egypt's outlook on Israel and the notion of settlement. He rejected Shiloah's suggestion to conduct military talks by stating that "the problems are political and the politicians have the say." Egypt's policy, as he put it, rested on

(1) the establishment of a partition [buffer] between Egypt and Israel and Egypt and Jordan. The way to achieve it would be to turn the whole Negev, north and south, into an Arab, but Palestinian Arab, territory. (2) a gradual improvement of relations with Israel. Thus Israelis would be allowed to enter Egypt; searches in ships would stop; "and so within a few years ordinary relations would be established between the two countries. As time goes by, Egypt would realize that Israel had become a viable state and that it had no aggressive intentions. Likewise, the Egyptian public would forget last year's tragic events."

These sentences are also reflected in the evaluation written by Sasson for Sharett in September 1949. (See the final paragraphs of Chapter 2.)

Mustafa added that the establishment of a buffer in the Negev would have two other positive consequences: The refugees, or some of them, would be repatriated to Palestine itself, and the Arab state in Palestine would become viable; the West Bank would not be annexed to Jordan; and the status quo in the Arab world would not be altered.

When Shiloah and Sasson remarked that according to the partition plan, the Negev was to form part of the Jewish state, Mustafa replied, predictably, that Israel had already acquired Galilee. When they then explained that it was unrealistic to expect Israel to give up a single square foot in the Negev, he stated that "if this was the situation, there was no basis for a direct understanding between Egypt and Israel and that it was thus preferable to bring the issue before the UN's General Assembly and have it decided there." If Egypt lost, it would withdraw into its own affairs, evacuate Gaza and its hinterland, and continue the "cold war" with Israel. At that point he made a brief and telling outburst:

> You must understand, Egypt does not want a common border with Israel. Egypt would have been happy if Israel had not come into existence. It did everything in order to prevent it. Egypt is convinced that an Israeli state, foreign in all respects, in the midst of the Arab ocean, will necessarily continue to generate conflicts, complications, and instability in the East. . . . Egypt's assessment of Israel may be wrong, but talk alone is insufficient at this time for uprooting the erroneous convictions that obtain in Egypt.

Mustafa informed Shiloah and Sasson that he had told the Americans:

> For the United States to regain the confidence of the Arab world and secure long-term stability in the Middle East, it must make sure that Israel not become large, strong, and heavily populated with Jews. Egypt will not feel safe and secure with three or four million Jews residing on its Negev border, all of them educated and possessing initiative and high motivation.

Without an agreement on the Negev, the discussion came to a virtual end, thereby marking the end of a phase, in that another such meeting was not held until March 1950. On the basis of the 1949 talks the Israelis could see that there was no prospect for a separate settlement with Egypt, that for Egypt a perpetuation of the status quo was preferable to the complexities of a political settlement, and that both Egypt's claim to the Negev and its hostility to Abdullah were deeply entrenched. It is difficult to know how seriously the Egyptians considered the idea of reviving a Palestinian Arab state in the West Bank and the Negev, but they were clearly interested in any plan that would deny Abdullah control of the West Bank.

## Egypt and the Jordanian–Israeli Negotiations

When the Israeli government decided in the fall of 1949 to seek a peace agreement with an Arab partner, it approached Egypt first. Given their experience in the spring and early summer of 1949, however, the Israelis were probably not surprised when their direct (to Ismail Shirine) and indirect approaches were either ignored or rebuffed. Egypt was aware of the opening of the Israeli–Jordanian negotiations and monitored their progress. It was particularly worried that Israel and Jordan might reach an agreement that would consolidate Israel's position on the Red Sea coast, and Egypt's direct and indirect pressure on Jordan in this matter must have convinced it to insist on an Israeli territorial concession in the southern Negev. Later, in March 1950, during the internecine conflict in Jordan over the nonaggression pact with Israel, Egypt criticized King Abdullah's position but did so less harshly. As the dominant actor in the Arab League, Egypt played an important role in shaping the compromise that was finally reached between Abdullah and the Arab system—a de facto acceptance of the West Bank's annexation to Jordan in return for Jordan's abandonment of the idea of a separate settlement with Israel.

It is in this context that the thesis raised by the American historian

C. E. Dawn in 1971 should be considered. In an essay entitled "Pan Arabism and the Failure of the Israeli–Jordanian Peace Negotiations,"[16] Dawn argued that Egypt had supported or had at least refrained from criticizing the Israeli–Jordanian negotiations as long as it expected Jordan to obtain the Negev from Israel. The Negev, Dawn explained, was important to Egypt not as a land bridge to the eastern Arab world but as an alternative site for the canal zone's bases. If Jordan could persuade Israel to give up the Negev and let the British build there the bases they needed in the region, the British could leave the Suez Canal zone, and Egypt's most pressing problem would be resolved. But, wrote Dawn, when the Egyptians realized that the negotiations were not about to lead to an Israeli evacuation of the Negev, they changed their mind and mounted a propaganda attack against Abdullah that made his position untenable. Dawn's essay is an impressive illustration of what a professional historian can achieve through analysis of open sources, but it also illustrates the limits of such efforts in the field of diplomatic history, for the material now available in several archives clearly does not sustain Dawn's interpretation of the Egyptian position in 1950.

In Egypt several governments came and went during this period. In January 1950 Mustafa Nahhas Pasha formed a comparatively durable government; it lasted until January 1952. Muhammad Salah al-Din, whom at least the Israelis viewed as hostile and not interested in a settlement, was appointed foreign minister. The Israelis were then preoccupied with the interplay between Egypt's domestic politics and its Israeli policy. In any case, Abdul Mun'im Mustafa was replaced by Mahmud Azmi as the liaison with Israel. Unlike his predecessor, Azmi was not a professional diplomat but a political figure associated with the Wafd party. Azmi had a Jewish wife and thus empathy for Israel's concerns.

Abdul Mun'im Mustafa had one more discussion with the Israelis, meeting on February 27, 1950, with Abba Eban and Gideon Rafael in Lausanne. All three attended a special conference convened by the PCC in an effort to break the deadlock it had reached. The Israeli account of the meeting was that an agreement with Jordan, albeit limited, was around the corner and that it would be important and possibly feasible to buttress it with some sort of settlement with Egypt, even though the Egyptians felt that such a settlement was unnecessary.

Eban was the principal spokesman on the Israeli side, and his chief argument was that a review of Arab–Israeli relations since 1947 would readily show how much the Arabs had lost by rejecting Israel's compromise proposals. He reminded Mustafa of the argument raised by the latter in a meeting held with the Israelis several months earlier, that time was on Egypt's side, whereas Israel was operating under the pressure of a need for a settlement. Furthermore, the assumption that either the United States or the United Nations would force Israel to make concessions had been proved wrong. Mustafa did not try to refute Eban's arguments or to contend with his eloquence but repeated the already familiar assertion that Egypt would not give up its demand for the southern Negev. Speaking more personally, he revealed for the first time that he belonged to the school of thought in Egypt that opposed intervention in the Palestine war, which he explicitly defined as an adventure. He also observed that the Gaza Strip and the refugees living there did not pose a problem for Egypt and that as far as it was concerned, relations with Israel could continue for many more years to be governed by the armistice agreement. If Israel wanted peace it should pay the cost. He asked whether Israel was willing to abide by the May 12 protocol (signed on May 12, 1949, in Lausanne) and was told that neither the protocol nor the partition boundaries could serve as a premise for negotiations.

When all efforts to circumvent the question of the southern Negev proved futile, Eban and Rafael tried to apply what still appeared as Abdullah's magic formula to Israel's relationship with Egypt. Thus Eban suggested that ''it may very well be possible to find an interim phase between armistice and final peace; at this stage the present arrangement would be stabilized but the door would be left open for changes shortly thereafter.'' Mustafa reacted cautiously. He neither rejected nor endorsed the idea but expressed great interest in it and asked that contact be maintained with him in the future.[17]

Eban's and Rafael's exchange with Mustafa becomes all the more interesting because at about the same time Israel gained access, through an intelligence source, to Mustafa's correspondence with his superiors in Cairo. This correspondence presented him in a rather different light from that familiar to his Israeli counterparts. His memorandum cast doubts on Israel's peaceful intentions and contended that only "forceful action" by the Arabs could change Israel's position. The guidelines issued by Mustafa's superiors stated that Egypt was opposed to direct peace negotiations with Israel as well as to any meetings with Israeli representatives. Secret meetings were unacceptable too, lest Israel publicize them. Still, the Foreign Ministry was interested in hearing about any new trends or developments regarding direct negotiations. The Egyptian Foreign Ministry also advised Mustafa that Egypt was trying to persuade Jordan to avoid a "real" separate agreement with Israel. Like their emissary to Lausanne, Egyptian Foreign Ministry officials were suspicious of Israel's peaceful intentions, and they countered by telling Mustafa that Egypt, too, was not inclined to make peace with Israel. But they attributed great importance to international public opinion:

> Egypt should show how seriously it was considering any peace proposal and bear in mind that international public opinion is not ripe for agreeing to a forceful action. Time is on Egypt's side and military preparations should continue, but the time has not come for a decision on war, peace, or a continuation of the status quo.[18]

In March 1950, following the failure of the talks initiated by the PCC, Israel decided to launch a "peace initiative" designed to prove that it was not to blame for this. On March 21 Gideon Rafael wrote to Eytan and suggested that the correspondence between Mustafa and his superiors be used to improve Israel's standing. Rafael's initiative thereby raised a problem that other governments—and the Israeli government itself on other occasions—have had to contend with: releasing sensitive intelligence material in order to advance a diplomatic effort. Some of the dilemmas inherent in the issue were handled by Rafael himself:

> In addition to the proposals summarized in Aburey [Eban's] telegrams 41 and 42 which you had accepted, I propose that we make

the most practical use of the Egyptian material that has reached us recently. We think that the material regarding Israel should be submitted together with a memorandum to [U.S. Secretary of State Dean] Acheson personally. There is no reason to be bashful about it. Quite to the contrary, it is an acceptable norm in a world governed by such tense relationships. These documents may already be in the hands of a certain American service, but I doubt whether they have been submitted to Acheson and whether appropriate commentary has been provided. And even if he had received the documents through his own channels, it would be better if he knew that we also have them and that we are in a position to prove that our claims are well founded. In my opinion, handing over the documents would not jeopardize our informant, as I know that he is not the only one who buys the merchandise. In our political activity we must take advantage of the contradiction inherent in Egypt's attempt to draw close to the United States while keeping its distance from Israel without making a sincere effort to bridge the gap.[19]

Rafael's memorandum reflected an assumption that became increasingly central to Israeli political thought and that had, in the early 1950s, a particular influence on Israel's relations with Egypt— the assumption that the growing importance of the United States' position in the region and Israel's special position in the United States might be used to persuade Egypt to improve its relations with Israel.

This same theme appeared also in the debate between Sharett and two of his senior aides, Eban and Rafael, in late February and early March. Only part of the written exchange was kept in the archives, but the main arguments can be reconstructed. Eban and Rafael had determined from the PCC's deliberations and their discussion with Abdul Mun'im Mustafa that in the prevailing circumstances not even a partial settlement with Egypt was feasible. In his letter to Sharett dated March 2, 1950, Rafael pointed out that Egypt's position might be altered in two ways: by having the Americans put pressure on the country and by bringing to bear the discomfort inherent in Egypt's control of Gaza. Because the United States could not then be mobilized to exert such pressure, Eban's and Rafael's initiative focused on Gaza. They suggested reviving Ben-Gurion's idea of April 1949 of absorbing Gaza and its refugees into Israel as the basis of a limited Egyptian–Israeli agreement. But Sharett rejected this idea with some irritation. His two aides were puzzled and retorted that his unwillingness to discuss the fate of Gaza and its refugees with Egypt was tantamount to refusing to discuss a settlement with Egypt. This offended Sharett, who claimed that he had never objected to talking about the Gaza Strip, and the refugees residing there, in the negotiations with Egypt. He was merely opposed to the possibility that such negotiations might

> be limited at this phase to just the question of the Gaza Strip and the refugees. On the other hand, I proposed in the same telegram [considering] comprehensive negotiations even if such negotiations were aimed at an interim phase of settlement, such as a nonaggression pact, and not at the final phase of a peace agreement. [Sharett's thinking was clearly influenced by the negotiations then being conducted with Jordan.]

Sharett did admit that he did not support the idea of a settlement based on "transferring all of Gaza's refugees to us" and argued that because negotiations based on these notions were bound to fail, they should, therefore, be avoided in the first place. He saw a way out of this dilemma, however, by expanding the premises of the negotiations. Sharett seized on a statement made by Mustafa first to Eban and Rafael and then, separately, to the journalist Jon Kimche, in order to show that there was a prospect of "discussing a nonaggression pact as an interim phase on the road to peace." In his view, additional issues could be explored in the framework of these negotiations, such as the demarcation of the border, the extension of the scope of the armistice, and possibly even the beginning of commercial and maritime relations. When an agreement had been reached on some of these issues, an accord on Gaza might be obtained without causing the negotiations to collapse, "by leaving the question of Gaza and the refugees as an open issue whose time has yet to come." And he challenged Eban and Rafael with a question: "While you are hard put to accept my rejection of this precondition, I am hard put to accept you willingness to comply with it. Where would you settle the Strip's 200,000 refugees?" Finally Sharett determined that the answer to this question is clear—it is impossible. Even if peace with Egypt depended on this issue, this could not make the impossible possible. The final fate of these refugees is a matter of the future, but in the meantime all those who deal with the problem must not indulge in illusions.[20]

It is difficult to avoid feeling that Sharett's bitterness toward his subordinates was nurtured by the fact that they had come to adopt an idea so clearly identified with Ben-Gurion.

Eban and Rafael were not the only ones seeking at that time a formula that would enable the opening of Egyptian–Israeli negotiations. In early February, General William E. Riley experimented with an initiative of his own. On February 1, 1950, he met with Ismail Shirine in preparation for the anticipated meeting of the Egyptian–Israeli mixed armistice commission. The meeting generated a spurt of political activity owing to the uncertainty whether the armistice agreement had been signed for just one year. If this turned out to be the case, an extension would have to be discussed. Riley therefore took advantage of this uncertainty to ask Shirine whether Egypt would consider political negotiations with Israel. Shirine's answer was that an Israeli withdrawal from Um Rashrash and Bir Qattar (on the Red Sea coast) had to come first. On February 2, Riley met with Sharett and Eban and recommended that Israel accept Egypt's demand. The Israeli government's negative reply was given to him by Shiloah on February 2. Riley's personal position, as he explained it to the British, was that if the matter had been raised formally in the meeting, he would have sided with the Egyptians on Bir Quttar but that the issue of Um Rashrash pertained to Israel's relationship with Jordan and not with Egypt.[21] Judging by Riley's actions on similar occasions in the past, his initiative was probably taken with the blessing of the State Department. It is also interesting to juxtapose Riley's discussion with Shirine with Sharett's and his aides' hair splitting over Gaza. The latter seems futile, as Egypt continued to insist on Israel's withdrawal from the Red Sea coast as a precondition for any political negotiations.

As a dispatch sent by Britain's ambassador in Cairo, Edwin A. Chapman-Andrews, to London in late December indicates, Britain, too, examined in the same period the possibility of initiating political talks between Israel and Egypt. This correspondence has not been found, but a later discussion held between Chapman-Andrews and Shirine on December 4, 1950, referred to the effort made during the previous winter and abandoned by April. On December 4 Shirine did most of the talking. As he put it, peace with Israel should be accomplished through a series of gradual measures, in the following order:

1. Agreement by the Jews to retire from the coast of the Gulf of Aqaba. This was an essential prerequisite in Egyptian eyes. The Jews have no need for an outlet to the Red Sea, having a long Mediterrean coastline. Their establishment there would be a threat to the Egyptian Red Sea coast. Moreover, if the Israelis were to establish themselves there, the Egyptians would claim that the Jews, having their own overland route from the Red Sea to the Mediterranean, would have no need to use the Suez Canal, and so the Egyptians would continue to bar use of the canal by Israel and for merchandise consigned to Israel.

2. Jewish agreement to give up part of the Negev. In this connection Ismail Cherine Bey said that the Egyptian government had now come around completely to the view that as far as it was concerned, the entire Negev and the rest of Arab Palestine should become part of Jordan. Egyptians wanted no Palestine territory. . . .

3. Recognition by Egypt of an Israeli frontier.

4. A permanent peace treaty with international guarantees of frontiers.

5. [This very much later] Exchange of diplomatic representatives.

Edwin Chapman-Andrew's response was chilly:

I told Shirine that, as he knew, we here had represented his views regarding Aqaba and the Negev to the Foreign Office nearly a year ago. They had been carefully considered by the British government who, however, had come to the conclusion that there was nothing they could do about the matter which was, and must remain, in the hands of the United Nations.

But Shirine did not give up easily. He lectured the British ambassador on the Middle East's strategic importance to Britain as well as on the vital interest Britain had in land communication between Egypt and Jordan and in the region's stability.[22] It is interesting that in the minutes appended to the dispatch from Cairo the Foreign Office experts in London remarked that Shirine's views in this matter were not to be taken too seriously.

## Egypt, Israel, and the Western Defense Plans

For a comparatively long period, between the spring of 1950 and the fall of 1951, no significant discussions were held between Egypt and Israel. Such Israeli diplomats as Shmuel (Ziama) Divon continued to meet and talk with Egyptian politicians considered sympathetic to Israel, and the Foreign Ministry's Middle East Department prepared a plan for tilting Egyptian public opinion in the direction of peace, but in reality the patterns of the Arab–Israeli conflict had been set, and Israel's various initiatives failed to affect the course of events.

A change occurred in this state of affairs in October 1951 that was a result of the American and British decision to take measures to establish a Middle East Command. The idea had been raised earlier, but it had been impeded by a number of difficulties, mainly the failure to reach a British–Egyptian agreement. In the fall of 1951 a deadlock seemed to have been reached, which neither the attempts at a direct British–Egyptian dialogue nor an Egyptian complaint to the UN Security Council could break. Egypt and the Suez Canal were essential to the region's defense in the event of a conventional war, and the United States came to endorse Britain's view that it might be possible to resolve the Suez question by internationalizing it. Instead of drawing up a mutually acceptable British–American treaty or finding a site for an alternative British base in the canal's vicinity, it might be easier to keep Egypt and the Suez Canal within the Western defense orbit, by having Egypt join a pro-Western Middle Eastern defense system—the Supreme Allied Command Middle East (SACME). As a courtesy to Egypt and in recognition of its seniority in the Arab world, the United States and Britain decided to begin by asking Egypt, first, to join the three Western powers and Turkey as a "founding member." They assumed that if Egypt accepted, it would soon be joined by the other Arab states. The invitation was issued on October 13, 1951.[23]

The United States and Britain decided also not to invite Israel to join the planned defensive alliance. During the consultations preceding the October 13 invitation, they resolved that if Israel asked to join, they would state that direct Israeli participation was not being considered and that the relationship between Israel and the new command would depend on the results of discussions with the other states concerned.[24]

Britain, whose relationship with Israel at that stage could be defined as correct, informed Israel of the command's establishment in a formal meeting held between Eytan and the British minister Knox Helm. The United States and Israel had earlier talked about the repercussions of the command for Israel and for its relations with the United States. George McGhee met first with the Israeli ambassador, Abba Eban, and then with Sharett, who was visiting the United States. The ambassador in Tel Aviv, Monte Davis, met on October 13 with Ben-Gurion, not in Ben-Gurion's capacity as acting foreign minister but in his capacity as prime minister, as the subject "had a direct bearing on the whole future of the state."[25]

Israel's leadership had, indeed, been preoccupied for a long time with this issue. In 1950 the Israeli government abandoned its original attempt to maintain a quasi neutrality between the two blocs and placed itself squarely in the Western camp. In January 1951 Ben-Gurion rejected a semiofficial British initiative to integrate Israel into a Western defense system in the region. At the time the British must have despaired of their inability to form a defense pact with the Arab states, and this led them to explore using Israel's territory and resources informally. On January 15, 1951, Sir William Strang, the permanent undersecretary in the British Foreign Office, invited Israeli Ambassador Eylat to what he defined as a "private talk in the Travellers Club." Strang told Eylat that he had been instructed by British Foreign Minister Ernest Bevin to establish contact with him but that he still regarded the conversation as personal and informal. He also explained that the British government had informed Knox Helm that General Brian Robertson of the Middle East Command was prepared to visit Israel on February 19 and to establish personal contact with the Israeli General Staff but not to discuss any political issues. Strang proceeded then to provide the political background of Robertson's prospective visit. According to Eylat's report to Ben-Gurion, Strang explained to him:

> The international situation was severe, and the Near East in the event of a Russian attack is a crucial area. It houses England's oil sources and the Suez Canal. The Suez Canal is the lifeline of the Commonwealth, and the Near East is Africa's defense. The arrangements that England has with Egypt, Iraq, Jordan, and Turkey (more limited ones) are not satisfactory. He raised this question after being encouraged by the U.S. government, which, following its own discussions with the Israeli minister, had informed the British government that Israel was ready for such talks. The British plan to make a pact on either a regional or a bilateral basis. He [Strang] does not know whether the Arabs would agree to a regional pact, and it is doubtful with regard to both Egypt and Jordan, but Egypt had informed the British that it would not oppose a British–Israeli understanding. Britain is considering two possibilities: (1) an Israeli consent to the establishment of a British base in Gaza (with a corridor to Jordan) and (2) bases in Israel.

Ben-Gurion's reaction was negative, as he interpreted the British initiative as an attempt to gain a foothold in Israel. In his view, Britain had not altered its Middle Eastern policy but remained hostile to Israel. His estimate was that this maneuver was carried out with the United States' knowledge and encouragement, and he noted in his diary that "with America, we are willing to discuss everything; not so with England." Ben-Gurion also maintained that "giving bases will present us as an enemy to Russia, may affect immigration;

and will tie our hands with regard to the Arabs.''[26] Ben-Gurion did not comment on it in his diaries, but he must have felt that the ideas that Strang raised also demonstrated the extent of Britain's influence on Jordan's line in the negotiations of November–December 1949.

The British overture in February 1951 reflected its willingness to secure a minimal military infrastructure as required in case of a confrontation with the Soviet Union, with Israel being perceived as a possible alternative to a recalcitrant Egypt. But it did not mark a lasting change in a British policy that sought to organize the region into a system that would preserve its relations with and position in the Arab states. That policy and the British and Western quest to develop a regional pro-Western alliance confronted Israel with a clear challenge. Having abandoned its semineutralist policy, Israel wanted to join the new alliance but soon discovered that it was not wanted. Although the Western powers recognized Israel's military value and geopolitical importance, given the need to choose between it and the Arab states, their choice was obvious. From Israel's perspective this turn of events had several negative consequences: It revealed Israel's isolation and the anomaly of its position; the military potential of the Arab states was about to be increased considerably without a comparable addition to Israel's military strength; and the United States could be expected to draw away from Israel and toward the Arab states. By October, Israel had information that Egypt was about to reject the Western overture, but the Israelis felt, correctly, that even if this turned out to be the case, the pressure on Israel would not be reduced. The question would be raised as to why Egypt refused to join a pro-Western alliance, and some, at least, would reply that Israel and the Arab–Israeli conflict were the chief obstacles to an otherwise natural American–Egyptian understanding. Ten years later a member of the American foreign policy establishment wrote:

> It was clear from the reaction of both sides that, quite aside from Suez and all the tangled problems of Anglo-Egyptian relations, the great unsettled questions of Palestine stood as a mountainous barrier in the way of all Western efforts to win the cooperation and support of the peoples of that part of the Middle East.[27]

The Israeli leadership was aware of this problem and its ramifications, and so it strove to demonstrate to the United States that Egypt's hostility derived from other sources, to prove that the Arab–Israeli conflict could be resolved by the parties themselves, or, on other occasions, that the United States should try to help resolve it. Whatever the argument, the question of organizing the Middle East and its consequences for Israel's position and its relations with the United States became a central issue of Israel's foreign policy.

A similar development occurred for entirely different reasons in Egypt's foreign policy. Egypt wanted the British to leave and also wanted a comprehensive settlement of its relations with Britain. If Egypt decided not to join the planned organization, it wanted to foil any attempt to form it without Egypt. Its ability to do this became an important test of its position of leadership in the Arab world and of its ability to mobilize the Arab states.

It is against this background that the account of the first talks between the Israelis and their new contact, Mahmud Azmi, which took place in early November 1951, should be interpreted.[28] Azmi came to the UN's General Assembly as a member of the Egyptian delegation and was characterized by Divon as "an informal and influential adviser to the Egyptian foreign minister." The initial contact was made by Divon, who suggested that they meet again for a "serious discussion." He was joined by Gideon Rafael.

Azmi began by explaining that he came to the meeting with his minister's knowledge and that he trusted that this was also the case with the Israelis. He spoke mainly about Egypt's relations with Britain and the possibility of a defensive alliance. Azmi was opposed to a pro-Western alliance and asserted that the only course to follow was the establishment of a UN force. Azmi said also that the Egyptians had taken into account the possibility that Israel would take advantage of the situation and launch an attack in Gaza and possibly even in the Sinai. But Egypt did not regard the loss of Gaza as disastrous and "should an appropriate formula be found, they would even be willing to hand it over to Jordan." In any event, he thought that "in view of what has been created, there is some prospect of

an Egyptian–Israeli rapprochement." Such an Egyptian–Israeli relationship would be determined by the serious test currently facing
the Arab League. If Egypt failed to receive the expected degree of
Arab support, the "Pharoanic" school would be strengthened, and
Egypt would adopt a position similar to that of Turkey and would
"reexamine its position on a number of problems, including the
problem of Israel." Divon and Rafael tried to channel the discussion
into a more constructive direction by explaining that Israel was reev-
aluating its Middle East policy. Azmi promised a reply "after the
meeting of the Arab representatives scheduled for Friday . . . and after
a talk with the Egyptian foreign minister." Divon and Rafael explored the possibility of organizing a meeting between Sharett and
Salah al-Din. Azmi explained that although there had been "no
possibility" of organizing such a meeting the previous year, "there
may be a prospect of such a meeting taking place this time." In
practical terms this was, of course, a negative reply.

The Israeli archives for that period also contain a puzzling document that seems to be the draft of a treaty designed to expand and
develop the armistice agreement with Egypt.[29] This would not have
been warranted by the actual state of Egyptian–Israeli relations, and
the document seems to have been the result of another initiative taken
by General Riley, who proposed to the Israelis, first in Jerusalem
and then in Paris, to consider negotiating with Egypt an expansion
of the armistice agreement. With Riley's consent the Israelis checked
with Azmi, who replied that the Egyptian government was not interested. Sharett interpreted the episode as an attempt by Riley "to
raise his stock and to present himself as a central factor in the quest
for peace in the Middle East taking the place of the unsuccessful
PCC." The Israelis were by then sufficiently familiar with the inner
workings of the Egyptian government to assume that Riley had
sounded out Shirine and was given a somewhat positive answer.
Sharett also commented that a more moderate Egyptian line had been
apparent in the UN General Assembly, reflecting Egypt's reluctance
"to widen the gap between them and us, but also a reluctance to
narrow it. They need the Arabs in their conflict with Britain." It is

curious that having said all this, Sharett still devoted time and space to a purely academic analysis of the possibility of Israel's expanding the armistice agreement with Egypt.[30]

## From "Black Saturday" to the July 1952 Revolution

January 1952 was a month of many important events in Egypt's political history. On January 26, the outburst known as "Black Saturday" began when a mob in Cairo went on a rampage, destroyed and burned more than 750 businesses, and caused the death of dozens and the wounding of hundreds. More than any other single event, this eruption marked the bankruptcy of the old order and, in retrospect, can be viewed as a harbinger of its imminent collapse and replacement. In more immediate terms the events of January 26 gave the king an opportunity to dismiss Nahhas Pasha and the Wafd government and to entrust one of the "strong men" of Egyptian politics, Ali Maher, with forming a new government. One of Maher's primary tasks, from the king's perspective, was to control the Wafd and sap its power. But he lasted barely over two months and was replaced on March 1 by Nagib Hilali. As the July 23 revolution drew nearer, Egyptian politics grew increasingly tumultuous, with one cabinet succeeding another in a useless effort to stabilize the political system.

Egypt's political agenda was still governed by the same problems: the conflict between the political establishment's main wings (the king, the Wafd, and the other traditional parties), the pressure of the radical forces that threatened to topple the establishment, and the fundamental foreign policy issues—the conflict with Britain, the questions of the treaty and evacuation, the future of the Sudan, and Egypt's international orientation. Egypt's relationship with Israel was not a particularly important issue at this time, though it was clearly linked to the more pressing problems with which Egypt's leaders were preoccupied. Indeed, the change of governments in January 1952 reinforced the line detected by Moshe Sharett in November 1951—a cosmetic improvement, at least, of Egypt's position toward Israel. The principal manifestation of further change was a series of articles published in the Egyptian press in early 1952 that were written in a tone more sympathetic to Israel and alluded to the possibility that a settlement was in the offing.

The Israeli experts were divided over the significance of these changes, but the Israeli government seems to have decided at some point in February to take advantage of the new situation, such as it was, in order to persuade the U.S. government that an Israeli–Egyptian agreement was a real possibility. The decision was translated into several plans of action. On March 6, Eban met with Secretary of State Dean Acheson, handed him a memorandum dealing with Israel–Egyptian relations, and reinforced it with an oral briefing. The memorandum stated: "There is evidence to show that Egyptian public opinion is increasingly aware of the need to reach a settlement with Israel. Israel's government has reached this conclusion on the basis of talks and contacts as well as of a study of the Egyptian press."[31] The Israelis also asked that the U.S. embassy in Cairo inquire as to whether there was any real substance to the various articles in the Egyptian press on the Arab attitude toward Israel. But Ben-Gurion did not wait for the inquiry's results when he told a group of some fifty American reporters that "peace between Israel and Egypt has [so far] been hampered by internecine squabbling in Egypt, but I hope that a peace [agreement] will be signed in the near future and that in its wake, peace will be established with the other Arab states." He added that "wide circles in Egypt want peace with Israel, but they are afraid of their political rivals."

Ben-Gurion's statement and the memorandum submitted by Eban to Acheson rested on a flimsy factual basis and, in fact, ran counter to the evaluation of at least some of the Israeli Foreign Ministry's experts. It was, therefore, hardly surprising that Eliyahu Sasson, in Ankara, was brought to his feet by press accounts of Ben-Gurion's statement, and on March 28 he wrote to Eytan expressing "puzzlement and dismay." Sasson knew that Divon had held meetings with

Egyptian representatives and that a number of positive statements and news items had appeared in the Egyptian press, but he saw no foundation for Ben-Gurion's statement. In his view such statements, when lacking a factual basis, were counterproductive.[32]

Ben-Gurion did not really believe that peace with Egypt was around the corner, but he apparently had decided that for the sake of Israel's relationship with the United States, it was essential to create the impression that the Arab–Israeli conflict was not a hopeless dispute but that a settlement was possible. This interpretation is supported by an analysis of the memorandum submitted by Eban to Acheson. It should also be borne in mind that the State Department was hoping at this time that the consolidation of Shishakli's regime in Syria would enable some sort of a Syrian–Israeli agreement, so that a general stabilization, if not a settlement of Arab–Israeli relations, could be achieved.[33]

When Rafael (on March 4) and Eban (on March 31) met with Azmi, their minds were, indeed, focused on the Americans. Rafael met with Azmi twice, in Paris in February and then in New York in March when Azmi came to the UN Conference on Freedom and Information. Before coming to New York Azmi spent two weeks in Egypt, and so he arrived fully briefed on the political mood in his country.

Azmi reacted to Ben-Gurion's statements by saying that

> judging by the echoes that had reached him, he had the impression that we overestimated the statements made recently in Egypt with regard to the establishment of relations with Israel. No one has dared and no one will dare say anything positive in this matter as long as the king persists in his stubborn hatred of Israel. Azmi has authoritative information that the king keeps insisting that Egypt must not settle its relations with Israel. To the same extent that the king was responsible for Egypt's joining the war against Israel, he remains responsible for preventing any progress in settling the two countries' relations.
>
> According to Azmi, the king's main purpose is to eliminate the Wafd, and Hilali's government is his chief instrument. Yasin Pasha will be denounced for corruption and possibly also for his ties with Israel. There are groups in Egypt that would like to rid the country

of "the Israeli legacy," and there also are elements in the army's high command who are disposed toward a settlement with Israel, but without a visible change in the king's position nothing will happen.[34]

When analyzing Azmi's statements, the Israelis must have assumed that his negative portrayal of the king's role and position was, to some extent at least, colored by the Wafd's hostility to Farouk.

In Azmi's talk with Eban, more general aspects of Egypt's foreign policy were discussed. When Azmi emphasized the authenticity of Egypt's neutralism, Eban commented (to himself as well as to the Foreign Ministry in Jerusalem): "Azmi performed our task for us. It was about two weeks ago that we decided to plant the idea in the State Department's mind that Egypt's recalcitrance was a frame of mind well entrenched in the Egyptian consciousness and not a mere political maneuver." Later in the conversation Azmi explained that Egypt was simply incapable of joining a pro-Western alliance. The only way to square this circle, he said, would be through the UN, which would recognize the Arab collective security pact as a regional defense organization. When he first had proposed this idea to the State Department, it had ruled it out as a possibility, owing to the pact's anti-Israeli character. This point seemed to Eban to offer an opening for Israel's policy: to persuade both the United States and Egypt that the problems on the agenda were closely linked and that it would be preferable to begin by solving the Egyptian–Israeli problem and to rely on its resolution to overcome the difficulties concerning Egypt's international policy. Indeed, the next day when he was invited to the State Department for a meeting with S. Wells Stabler, one of its senior Arabists, Eban did use this argument.[35]

Gideon Rafael's impressions of the discussions with Azmi were similar to Eban's: (1) Israel must disprove the view current in the State Department "as if in certain conditions Egypt could be wooed to join the West's defense mechanism." (2) We must act against the trend that has been manifested by the important U.S. press and that may also have its impact in the State Department "as if salvation could come from King Farouk." Pressure on the king in person should be increased.

The trilateral American–Israeli–Egyptian relationship during that period is seen somewhat differently in light of the mediation attempt made by the American Jewish leader Jacob Blaustein.[36] Blaustein began his attempt after meeting the Egyptian ambassador in Washington. He worked through the ambassador himself and achieved very modest results. But in mid-March 1952, upon returning from a trip, he decided to try his hand again and, in the best tradition of mediators, suggested that Israel modify its opening position as a gesture designed to start the process. Eban was doubtful about the usefulness of Blaustein's efforts but stated all the same that if the discussions were renewed, he would instruct Blaustein to do the following: (1) to direct the Egyptian ambassador's attention to the Americans' positive reaction to the rumors concerning Egypt's new moderation vis-à-vis Israel; (2) to allude to the possibility that peace with Israel could lead to considerable American support of Egypt's "national demands" (in regard to Britain); (3) to explain that the entire Negev was vital to Israel but that Egypt's passage under Israeli sovereignty in peacetime could be arranged—such a formula would solve the problem of the "wedge," namely, Egypt's claim that Israeli control of the Negev would drive a wedge between Egypt and the eastern Arab world; and (4) to explain the Israeli line regarding the security pact and SACME.

## Israel and Egypt's Domestic Politics

The rapid and sharp changes that occurred in Egypt during the early months of 1952—Black Saturday, the successive changes of governments, and the other symptoms of Egypt's political crisis—led Israel's Arab experts to devote greater attention to the interplay between the dominant trends in Egyptian politics and Egypt's position on Israel.

Underlying the Israeli thinking on Egyptian–Israeli relations was the assumption that although the question of Palestine and the Israeli issue were important to Egypt, they were not at the top of its national agenda. Other issues, such as the conflict between the royal court and the Wafd, personal and factional considerations, and the problem of relations with Britain, were uppermost in the minds of the Egyptian politicians, and their position on Israel at any given moment was determined by both the merits of the issue and its barring of the other, more important concerns from Egypt's political system. The Israelis viewed King Farouk as the single most hostile actor. According to this interpretation, the king was seeking revenge for the Egyptian army's defeat in the 1948 war, which he had personally launched. The king also regarded his aggressive attitude in the conflict with Israel as crucial to the advancement of his ambitions for Arab and Islamic leadership.

Among Egypt's political parties, the Wafd's position was, naturally, the most influential. The Israelis did not treat the Wafd as a monolithic bloc; they distinguished between a rigidly anti-Israeli faction represented most prominently by the foreign minister, Salah al-Din, and a Wafdist group that advocated moderation toward Israel: economic and commercial circles that believed that a settlement would advance the Egyptian economy and "progressive" circles that sought social and economic reforms in Egypt and believed that an adventurous foreign policy could jeopardize such reforms.

In the early 1950s Israeli representatives met with various members of the Saraj al-Din family, headed by Yasin Saraj al-Din, to discuss the possibility of improving Egyptian relations with Israel. In these discussions a familiar theme appeared, the expectation that Jewish influence in the world, particularly in the United States, could be mobilized for Egyptian interests once relations improved. But as a rule, the Israelis had no illusions regarding the actual significance of such factors and calculations. They estimated that it was the main political issues of the day (especially British–Egyptian relations, inter-Arab relations, and the domestic balance of forces) that determined the position of a party or a government at a given moment. The Israelis found out also that not everything they had heard in Europe from Egyptian politicians out of power would be translated into concrete policy when one of these politicians regained power.

The lessons that the Israelis learned from their observation of the Wafd they applied to the study of the other political parties. They knew that the Liberal party did not have a uniform position on Israel. Hussein Haykal, the party's president, was considered moderate toward Israel and had met Sasson and other Israeli representatives several times, even during the 1948 war. However, his deputy, Desouki Abaza, was regarded as particularly hostile to Israel. Egypt's two main radical movements in that period, the Muslim Brotherhood and the Communists, were, each for its own reasons, hostile to Israel, but both stood outside the established political system, and their influence was manifested mainly through mood and atmosphere rather than on concrete political steps.[37]

A characteristic example of the traditional Israeli approach to these issues can be found in the telegram sent by Sasson from Ankara to Director-General Eytan on January 30, 1952, when Ali Maher's government was formed in the aftermath of "Black Saturday." Sasson commented:

> To the extent that I know Ali Maher, it would seem that the prospects of direct contact and settlement with him are greater than with the Wafd people. He is stubborn and an extremist but more realistic, positive, and courageous. I propose that Divon will strengthen his ties with Shirine and will promise to support court policy without informing Mahmud 'Azmi and his Wafdist acquaintances about it. I also propose that the Voice of Israel in Arabic will now maintain strict objectivity in its broadcasts concerning Egypt."

Sasson went on to explain that he did not recommend the establishment of immediate contact with Ali Maher but that it would be better to wait and see how things developed. He elaborated further on the importance of the ties between Divon and Isma'il Shirine. Sasson's reference to Israel's radio broadcasts in Arabic is particularly interesting. As direct contact between Israeli representatives and Arab politicians diminished and the gap between Israel and its neighbors widened, Israel's Arab experts came to view the Arabic-language broadcasts as an even more important instrument for shaping Arab opinion and politics.

Two other prominent issues were reflected in Sasson's telegram. He noted that he himself had no doubts that Western policymakers would try to grow closer to Ali Maher and to encourage him to help them resolve in one way or another the British–Egyptian dispute and to form the Middle East Command. Sasson thought that Israel must not appear as an opponent of such moves. Still more interesting was what Sasson defined as a "modest proposal for the preparation of a ground for direct contact with Ali Maher." His recommendation was

> to avoid to the extent that it was possible during the next two months any military activity on the Egyptian border that might hurt Egypt's prestige, further complicate the relations with Egypt, provoke the Egyptians to react and complain, and so forth. Any activity would necessarily lead Ali Maher's government to make such public statements that it would subsequently find difficult to retract or contradict by action.[38]

As has already been seen, the Israelis had formed by late 1951 the impression that Egypt's position on Israel had been moderated, and that moderation was reflected in Egypt's conduct during the UN General Assembly sessions and in the Egyptian press. Egyptian newspapers published items informing their readers that Israel was drawing away from the West in order to improve its relations with the Arabs. A new thesis appeared in these papers—the call to learn from the effectiveness displayed by the Israelis during their period of struggle against the British.[39] The Israelis' interpretation at the time was that the change in the Egyptian position derived primarily from the fear that Israel might take advantage of Egypt's problems in order to stage a military action in the Gaza area and then from Egypt's hope of relying on "the Jewish influence" on American public opinion against Britain.

Ali Maher's tenure of power vindicated Sasson's prediction, and Egypt's line toward Israel was moderated even more. The memorandum submitted by Ambassador Eban to the American secretary of state on March 15, 1952, included an appendix in which the Israelis enumerated six manifestations of Egyptian moderation, in order to buttress their argument that an Egyptian–Israel settlement was possible. The Israeli memorandum quoted the Egyptian weekly *Ruz al-Yusuf* of February 11 to the effect that "diplomatic circles confirmed that the Arab states had decided to conclude peace with Israel. . . . [T]he Arab states have expressed officially their consent to negotiate with Israel directly in order to settle the outstanding questions. These negotiations will constitute a first step toward peace," but a closer look at the original material reveals the limitations of the changes in the Egyptian position. The Israelis had seized on the statement made on February 16 by Yasin Sarag al-Din, chairman of the Egyptian Parliament Committee, formulations according to which "negotiations with Israel do not mean recognition of Israel; an armistice exists between us and Israel, and we are in a position to start negotiations to solve outstanding problems within the limits of the armistice and the United Nations' resolutions."

The statement itself is not particularly impressive, and when read in the context of the original item as it appeared in *al-Ahram*, it appears even less impressive. It is included in a report on the forthcoming Arab–Israeli (and not Egyptian–Israeli) negotiations, which had been approved by the Arab League within the limitations of the Arab consensus. Even the Palestinian activist Ahmad Shuqayri, who was then the Arab League's assistant secretary-general, did not object to the framework of the negotiations. Against this background, therefore, the statement by Yasin Sarag al-Din, who was seen by the Israelis as their closest ally in the Wafd, does not appear particularly bold.

The Israeli observation that the actual policy pursued by an Egyptian government toward Israel was only loosely related to the personal position of the man heading it was reinforced after Nagib al-Hilali's assumption of power. Hilali was considered by the Israelis to be more moderate than Ali Maher, but during his reign he adopted a tougher attitude toward Israel. The Israelis attributed the change to Hilali's very moderation and felt that he was under pressure to demonstrate to the Egyptian public that he was not making concessions in this sensitive matter. In addition, Israelis argued that the lack of progress in the deliberations with Britain and the ensuing frustration contributed to the abandonment of Egypt's comparatively moderate attitude toward Israel that it had displayed during the previous months.

A study of the archives and interviews with some of those who wrote the papers stored in the archives lead to another important conclusion. Neither the Israeli leaders nor the experts anticipated the revolutionary political change that took place in Egypt on July 23, 1952, which, among other things, transformed the Arab–Israeli conflict. Indeed, some time had elapsed before the Israeli leadership came to realize that the July revolution had brought to power in Egypt a leader and a group that were radically different from the military factions that had been intervening in Syrian politics since 1949 and that this new regime was destined to expedite the transition of Egyptian and regional politics to a new phase.

The traditional channels of contact between Israel and Egypt were reactivated soon after July 23, and the moderate nature of the messages transmitted by the new Egyptian government reinforced the Israelis' feeling that the changes in Egypt were not far-reaching. But in fact new forces had already been at work that were destined to give Israel's relations with Egypt and with the larger Arab world an entirely different character.

Some experts in Israel recognized the ramifications of the developments that took place in Egypt in July 1952. In September of the same year the Intelligence Department of the IDF's General Staff inaugurated a new series of publications entitled "Brochures for Middle Eastern Knowledge." The publication was defined as "internal" but was not given a security classification. The first brochure, on British–Egyptian relations, had been written by Yitzhak Oron Sokolovsky before July 23 but was updated in August. The author began the epilogue by arguing that "it should first be stated that the coup in Egypt has transcended during its early days the boundaries of a mere coup d'état and is assuming the character of a fundamental social revolution—an expression of the revolutionary potential whose sources have been described in this brochure." Having noted that both the United States and Britain, for different reasons, had sent positive signals to Nagib's regime (as seemed to be the case then) Sokolovsky estimated, correctly, that it was a transitional stage. As he saw it, the social and political tensions that had accumulated in Egypt, the Soviet–Western competition, Britain's weakness, and the erroneous American assumption that cooperation with military dictatorships could neutralize the tensions inherent in the situation were bound to breed more ferment and conflict. His analysis was amply vindicated by the subsequent course of events. The ''Free Officers'' coup in Egypt did lead to a far-reaching reshuffling in the regional and international politics of the Middle East. It also contributed more than did any other single event to shifting Israel's relationship with the Arab world from the transitional phase of the years between 1949 and 1952 to the full-blown Arab–Israeli conflict of the later 1950s.

6

# Conclusion

In July 1953 Eliyahu Sasson, on vacation in Geneva from his post in Ankara, ran into an old acquaintance, Syria's former president Shukri al-Quwatli. Sasson took full advantage of the unplanned encounter. He telephoned Quwatli at his hotel and was invited to a lengthy discussion, during which his Syrian host laid out an elaborate plan for organizing the region's future. Quwatli's scheme was based on the Arab world's partition into two blocs. Israel was perceived as a buffer between the two blocs, as a sort of a Middle Eastern Switzerland, and as the target of an Arab offensive when the right moment came. In his report to the Foreign Ministry in Jerusalem, Sasson explained his purpose: "I wanted to check whether a famous leader like al-Quwatli was willing to talk to us despite recent developments in Syria and the unfolding of the Syrian–Israeli conflict."[1]

Even though the efforts by Sasson and his colleagues in the 1940s to reach an agreement with Syria's Arab nationalist leaders had failed, their discussions had been civilized and, in a way, cordial. The idea of a Jewish state in Palestine was unacceptable to the Syrian leaders, but they were willing to meet and talk without acrimony. It therefore was important to find out whether this was still true or whether the 1948 war and the changes since then that had occurred in Syrian and Arab politics had also altered the attitude and conduct of the Syrian leadership. Sasson established that they had not. Although Israel, and the idea of Israel, remained unacceptable to Quwatli, he was still glad to meet with Sasson and have an amicable, albeit futile, discussion with him.

What had changed was Quwatli's position in Syrian and Arab politics. The 1949 military coups d'état in Syria had set in motion a process that sapped and then eliminated the power of Shukri al-Quwatli, his generation, and his social class. Later in the 1950s, he enjoyed an apparent Indian summer as Syria's president, but the real power had shifted to the military and their allies in the ideological parties who radicalized Syria's politics and led the country first to an alliance with Egypt and the Soviet Union and then to an ill-fated union with Egypt. The army's intervention in Egyptian politics came later, in July 1952, and its consequences for the region were far greater. The emergence of a radical and ideological regime that transformed inter-Arab politics and Israel's reactions to it soured Arab–Israeli relations and paved the way to the full-blown Arab–Israeli conflict of the mid-1950s.

From this perspective it seems important to reexamine Israel's and the Arab countries' failure to reach a peace agreement at the end of the 1948 war—before the conflict itself was embittered and ideologized, before the radicalization of Arab politics, and before the intensification of inter-Arab and international conflict in the region. Why was it that peace could not be achieved in 1948 or 1949?

Several writers have addressed this question as well as the significance of this phase in the larger history of the Arab–Israeli dispute. One of the first scholarly studies of the conflict was Rony Gabbay's 1959 *A Political Study of the Arab–Jewish Conflict: The Arab Refugee Problem (A Case Study)*. Based on a doctoral dissertation, the book concentrates on the problem of the Palestinian refugees, but it deals also with the broader aspects of the conflict. In a section entitled ''The Failure of Political Attempts,'' Gabbay wrote:

The experience gained during the period 1948–1951 showed that the conflict was deeper than previously thought. Hatred of Israel had intensified and the Arab world was in no way ready to accept Israel as a sovereign state. The perpetuation of the Arab–Israeli conflict was a direct result of the political instability of the Middle Eastern countries. It revealed many fundamental defects of a social, political, psychological and economic nature for which no one could be blamed.[2]

He went on to elaborate on the exacerbating effects of domestic instability in the Arab world, of inter-Arab rivalries, of the significance of the psychological blow dealt to the Arabs, and of the compromising nexus between the traditional Arab elites and the Western powers. But Gabbay allocated some of the blame to Israel, concluding that with some magnanimity, Israel could have made peace with Jordan and Egypt in early 1950:

Israel's policy of unlimited immigration, coupled with the economic crisis and, above all, her over-confidence, made it difficult, if not impossible, for her to assume a generous attitude and meet some of the Arab demands, such as the repatriation of the refugees. Moreover, the internal rivalry and the split in the Arab world were utilized very wrongly to serve its own interests. Indeed much of its success— perhaps even its survival during the War of Independence—was due to this split and rivalry among the Arab leaders and states; but to continue to rely on this miracle and even to utilize it in seeking a final political settlement was a very dangerous game. Thus Israel, on the brink of some kind of settlement with King Abdullah entailing very little sacrifice on its part, became intransigent towards Egypt's demands for territory and other concessions in exchange of a final settlement. The result was that Egypt alarmed at the possible double gains of King Abdullah in concluding peace and annexing the Arab part of Palestine, undertook an energetic campaign throughout the Arab world to frustrate any peace settlement with Israel, and finally succeeded. In reality, the damage was even greater. It was not only the prospect of a final settlement with King Abdullah that had been frustrated, but the whole possibility of concluding peace with the Arab states had been lost. Egypt had been the originator of the slogan "no separate peace with Israel" and could not retreat easily.

> Had Israel been able to conclude a peace settlement with Egypt . . .
> the situation would have been entirely different. . . . That was the
> golden opportunity of Israel, but it was lost due to serious
> miscalculations.[3]

The Suez–Sinai war of 1956 generated a series of books that
focused on the British–French–Israeli collusion and other diplomatic
and military aspects of the 1956 crisis. The 1967 Six-Day War then
had an even greater and more diverse effect on the literature dealing
with Arab–Israeli relations. The magnitude of the Israeli victory and
the Arab defeat was reflected in the difference between the smugness
that characterized much of the Israeli postwar writing and the chest
beating and despair of most Arab writers. A slew of academic and
popular books interpreted the events of 1967 as part of a general
history of the Arab–Israeli conflict. Within this larger context the
first Arab–Israeli war and the failure to reach peace in its immediate
aftermath were addressed.

In *The Road to War* Walter Laqueur explained:

> At the time it was widely thought in Israel that the armistice would
> soon give way to real peace but the hostility of the Arab states
> toward Israel had by no means diminished as a result of their military
> defeat. They had not the slightest intention of recognizing the
> "gangster state." . . . The Arabs confidently expected that this first
> round would soon be followed by a second which would restore
> Palestine to its rightful owners. . . . The Arab leaders simply refused
> to accept the status quo which in their eyes perpetuated a crying
> injustice. . . . So the weary truce lingered for years until a process
> of escalation (or deterioration) led to another round of fighting.[4]

Writing from a very different vantage point, Maxime Rodinson,
an ideological and emotional critic of Israel, produced a remarkably
similar paragraph in his *Israel and the Arab World:*

> The Zionists had achieved their aims. . . . As for the Arabs a foreign
> colony had succeeded in seizing a part of their territory and driving
> out a number of its Arab inhabitants and this with the support of
> the entire Western world. . . . The Arabs, full of bitterness and ran-

cor, refused to recognize this European *diktat*, this colonial amputation which had been imposed on them—hostilities were only broken off because of their own impotence, which they hoped would be temporary. One way or another, for them the war would go on.[5]

Fred Khouri, offered a more ambitious and complex interpretation that added, correctly, an important psychological dimension but managed also to lay much of the blame on Israel and its "supporters."

> Certain aspects of Israel's military achievements were to have a deleterious effect upon Arab–Israeli relations. On the one hand, the extent of their war victory created such a great increase in the pride and self-confidence of the Israelis that they became less willing to make those concessions which were needed if there was to be any hope of reconciliation with the Arabs. On the other hand, the extent of the Arab defeat brought about such a blow to the pride and self-reliance of the Arabs that they became more opposed than ever to acknowledging the existence of the enemy who had so deeply humiliated them. In the long run, a lesser Israeli victory, even military stalemate would have netted Israel less territory but might have provided a better and more practical basis for meaningful and lasting Arab–Israeli peace.
>
> By tending to belittle Arab courage, character and way of life, to gloat unduly and even to inflate the extent of their victory, the Israelis and their supporters merely helped intensify Arab bitterness and foster the conviction among many Arabs that they could regain their self-respect only by proving themselves successsful in a future battle.[6]

After criticizing the Western powers, the Soviet Union, and the United Nations for failing to impose their authority, Khouri argued: "As a result Arab–Israeli hostility was not reduced, their differences were not resolved and, as future events were to demonstrate, the course of peace was not served during this critical period."[7]

A particularly perceptive and sympathetic student of Arab politics, Malcolm Kerr offered a two-tiered interpretation:

> From 1948 onward, it was the Jewish side whose claim to inhabit and govern most of Palestine was largely satisfied and who therefore

was ready for a peace settlement on the basis of the status quo. The Palestinian Arabs and their brethren in the surrounding states were left to chew on their own frustrations. . . . What compromise if any should they resign themselves to?

As Kerr saw it, "In a way it hardly mattered which of these lines they took since none of them were remotely acceptable to the victorious Israelis." The Israelis, of course, had their own point of view and their own version of events, and their conclusion was to "let the Arab governments accept the reality and inevitability of Israel's existence and enter into peaceful relations with it."

The second level of Kerr's analysis went far beyond the standard interpretation of the subject. On this level, he contended, it did matter what claims the Arabs directed to Israel. To Kerr, a compromise would have been possible only if Palestinian refugees had been allowed to return, as this would have "diluted the Jewish character of the society and made more than a trickle of Jewish immigration from abroad highly unlikely." Such ideas would have encountered strong Israeli opposition, but "if such compromise carried the prospects of peace it might have won acceptance, perhaps with the aid of pressure on Israel from the United States and others." And yet a moderate consensus in the Arab world did not emerge, and those Arab leaders who believed in the notion of a compromise based on the refugees' return could not come forward and propose it.

Kerr did not attach particular importance to the war's immediate aftermath. Instead, he examined the whole postwar decade and discovered in Israel

> people who were in favor of making major conciliatory gestures but the prevailing attitude reflected in official policy was such that it would be unthinkable to exchange the reality of an almost exclusively Jewish state, providentially secured in 1948 after Jews had hardly dared hope for it, for a polyglot backwater Jewish Arab state in which Jews might again become the minority—even with a full peace settlement thrown into the bargain.[8]

Although Kerr did not state it explicitly, clearly he would have welcomed a combination of Arab flexibility and American pressure in Lausanne that would have resulted in an imposed settlement along the lines of the Lausanne protocol of May 12.

It was precisely on this protocol that Nadav Safran based his interpretation, which took him in an entirely different direction.[9]

> Because the only open and formal peace attempt between Israel and its neighbors failed on account of the refugees and boundaries questions, most people concerned with the Arab–Israeli conflict academically or diplomatically have come to view these two problems as the real issue between the Arab states and Israel. Countless efforts have been made by well-meaning mediators especially American to resolve the conflict between Arabs and Israelis on the basis of this premise and when all these efforts failed the conclusion was drawn that the problems were intractable rather than that the premise was wrong.

To Safran "the conflict has persisted because key Arab countries had no desire for peace for reasons which have varied over the years and they could not be compelled to make peace. . . . The problems of the refugees and the boundaries in other words have been symptoms rather than causes."[10]

Safran found evidence to support his argument in the text of the Lausanne protocol and "in the more interesting attempt at peace between Israel and Jordan." The Jordanian and Israeli negotiators

> thrashed out the terms of a peace treaty between the two countries including a settlement of these two issues. . . . [Safran wrote erroneously that Jordan was to be given an outlet to the Mediterranean through free-port rights at Haifa.] The treaty did not come to fruition because the opposition to peace at home and in other Arab countries deterred any Jordanian prime minister from putting his signature to the agreement and because King Abdullah was assassinated in July 1951 for pursuing the attempt.
>
> As far as the Arab governments other than Jordan's were concerned, the problems of the refugees and the boundaries may have been the real issues for perhaps a few months right after the termination of the war. They as everyone else assumed at the time that peace followed after armistice and they wanted some concessions on these questions in order to preserve their self-respect and to justify

themselves before home public opinion from which they had endeavored to hide the magnitude of the disaster.

While seeking these concessions through UN mediators, the Arab states discovered yet another dimension of the Arab–Israeli conflict: The victorious party was hamstrung by the UN and other parties and could not consummate its victory and impose peace. At the same time, the Arabs' balance sheet showed that the gains to be derived from a peace settlement were considerably outweighed by its costs.[11] These calculations were confirmed by the psychological difficulty of admitting defeat, the paralyzing effect of inter-Arab rivalries, and the ambivalent view of the balance of power between the Arabs and Israel—on the one hand, fear of Israeli expansion and, on the other, hope that in the future the demographic gap would enable the Arabs to take advantage of their larger numbers and defeat Israel. Safran rightly observed that "the same ambivalence only with a confident arrogance feeding on the future is to be found on the Israeli side."[12] But in the early postwar period, Arab expectations for a reversal of the balance of power were a vague hope rather than a blueprint for action. The actual pressure to resume hostilities came a few years later when the failure to make peace and the ensuing friction resulted in "the festering of the conflict."[13]

The third wave of studies of the early Arab–Israeli conflict came in the latter half of the 1980s, primarily as a result of the opening of the Israeli, British, and American diplomatic archives for the late 1940s and 1950s. Works by Sela, Gazit, Pappé, Ilan, Oren, and Schueftan[14] fall in this category. Another category is sometimes defined as the "revisionist school of early Israeli history,"[15] and these self-styled "new historians"[16] consist primarily of Avi Shlaim, Benny Morris, the late Simha Flappan, and, to some extent, Tom Segev.[17]

The members of this group departed from an explicit contemporary political premise and sought to demolish an orthodox version of the past that, as they saw it, was part of the mythology propagated by the Zionist and Israeli establishments. This was stated most explicitly by the least academic (and professionally most vulnerable) of the group—Simha Flappan, who first formulated the principal myths propagated by Israeli "official" or "semiofficial" versions and then tried to demolish them. Flappan was concerned mainly with the establishment of the state of Israel, the conduct of the first Arab–Israeli war, the problem of the Palestinian refugees, and the failure to reach peace at the war's end. On this last issue Flappan argued that contrary to its own propaganda, during the war's final phases Israel rejected several Arab offers to make peace, principally because it believed that it could achieve its objectives by means of military superiority and without concessions.[18]

Benny Morris's work focuses on the Palestinian refugees, but his review essay addresses the larger questions. He was critical of Flappan's research but relied on Shlaim and Pappé to demonstrate that Israel's recalcitrance was mainly to blame for the failure to make peace at the war's end and afterward. Shlaim's argument is not made all that clearly in Pappés book, but it certainly occupies a central place in Shlaim's work. (Reference has already been made to his criticism of Ben-Gurion's "spurning" of Husni Zaim's overture.) Shlaim's study of the Israeli–Jordanian relationship concludes in a similar vein:

> Two principal factors were responsible for the failure of the postwar negotiations: Israel's strength and Abdullah's weakness. Israel's resounding victory . . . lessened her interest in accomodation and compromise. So confident was the fledgling Jewish State in her military superiority over the Arabs that her willingness to make concessions for the sake of a settlement of the conflict was seriously curtailed. . . . Israel adopted a tough stance, offering little by way of concessions to the Arabs and insisting that peace be based substantially on the territorial status quo and without repatriation of the Arab refugees. Such a stance compounded by hypocrisy and double dealing was bound to have a negative effect on the negotiations with Abdullah.[19]

Shlaim's argument was refuted by some reviewers of his book and some participants in a colloquium organized in 1989 at Tel Aviv University on the new sources for and approaches to the study of the 1948 war. Some of the harshest criticism of Shlaim's (and Morris's) work was that by Shabtai Teveth, Ben-Gurion's biographer, at the colloquium and in the Israeli newspaper *Haaretz* and the American-Jewish monthly *Commentary*.

In his response, in *Commentary*, Shlaim reformulated his argument:

> The principal bone of contention between the "old" historians and myself concerning the responsibility for the political stalemate that followed the 1948 war is not even mentioned by Mr. Teveth. According to the "old" historians, Israel's leaders did everything in their power to come to terms with the Arabs but found no willing partner. I list the peace efforts made by Egypt, Jordan and Syria, each of which carried a different price tag, and conclude that in the aftermath of the first Arab–Israeli war Israel's intransigence was greater than that of the Arabs. Ben Gurion in particular preferred the status quo enshrined in the armistice agreements to a formal peace that entailed Israeli concessions either in territory or on the refugee question. Whether he made the right choice is a matter of opinion.[20]

To this and to some of Shlaim's other arguments Teveth replied:

> No less shaky than the collusion thesis is Mr. Shlaim's preposterous allegation that the Arab governments of Egypt, Syria and Jordan "stood in line"—as he put it at Tel Aviv University—to make peace with Israel only to be rejected out of hand. In the case of Egypt and Syria, Mr. Shlaim's thesis has already been proved totally unfounded by others . . . but what of Abdullah? Was he, too, pressuring Israel to accept peace?[21]

This debate indicates the direction of the revisionist school's approach to the early years of the Arab–Israeli conflict. The new source material that became available in the 1980s enabled a review of the formative phase of the Arab–Israeli conflict. Some of the first studies that drew on this material sought, first, to bring to the surface new facts and thereby to present a fuller picture of the past, in contrast with the somewhat schematic picture that emerged from the literature in earlier stages. The revisionist school focused its research on the following questions: Were opportunities missed for making peace? Who is to blame for the failure to make peace? What are the myths and accepted truths that can and should be debated? The revisionist school, however, was hampered by several flaws—its point of departure was political and moralistic rather than academic; it relied almost exclusively on Israeli and Western rather than Arab sources, thereby presenting an unbalanced picture; and it introduced emotional issues that were not always the most important ones. In the course of the controversy and debate a process of refinement occurred. The line presented by Shlaim in the pages of *Commentary* was much subtler than his conclusions in his piece on Husni al-Zaim. But the revisionists also made at least one important contribution: They revealed significant weaknesses in the traditional historiography and orthodox version of Arab–Israeli relations that were dominant in Israel. All arguments made by revisionist historians need not be accepted in order to recognize the need to correct and refine the orthodox version.

The study of the Arab–Israeli conflict should be moved beyond this controversy and the mere presentation of new facts. The three sets of negotiations we have considered in this book reveal the extent to which the conflict with Israel had already been internalized in the Arab consciousness by the end of the 1948 war. Samir al-Rifai, who was considered a moderate and pragmatic politician, a loyal subordinate of Abdullah, and a man with many ties to Israel, is an excellent example. In February 1950, you may recall, he refused to write down the text of a proposed nonaggression pact that Abdullah wanted to dictate. Al-Rifai was willing to meet with the Israelis and to negotiate with them, but he did not wish to leave written evidence or to be the person who actually wrote down the text of the agreement. Rifai's conduct was also a manifestation of the distinction made by many Arabs among their official, symbolic, and practical dealings with Israel.

This distinction was already being made before the 1948 war, was reinforced by it, and was developed to its fullest in its aftermath. Arab resistance to the notion of Jewish sovereignty over Palestine or part of it was too intense to be confronted by Arab governments or individual politicians, and yet powerful interests were also at stake that required contact, cooperation, or settlements with Israel. The solution that was devised led either to secret contacts with Israel or contacts through channels that were defined as legitimate. The armistice mechanism is the best example. The fact that the armistice agreements were defined at the war's end as an inferior substitute to peace agreements gave them legitimacy in Arab eyes. It was thus possible to discuss new agreements as long as they were presented as an expansion of the armistice agreements. Likewise, Israeli and Syrian officers could maintain good and even cordial relations through the mixed armistice commission.[22] But any departure from these unwritten rules that implied acceptance of Israel's legitimacy or official or open contact with that nation was prohibited.

The partition plan remained illegitimate in Arab eyes even at the war's end when a Jewish state had been established over a larger territory. The most accommodating Arab position in 1948 was the idea of a secular state in Palestine. Indeed, this idea had appeared, if amorphously, as early as 1949.[23] And the notion of a secular (democratic) state was a central theme in Palestinian thought and activity immediately after the 1967 war. ("Secular" in this context means not Jewish and also not Arab, that is, binational.)

In 1971 the English-language version of Y. Harkabi's book, *Arab Attitudes Towards Israel*, was published, and twenty years later it still is the most thorough and comprehensive study of this issue. Harkabi's work was undoubtedly nourished by his experience and firsthand knowledge, but it relied in the main on a textual analysis of Arab writings and statements regarding Israel. The documents that I have used in this book show that now the archives have been opened, Harkabi's work can be further developed and the positions and attitudes of both Arabs and Israelis can be studied on the basis of their conduct during their negotiations.[24]

The negotiations with Husni al-Zaim were the most instructive of the three cases we studied. It is not a new idea to state that it was impossible to reach a peace agreement with Abdullah, who had lost control of his kingdom after the de facto annexation of the West Bank, nor is it surprising to discover the great degree of continuity in Egypt's position in its conflict with Israel. Although this continuity was later broken during Gamal Abdul Nasser's time in power, the similarity between Sadat's policy and Egypt's conduct under the monarchy is considerable.

As for the negotiations with Husni al-Zaim: Even if he is seen as an eccentric and exceptional figure with no real roots in Syrian politics and even if Adel Arslan is seen as Syria's true representative regarding the conflict with Israel, the fact remains that Zaim's Syrian enemies generally did not denounce him for his dealings with Israel and for his efforts to come to terms with that country. The problem of Palestine, as the British representative in Damascus then observed, did not occupy a central position in Syrian consciousness during the latter part of 1949. This observation, which ties in with the new facts regarding Syrian–Israeli relations in the late 1940s and early 1950s, calls for a revision in the traditional perception of the Syrian–Israeli conflict as bitter and hopeless. Syria was indeed the quintessential Arab state, committed to pan-Arab nationalism and the Palestine question. But Syria nonetheless maintained a streak of pragmatism: Khaled al-'Azm, who was prime minister when Syria decided to enter armistice negotiations with Israel, reveals this in his memoirs.

According to his own description 'Azm concluded in the spring of 1949 that after Egypt, Jordan, and Iraq had departed and left Syria exposed and isolated vis-à-vis Israel, it had no choice but to negotiate. But 'Azm understood that this was not a decision he could make on his own and so sought parliamentary support. Realizing that in an open session of parliament dedicated to this issue, the delegates would speak to the crowd and the protocol, 'Azm held a closed session during which he demanded that Faris al-Khouri review the facts "free from any reprehensible duplicity." He made it clear to the parliament that Syria alone—and in fact even with its fellow Arab states—could not defend its own lands if it were attacked by the Zionist forces. The parliament thereupon permitted the government to enter into the armistice negotiations.

With this approval, 'Azm instructed his representative to inform Ralph Bunche that Syria was ready to negotiate and announced his two principal conditions: Syria would remain in the cease-fire lines, and the border would be drawn in the middle of the Jordan River and Lake Tiberias and not according to the international boundary between Syria and Mandatory Palestine.[25]

'Azm took advantage of the concessions that Zaim had made, in order to disparage the man who deposed him from power, and in so doing he followed the same pattern of political overbidding on the question of Palestine and Israel that constrained him when he sought to end the war and enter into the armistice negotiations.

'Azm's memoirs thus point to two important elements: Even the most committed position on the question of Palestine could be mitigated by pragmatic considerations. One wonders, therefore, what could actually have been achieved had all those concerned taken a much bolder stance at the end of the 1948 war. In any case, it took another two decades to reach a similar degree of flexibility that made possible the partial breakthrough of the 1970s.

# Notes

## Chapter One

1. Two essays offer frameworks for analyzing the Arab–Israeli conflict: Shimon Shamir, "The Arab-Israeli Conflict," in A. L. Udovitch, ed., *The Middle East: Oil Conflict and Hope* (Lexington, Mass.: Lexington Books, 1976), pp. 195–231; and Elie Kedourie, "The Arab–Israeli Conflict," in E. Kedourie, ed., *Arabic Political Memoirs* (London: Frank Cass, 1974), pp. 218–31.

2. David Ben-Gurion, *From Ben Gurion's Diary—The War of Independence*, ed. G. Rivlin and E. Oren (Tel Aviv: Ministry of Defense, 1986), p. 435. All translations are mine unless otherwise noted, and all translations have been edited for clarity.

3. Moshe Sharett, "Israel and the Arabs: War and Peace," *Ot*, October 1966, pp. 8–10 (in Hebrew). This text was based on presentations made by Sharett at Beit Berl, a Labor movement institution, in October–November 1957.

4. Yemima Rosenthal, "David Ben-Gurion and Moshe Sharett Facing Crucial Decisions in Israel's Foreign Policy," *Skira Hodshit* 35, no. 11 (1988): 15–22 (in Hebrew); Ya'acov Bar-Siman Tov, "Ben Gurion and Sharett: Conflict Management and Great Power Constraints in Israeli For-

eign Policy," *Middle Eastern Studies* 24 (1988): 330–56; Avi Shlaim, "Conflicting Approaches to Israel's Relations with the Arabs: Ben Gurion and Sharett, 1953–1956," *Middle East Journal* (Spring 1983): 180–202.

5. Sharett, "Israel and the Arabs," pp. 8–10.

6. The Israeli Foreign Ministry's approach to the issues is reflected in memoirs published by several veteran Israeli diplomats. See especially Walter Eytan, *The First Ten Years* (New York: Simon & Schuster, 1958); Abba Eban, *An Autobiography* (London: Weidenfeld & Nicholson, 1977); and Gideon Rafael, *Destination Peace* (London: Weidenfeld & Nicholson, 1981), p. 74.

7. Rony E. Gabbary, *A Political Study of the Arab–Jewish Conflict: The Arab Refugee Problem (A Case Study)* (Geneva: Librairie E. Droz, 1959), pp. 220–67.

8. David Forsythe, *United Nations Peacemaking: The Conciliation Commission for Palestine* (Baltimore: John Hopkins University Press, 1972).

9. Malcolm Kerr, ed., *The Elusive Peace in the Middle East* (Albany: State University of New York Press, 1975), pp. 1–18.

10. Avi Shalim, "Husni Zaim and the Plan to Resettle Palestinian Refugees in Syria," *Middle East Focus* (Fall 1986): 26–31.

11. For the standard description and analysis of the American and British efforts to bind the Middle East in a framework of defense pacts, see John Campbell, *Defense of the Middle East—Problems of American Policy* (New York: Praegar, 1960), pp. 39–62. For British policy in the region during those years, see Roger Louis, *Britain's Empire and the Middle East* (Oxford: Oxford University Press, 1984).

12. On inter-Arab relations of the period, see Malcolm Kerr, *The Arab Cold War 1958–1964, A Study of Ideology in Politics* (Oxford: Oxford University Press, 1968); Itamar Rabinovich, "Inter-Arab Relations Foreshadowed: The Question of the Syrian Throne in 1920s and the 1930s," Hebrew version of an article in *Zmanim* 3 (Spring 1980): 92–99; and Asher Goren, *The Arab League 1945–1954* (Tel Aviv: 'Ayanot, 1954) (in Hebrew).

13. On Syrian politics of the period, see Patrick Seale, *The Struggle for Syria: A Study of Post-War Politics* (Oxford: Oxford University Press, 1965). For additional details, see the memoirs published by several Syrian politicians: Nadhir Fansa, *Days of Husni al-Za'im: 137 Days That Shook Up Syria* (Beirut: Manshurāt dar el Āfāq al-Jadida, 1982) (in Arabic); Khaled al-Azm, *The Memoirs of Khaled al-Azm*. 3 vols. (Beirut: Al Dar al Muttahida Lil-Nashir, 1973) (in Arabic); and Adel Arslan, *The Memoirs of Emir Adel Arslan* (Beirut: Al Dar al-Taqadumiyya Lil-Nashir, 1983) (in Arabic). Nadhir Fansa was Husni Zaim's brother-in-law and personal secretary, and Khaled al-Azm was the prime minister deposed by Husni Zaim who later became Syria's president. Adel Arslan was Husni Zaim's foreign minister. On Shishakli's relations with the United States, see Miles Copeland, *The Game*

*Game Player* (London: Aurum Press, 1989), pp. 98–100. Material concerning Shishakli's ties with the Israeli diplomats later in 1950 can be found in Israel's state archive. Shishakli is not mentioned in these documents by name but is referred to as "the polite one," a code name that, in the best tradition of the Jewish Agency's political department, is based on his first name.

14. For a survey of Egyptian political history during those years, see P. J. Vatikiotis, *Egypt from Muhammad 'Ali to Sadat* (London, 1969).

15. The Jericho Congress has been studied in detail by Yosef Nevo, *Abdullah and the Palestine Arabs* (Tel Aviv University, Shiloah Institute, 1965) (in Hebrew).

## Chapter Two

1. Israel State Archive, File 4373/13.

2. Yemima Rosenthal, "Ben-Gurion and Sharett Facing Crucial Decisions in Israel's Foreign Policy," *Skira Hodshit* 35 (11) (1988): 15–25 (in Hebrew).

3. Ibid.

4. Mordechai Gazit, "The Israel–Jordan Peace Negotiations (1949–51): King Abdallah's Lonely Effort," *Journal of Contemporary History* 23 (3) (July 1988): 409–23.

5. Israel State Archive, File 2570/11.

6. Memorandum from Shimoni to Eytan, "On Political Problems in the Galilee and the Northern Border and on the Relationship Between the Ministry of Foreign Affairs and the Army's General Staff," November 18, 1948, Israel State Archive, File 186/17.

7. Israel State Archive, File 4373/13. Danin's statement during consultation on peace negotiations with the Arab states held on April 12, 1949.

8. Sharett to Ben-Gurion, January 22, 1953. Israel State Archive, File 2408/13.

9. On the Israeli Foreign Ministry, see Michael Brecher, *The Foreign Policy System of Israel* (New Haven; Conn.: Yale University Press, 1972), pp. 430–63.

10. Israel State Archive, File 250/11. Eytan published a book of memoirs dealing with his first decade in Israeli diplomacy: *The First Ten Years* (New York: Simon & Schuster, 1958).

11. See Gideon Rafael, *Destination Peace* (London: Weidenfeld & Nicholson, 1981).

12. Shiloah's career is described in the biography written by Haggai Eshed, *A One-Man Institution* (Tel Aviv: Idanim, 1978) (in Hebrew). A critical description of Shiloah and the political department by a bureaucratic rival is by Isser Harel, *Security and Democracy* (Tel Aviv: Idanim, 1989), chap. 9 (in Hebrew).

13. Shimoni's letter to Sasson, October 24, 1948, Israel State Archive, File 2570/11.

14. Moshe Sharett, *A Personal Diary* (Tel Aviv: Maariv, 1988), vol. 8, p. 2398 (in Hebrew).

15. Many of the reports written by Eilat and Sasson on their contacts and conversations with Arab leaders and diplomats were included in books published by them in the 1970s: Eliahu Elath, *Zionism and the Arabs* (Tel Aviv: Devir, 1974) (in Hebrew); Eliyahu Sasson, *On the Road to Peace* (Tel Aviv: Am Oved, 1978) (in Hebrew).

16. Ezra Danin's career is described in *Ezra Danin—An Unconditional Zionist*, ed. Gershon Rivlin (Jerusalem: Rivlin, 1987) (in Hebrew).

17. Shimoni to Sasson, July 12, 1948, Israel State Archive, File 2570/11.

18. Eytan to Shimoni, December 22, 1948, Israel State Archive, File 2565/13.

19. Eliyahu Sasson to Moshe Sasson, Israel State Archive, File A/4021, April 17, 1952.

20. On Ben-Gurion's Arab policy, see Shabtai Teveth, *Ben Gurion and the Palestinian Arabs* (Oxford: Oxford University Press, 1985); and Shabtai Teveth, *Ben Gurion: The Burning Ground 1886–1948* (Boston: Houghton Mifflin, 1987), esp. pp. 457–64, 535–47.

21. About these efforts, see Ya'acov Shimoni, "Jordanian Orientation, Egyptian Orientation, and Palestinian Orientation on the Eve of the Establishment of the State and During Its Early Years" (unpublished paper).

22. Two books published in recent years deal with Israel's relationship with Abdullah: Dan Schueftan, *A Jordanian Option*, 2nd ed. (Tel Aviv: Hakibut Hameuhad, 1987) (in Hebrew); and Avi Shlaim, *Collusion Across the Jordan: King Abdallah, the Zionist Movement, and the Partition of Palestine* (Oxford: Oxford University Press, 1988). Both books carry explicit or implicit political messages. Schueftan's book, as its title implies, seeks to place in its historical context what some view as a political option currently available to Israel. The title of Shlaim's book betrays a negative attitude toward the Israeli–Jordanian partnership. Indeed, in the book itself Shlaim goes further and refers to "an unholy alliance." In the introduction to his book Shlaim defines himself as a "revisionist historian" critical of Israel's policy of the time.

23. Shimoni, "Jordanian Orientation, Egyptian Orientation, and Palestinian Orientation."

24. David Ben-Gurion, *The War Diary, The War of Independence, 1948–1949.* 3 vols. (Tel Aviv: Ministry of Defence, 1982) (in Hebrew), pp. 953, 966, 963. Ben-Gurion's diaries of those years are available in three forms. The full diary is available for research in the Ben-Gurion Archives at Sdeh Boker. A slightly abridged and annotated text of the diary for the 1948 war period has been published in three volumes under the preceding title. The same editor published a slightly different selection under the title *From Ben Gurion's Diary—The War of Independence*, ed. G. Rivlin and Elhanan Oren. (Tel Aviv: Ministry of Defence, 1986) (in Hebrew).

25. Sasson to Abd al-Majid Haydar, Documents on the Foreign Policy of Israel (DFPI), vol. 1, doc. 416, p. 453, notes; and doc. 428, p. 490, note 1. It is curious to note that Muhammad Hussein Haykal mentions the episode in the third volume of his memoirs but presents a version that is quite different from Sasson's.

26. Foreign Relations of the United States (FRUS), 1948, pp. 1266–71.

27. See Schueftan, *A Jordanian Option*, p. 89; Shlaim, *Collusion Across the Jordan*, pp. 281–82. See also DFPI, vol. 1, doc. 437, p. 499, notes.

28. Israel State Archive, File 2570/11.

29. Israel State Archive, File 4373/11.

30. Yigal Alon's point of view is spelled out in two books, his own, *A Curtain of Sand* (Tel Aviv: Ovir, 1959) (in Hebrew), and a book written by his associate, Yeruham Cohen, *By Daylight and in Darkness* (Tel Aviv: 'Amikam, 1969) (in Hebrew).

31. Danin to Sasson, September 22, 1948; Israel State Archive, File 2570/11.

32. Sasson, to Shimoni, DFPI 1948, doc. 201, pp. 241–43.

33. Sasson, DFPI 1948, doc. 282, pp. 320–31.

34. Ben-Gurion, *From Ben Gurion's Diary*, pp. 852–53.

35. Ben Gurion speaking on April 12, Israel State Archive, File 4373/13.

36. Ibid.

37. *Divrey Ha-Knesset* (Minutes of the Knesset), 1949, pp. 306–7.

38. Ben-Gurion, *From Ben Gurion's Diary*, pp. 444–45.

39. Israel State Archive, File 4373/13, July 14, 1949.

40. Moshe Sharett speaking to department heads of the Israeli Foreign Ministry, May 25, 1949, Israel State Archive, File 2447/3.

41. Israel State Archive, File 2408/13.

42. Yusuf Haikal, *Meetings at Raghdan Palace* Amman: Dar al-Galil Lil-*Nashir,* 1988) (in Arabic), pp. 178–79.

43. Sharett to department heads, Israel State Archive, File 2447/3.

44. Israel State Archive, Files 2451/2, 2565/19.

45. Israel State Archive, File 4373/13.
46. Ibid.
47. Ibid.
48. Ibid.
49. Sasson to Sharett, September 27, 1949, Israel State Archive, File 2403/12.

## Chapter Three

1. For details of the discussions and conversations between representatives of the Jewish Agency's political department and the Syrian leaders and politicians, see Eliahu Elath, *Zionism and the Arabs* (Tel Aviv: Devir, 1974) (in Hebrew); and Eliyahu Sasson, *On the Road to Peace* (Tel Aviv: Am Oved, 1978) (in Hebrew). See also Philip Khoury, "Divided Loyalties: Syria and the Question of Palestine, 1919–1939," *Middle Eastern Studies* 21 (July 1985): 324–48.

2. For Syria's role in the 1948 war and its position on the question of the war's termination, see Abraham Sela, "Syria and the Palestinian Question from the Establishment of the Arab League to the Armistice Agreement, 1945–1949," *Dapei Elazar*, no. 6 (Tel Aviv University), pp. 24–42 (in Hebrew). An intriguing version by the Syrian prime minister in the first months of 1949 can be found in Khaled al-'Azm's *The Memoirs of Khaled al-'Azm* (Beirut: Al Dar al-Taqadumiyya Lil-Nashir, 1973), vol. 1, pp. 379–90 (in Arabic).

3. The Soviet Union's attitude was determined by the fact that at this time it still believed that Husni Zaim was linked to Abdullah and the British. See Moshe Zak, *Israel and the Soviet Union—A Forty-Year Dialogue* (Tel-Aviv: Maariv, 1988), p. 216 (in Hebrew).

4. An excellent background to and summary of the armistice negotiations between Israel and Syria can be found in the introduction written by Yemima Rosenthal to the third volume of DFPI (Jerusalem, 1983) (in Hebrew), pp. 11–12, 27–32. See also N. Bar-Yaacov, *The Israeli–Syrian Armistice* (Jerusalem: Magnes Press, 1967) (in Hebrew); Aryeh Shalev, *Cooperation in the Shadow of Conflict* (Tel Aviv: Maarachot, 1987) (in Hebrew). Shalev was a member of the Israeli delegation to the Syrian–Israeli mixed armistice commission, and his book combines his memoirs with the fruits of archival research.

5. Ben-Gurion, *From Ben Gurion's Diary*, p. 3435.
6. Ibid.

7. Israel State Archive, File 4373/13.
8. See FRUS, 1949, vol. 4, p. 962, n. 3.
9. Ibid., pp. 965–66.
10. Ben-Gurion, *From Ben Gurion's Diary*, p. 436.
11. Ibid.
12. See FRUS, 1949, vol. 4, p. 990.
13. DFPI, vol. 3, doc. 303, pp. 562–63.
14. Shabtai Rosenne to Foreign Minister Sharett, May 8 1949, Israel State Archive, File 2454/10. See also Shalev, *Cooperation*, pp. 49–50.
15. Keeley to the secretary of state, May 11, 1949. National Archives 767, no. 90, D 15/5.
16. DFPI, doc. 310, pp. 581–82.
17. DFPI, doc. 312, p. 584.
18. DFPI, docs. 310, 320, 321, 323–27.
19. DFPI, docs. 332–37.
20. DFPI, doc. 328, p. 597.
21. Broadmead to the Foreign Office, June 1949, FO 371/E6804.
22. Adel Arslan, *The Memoirs of Emir Adel Arslan*, vol. 2, *1946–1950* (Beirut: Dar al-Taqadumiyya Lil-Nashir, 1983), pp. 839, 841–42, 844 (in Arabic).
23. For a summary of Arslan's articles in the Beiruti newspaper *al-Hayat* and their echoes in Damascus, see the report by the American Legation in Beirut on August 31, 1949, NA 890 D 00/8–3149, no. 217.
24. Ben-Gurion, *From Ben Gurion's Diary*, p. 445. Zaim indeed made his ideas public in an interview he granted to the correspondent of the *Gazette de Lausanne* in which he spoke broadly about his foreign policy. The Syrian newspaper *al-Inḳilab* published a translation of the interview, according to the American legation in Damascus. Zaim said the following with regard to Israel: "Syria and Israel are now bound by a cease-fire agreement. On my part I should like to conclude a permanent truce agreement, but if Israel does not abide by its pledges, I will proceed to take all the measures that the violation of these pledges might necessitate."
25. M. Sharett's guidelines to Israel mission abroad, DFPI, vol. 4, doc. 146, pp. 239–49.
26. DFPI, doc. 188, pp. 300–301.
27. See FRUS, 1949, pp. 1030–32; and Keeley to the secretary of state, May 11 and May 19, 1949, NA 767, N 90 D.
28. FRUS, 1949, pp. 1245–46, 1256.
29. On the social and ideological differences among the various age groups in the Syrian officer corps during those years, see M. van Dusen, "Intra and Inter-Generational Conflict in the Syrian Army" (Ph.D. diss., Johns Hopkins University, 1971). Zaim's lack of sensitivity with regard to the ideological sensibilities were analyzed by Ya'acov Shimoni, "Syria

Between the Coups," *Hamizrah Hehadash*, October 1949–50, pp. 7–21 (in Hebrew).

30. On June 20, 1949, the Israeli Foreign Ministry prepared a profile on Muhsin al-Barasi. See Israel State Archive, File 2565/13.

31. Khaled al-'Azm, *The Memoirs of Khaled al-'Azm* (Beirut: Al Dar al-Taqadumiyya Lil-Nashir, 1973), vol. 2, p. 380.

32. *New York Times*, August 19, 1949.

33. *New York Times*, July 26, 1949.

34. Miles Copeland, *The Game of Nations* (London: Weidenfeld & Nicholson, 1969), pp. 60–66. In 1989 Copeland published a second biography, entitled *The Game Players* (London: Aurum Press, 1989). This book, too, includes a chapter dealing with the "Syrian episode" of 1949, but it does not alter the main lines of the story told twenty years earlier. For a critical review of Copeland's first book, see E. Kedourie, "The Sorceror's Apprentice," in his *Arabic Political Memoirs* (London: Frank Cass, 1974), pp. 170–76.

35. Copeland, *The Game of Nations*, p. 42.

36. Ibid.

37. For Meade's reports to the State Department on his unusual discussions with Zaim, see, for instance, the memorandum he submitted to Minister Keeley on August 11, 1949. The report was released by the National Archives on May 4, 1984. For a summary of Meade's role in preparing for Zaim's coup, based on Meade's report to Washington, see Douglas Little, "Cold War and Covert Action: The United States and Syria, 1945–1958," *Middle East Journal* 44 (Winter 1990): 51–75.

38. FO 371/75529 E4–72, March 28, 1949.

39. NA, 350 Syria 3144.0501.

40. Integrated weekly report no. 60, March 18, 1949, Confidential File RG 130X.22.

41. FO 371/68810 E 15669 and NA 800A Moose to Washington, March 12, 1947.

42. See the report by the U.S. military attaché, Lawrence Mitchell, on November 1, 1949 (no archival number).

43. For the role of the U.S. oil companies in the formulation of U.S. policy in the region, see Little, "Cold War and Covert Action," pp. 53–54. The memoirs of Khaled al-'Azm and Nadhir Fansa echo the rumors current at the time that U.S. oil executives were involved in staging Zaim's coup, in order to secure the ratification of the Tapline agreement. See Nadhir Fansa, *Days of Husni al-Za'im: 137 Days That Shook Up Syria* (Beirut: Manshurat Dar el-Āfāq al-Jadida, 1982), p. 134. For 'Azm's insistence that during his period in power the Tapline agreement could not be ratified, see his memoirs, vol. 2, pp. 373–76.

44. Copeland, *The Game of Nations*, pp. 42–44.

45. For Keeley's discussions with the Syrian leadership regarding the termination of the war with Israel, see FRUS, 1949, pp. 637–39, 796–98.

46. On George McGhee's plan, see his memoirs, *Envoy to the Middle World: Adventures and Diplomacy* (New York: Harper & Row, 1983); see also Cyrus Sulzberger, *New York Times*, September 16, 1949.

47. See Minister Keeley's report to Washington on May 11, 1949, for his discussion with Zaim and Arlsan on this matter. FRUS 890 D/0–02/5–1149.

48. FO 371/75072 E702, 1949.

49. Acheson's cable to Keeley on May 13, 1949, FRUS, pp. 1007–8.

50. See Keeley's report in FRUS, 1949, pp. 1226–28.

51. Meade's memorandum to the chargé d'affaires, August 11, 1949 (no archival number).

52. Adel Arslan, *The Memoirs of Emir Adel Arslan*, vol. 2 (Beirut: Al Dar al-Taqadumiyya Lil-Nashir, 1983).

53. This description is based on Arslan's own version, as told in his memoirs and in *al-Ḥayat*. His version is confirmed by the dispatches sent at the time by British and American diplomats. See, for instance, the report by the British ambassador, Broadmead, on June 1, 1949, FO 371 E6804.

54. See essay by Shimoni, "Syria Between the Coups," and the memoirs of Khalid al-'Azm and Nadhir Fansa. Fansa was Zaim's brother-in-law and private secretary, a fact that accounts for the book's advantages and shortcomings. Fansa was clearly is familiar with the most intimate details of Zaim's regime and period, but he also is trying to defend Zaim's and his own records. 'Azm despised Zaim and held a grudge against him, but his memoirs abound in detail with regard to those months (see esp. vol. 2, pp. 179ff).

55. Israel State Archive, File 2447/3.

56. Ibid.

57. Ben-Gurion, *From Ben Gurion's Diary*, April 2, 1949.

58. Israel State Archive, File 33/11.

59. Israel State Archive, File 2570/11; Danin to Sasson, August 24, 1948.

60. Ibid.

61. Ibid.

62. Israel State Archive, File 130.02, file 22, box 2408.

63. Nasser was an Alawi officer, one of Zaim's brigate commanders and a key figure of his regime. See also the report by the U.S. military attaché, Mitchell, November 1, 1949 (no archival number).

64. See the text of an interview conducted by Shabtai Teveth with Major Itzak Spector. I am grateful to Shabtai Teveth for making this available to me.

65. Ben-Gurion, *From Ben Gurion's Diary*, p. 463.

66. McDonald to secretary of state, June 27, 1947, FRUS 7767N–90D/6/2749.

67. Sasson's telegram to M. Sharett, April 4, 1949, DFPI, vol 2, doc. 475, pp. 547–48.

68. Eytan on discussion with Abdullah al-Tal, in DFPI, vol. 3, doc. 267, p. 500, April 3, 19949.

69. Ben-Gurion, *The War Diary*, vol. 3, p. 984.

70. "The Character of the Coup in Syria, Primary Comments," Israel State Archive, File AS/20/2408.

71. The New Syrian Government, Israel State Archive File AS/20/2408.

72. Ben-Gurion, *From Ben Gurion's Diary*, August 14, 1949.

73. FO 371/82782 EY/1011.

74. J. Inis Claude, *Swords into Plowshares* (New York: Random House, 1971), p. 228. Claude relied here on Raymond Aron, *Peace and War* (Garden City, N.Y.: Doubleday/Anchor, 1973), pp. 116, 560.

## Chapter Four

1. In addition to Dan Schueftan, *A Jordanian Option*, 2nd ed. (Tel Aviv: Hakibut Hameuhad, 1987) (in Hebrew); and Avi Shlaim, *Collusion Across the Jordan: King Abdallah, the Zionist Movement and the Partition of Palestine* (Oxford: Oxford University Press, 1988); see Abraham Sela, *From Contacts to Negotiations—The Relationship of the Jewish Agency and the State of Israel with King Abdullah, 1946–1950* (Tel Aviv University, Shiloah Institute, 1985); and Uri Bar Joseph, *The Best of Enemies* (London, Frank Cass, 1987).

2. According to the report written by the Israeli diplomat Michael Comay on Ben-Gurion's meeting with McDonald, Israel State Archive, File 282/154/1.

3. David Ben-Gurion, *From Ben Gurion's Diary—The War of Independence*, ed. G. Rivlin and E. Oren (Tel Aviv: Ministry of Defence, 1986), February 13, 1951.

4. The text of Sasson's letter to Isma'il Shirin as transmitted to the British Foreign Office can be found in FO 371/75345 E 14875.

5. FRUS, 1949, pp. 1509–10.

6. See Kirkbride's important letter to the directors of the Eastern Department in London, Furlonge, July 14, 1950, FO 371/882179 E 1015/77.

7. A brief summary of the meeting between Abdullah and Novomeyski can be found in the Editor's Note in DFBI, vol. 4, p. 636.

8. FRUS, 1949, pp. 1483–86.

9. Ibid., pp. 1495–96.

10. Kirkbride to London, December 15, 1949, FO 371/75345 E 14982.

11. *DFBI*, vol. 2, doc. 422, p. 637.

12. Ben-Gurion, *From Ben Gurion's Diary*, November 26, 1949.

13. The summary of the meeting is available in DFPI, vol. 4, doc. 441, pp. 659–61. Kirkbride's report on the meeting, according to Samir al-Rifai's account, is available in FO 371/75344. The accounts complement each other; thus the argument raised by the Israelis on the importance of the Negev to Israel can be found in the Jordanian but not in the Israeli report. According to Kirkbride's report, Sasson had replied to Rifai's question on this matter that "the land of the Negev was the only territory in Israel capable of absorbing a really large number of new settlers."

14. According to the report of the British minister in Tel Aviv, Knox Helm, December 18, 1949, FO 371/75345 E 15050.

15. The Israeli account of the December 18 meeting could not be found in the archives, and so this version is based on the report by Kirkbride, FO 371/75345 E 14892 and E 14983, and Fritzlan, FRUS, 1949, pp. 1845–47; and on Shiloah's account to McDonald as recounted to Knox Helm, FO 371/75345 E 15050. A detailed description of the meeting can also be found in Moshe Dayan, *The Story of My Life* (Tel Aviv: Idanim Davir, 1982), pp. 89–90. But the Dayan description raises a problem: In his autobiography and article published in *Yedi'ot Aharonot* on February 28, 1975, Dayan stated that he took part in that meeting, but according to the American and British accounts and to Ben-Gurion's diary, it was Sasson who participated in the meeting along with Shiloah. It seems that Dayan's mistake was the result of telescoping earlier and later meetings. See Schueftan, *A Jordanian Option*, pp. 195–96.

16. Shlaim, *Collusion Across the Jordan*, pp. 528–30; Schueftan, *A Jordanian Option*, p. 127, also describes the agreement as "a breakthrough," but he does not criticize Israel's policy.

17. FO 371/75345 E 15051.

18. Ben-Gurion, *From Ben Gurion's Diary*, December 14, 1949.

19. Israel State Archive, File 2593/12.

20. See the reports by Kirkbride, FO 371/75345 E 15277, and McDonald, FRUS, 1949, p. 1561.

21. FRUS, 1950, pp. 691–92.

22. The Israeli accounts for the January 24 and 30 meetings can be found in DFPI, vol. 5, docs. 40 and 55, pp. 40–46, 75. Kirkbride's reports can be found in FO 371/82177 E 1015/10 and E 1015/13. Kirkbride also covers the domestic dimension of this meeting.

23. DFPI, vol. 5, doc. 73, p. 92; and FO 371/82177 E 1015/20, February 10, 1950; E 1015/27, February 18, 1950; and E 1015/28, February 20, 1950.

24. See FO 371/82177 E 1015/22, February 13, 1950.

25. See, for instance, the report of the conversation between the king and Kirkbride in FO 371/82177 E 1015/20, February 20, 1950.

26. See DFPI, vol. 5, doc. 73, p. 92; and 70 371/82177 E 1015/20, February 10, 1950; E 1015/27, February 18, 1950; and E 1015/28, February 20, 1950.

27. DFPI, vol. 5, doc. 74, pp. 99–100.

28. On the discussion in the Israeli cabinet, see DFPI, vol. 5, doc. 100, p. 135, n.4.

29. According to the minutes of Moshe Sharett's meeting with editors of the Israeli press on March 9, 1950, Israel State Archive, File 130.02.2453.3.

30. The Israeli version of the February 24 meeting can be found in DFPI, vol. 5, doc. 105, p. 140. A different Jordanian version was reported to Kirkbride; see FO 371/82178 E 1015/36, March 2, 1950; and see also the editor's note in FRUS, 1950, p. 766.

31. FO 371/82178 E 1015/34.

32. FO 371/82178 E 1015/36, March 2, 1950.

33. For the Israeli version, see DFPI, vol. 5, doc. 106, pp. 146–52.

34. FO 371/82704 ET 1016/4, March 15, 1950.

35. FRUS, 1950, pp. 796–97.

36. The summary of Jordan's radio broadcasts between March 8 and 13, 1950; Israel State Archive, no file number.

37. FRUS, 1950, pp. 781–82.

38. Ibid., pp. 782–83.

39. Ibid., pp. 787–88, 798–99.

40. FO 371/81930 E 1071/16, March 28, 1950; NA 785.003/3–2450, March 24, 1950; FO 371/81930 E 1071/18, April 1, 1950. FRUS, 1950, p. 818.

41. On Sasson's meeting with Karmi on April 24, see Israel State Archive, File 130.00.2453.2; and on the message transmitted by Shiloah to the king, see FO 371/8278 ET 1081/23, April 25, 1950.

42. The Israeli account of the April 27 meeting is given in DFPI, vol. 5, doc. 213, pp. 300–302.

43. Drew from Amman, NA 684.85/4–2650, April 27, 1950.

44. DFPI, vol. 5, doc. 217, pp. 306–7.

45. See Moshe Sasson's letter to Eliyahu Sasson, *ibid.*

46. Ben-Gurion, *From Ben Gurion's Diary*, April 3, 1950.

47. DFPI, vol. 5, doc. 213, pp. 300–302.

48. Moshe Sasson to Eliyahu Sasson.

49. Israel State Archive, File 2463/3, March 3, 1955; and Haggai Eshed, *A One-Man Institution* (Tel Aviv: Maarochot, 1988) (in Hebrew).

50. Report to the Israeli foreign minister on June 25, 1950, Israel State Archive, File 4021/A.

51. FRUS, 1951, pp. 735–36.

52. FO 371/82178 E 1015/37, February 22, 1950. For a description of Abdullah's court in the better days of the early 1930s, see Hector Bolitho, *The Angry Neighbors* (London: Arthur Barker, 1957).

53. Israel State Archive, File 4021/A, June 25, 1950.

54. FO 371/81930 E 1071/20 and E 1071/14. 'Abd al-Illah sent Abdullah a personal letter on March 28. He explained his position to the British in more direct terms.

55. A detailed description of this episode can be found in Bruce Maddi-Weitzman, "The Crystallization of an Arab State System: Inter-Arab Politics, 1945–1954" (Ph.D. diss., Tel Aviv University, 1987), pp. 327–55.

56. On the various positions in Egypt on these questions at the time, see the memorandum prepared in the U.S. embassy in Cairo for a regional conference of U.S. representatives in the Middle East dealing with Egypt's attitude toward a settlement of the Palestinian question. The memorandum was sent by Ambassador Jefferson Caffery to Washington on March 22, NA 784–003.2250.

57. See, for instance, the discussion between King Farouk's brother-in-law, Ismail Shirin, and the British diplomat Edwin Chapman-Andrews on this matter at the end of November 1947. FO 371/76345 E 14875, November 30, 1949.

58. British Foreign Office to Cairo, December 22, 1949, FO 371/75345 E 14984.

59. Dayan, *The Story of My Life*, p. 89. Dayan presented his version in starker terms in a public lecture delivered in February 1975. The text of the lecture was published in *Yedi'ot Aharonot*, February 28, 1975.

60. See Israel State Archive, File 2463/3, March 3, 1955; and Eshed, *A One-Man Institution*.

61. Record on a meeting with Furlonge, Kidron to Comai, Israel State Archive, File 2412.6.4307/15A May 16, 1950.

62. See M. Gazit, "The Israel–Jordan Peace Negotiations (1949–51): King Abdullah's Lonely Effort," *Journal of Contemporary History* 23 (3) (July 1988): 409–23.

63. At the end of February 1955 Kirkbride tried to calm down Tawfiq Abu al-Huda, who wanted to torpedo the negotiations for a nonaggression pact. See Kirkbride's report in FO 371/82178 E1015/36, March 2, 1950; and the report by his American colleague in FRUS, 1950, pp. 774.

64. FO 371/75344 E 14529, December 8, 1949.

65. Ibid.

66. FO 371/75345 E 14875, December 12, 1949.

67. FO 371/75345 E 14904, December 13, 1949.

68. FRUS, 1949, pp. 1533–34.

69. FO 371/75344 E 14367, November 29, 1949.

70. FO 371/75345 E 14897, December 13, 1949. For the text of the message transmitted by Knox Helm to Israel and for the Israeli Foreign Ministry's political and legal analysis of it, see Israel State Archive, File 430/202, 2408/12/15.

71. FO 371/75345 E 14984.

72. See Kirkbride's two books, *A Crackle of Thorns* (London: John Murray, 1956), and *From the Wings* (London: Frank Cass, 1976).

73. For a description of this episode, see Uriel Dann, *Studies in the History of Transjordan, 1920–1949: The Making of a State* (Boulder, Colo.: Westview Press, 1984), pp. 117–18.

74. Kirkbride to Furlonge, FO 371/82179, E 1015/77.

75. FRUS, 1950, pp. 763–66.

76. Ibid., pp. 680–82.

77. Ibid., pp. 699–702.

78. Ibid., pp. 804–5.

79. Ibid., pp. 807–8.

# Chapter Five

1. See Itamar Rabinovich, "Egypt and the Question of Israel Before and After the July Revolution," *Zmanim* (Tel Aviv University) (Winter 1990): 78–87 (in Hebrew).

2. *Al-Tali'a*, February 1975.

3. See Yemima Rozenthal, Introduction to vol. 3, DFPI, pp. 11–32.

4. On the discussions with Riyad, see DFPI, vol. 1, pp. 632–33; vol. 2, pp. 21–29, 306–7; and David Ben-Gurion, *The Restored State of Israel* (Tel Aviv: Am Oved, 1969), pp. 311–16.

5. Ben-Gurion, *The Restored State of Israel*.

6. Ibid.

7. Ibid.

8. Israel State Archive, File 4373/13.

9. Israel State Archive, File 2453/12.

10. Ibid.

11. Ibid.

12. See Sasson's report on July 29, 1949, Israel State Archive, File 2453/12.

13. Ibid.

14. Israel State Archive, File 4373/13, July 13, 1949.

15. Ibid., August 21, 1949.

16. Ernest Dawn, ''Pan-Arabism and the Failure of Israeli–Jordanian Peace Negotiations, 1950,'' in Girdhari L. Tikku, ed., *Islam and Its Cultural Divergence* (Champaign–Urbana: University of Illinois Press, 1971), pp. 25–51.

17. Israel State Archive, File 2453/12, February 27, 1950.

18. See Rafael to Eytan, Israel State Archive, File 2447/9, March 3, 1950. The material in this file was supplemented by discussions with former senior Israeli officials.

19. Ibid.

20. Ibid.

21. FO 371/8218 E 1017/13, February 2, 1950.

22. FO 371/82200.

23. J. C. Campbell, *Defense of the Middle East of American Policy* (New York: Praeger, 1961), pp. 39ff.

24. FO 371/91226 E 1192/241, August 13, 1951.

25. Israel State Archive, File 2453/12, a review of Western defense planning for the Middle East, August 24, 1951.

26. David Ben-Gurion, *From Ben Gurion's Diary—The War of Independence*, ed. G. Rivlin and E. Oren (Tel Aviv: Ministry of Defence, 1986), June 27, 1951. For Ben-Gurion's position on these matters, see also Uri Bialer, ''Ben Gurion and the Question of Israel's International Orientation, 1948–1956,'' *Cathedra* 43 (1987): 145–72.

27. Campbell, *Defense of the Middle East*, p. 47.

28. Israel State Archive, File 3043/15, August 11, 1951.

29. Israel State Archive, File 2453/12.

30. Israel State Archive, File 2565/19.

31. Israel State Archive, File 2453/12.

32. Ibid.

33. See Moshe Sasson to Eliav in Washington, Israel State Archive, File 2565/13, April 8, 1952; and Moshe Sasson to Eliyahu Sasson, Israel State Archive, File 2408/13, March 21, 1952.

34. Israel State Archive, File 3043/5, May 14, 1952.

35. Ibid.

36. Eban to Sharett, March 19, 1952, Israel State Archive, File 2453/12.

37. A typical analysis can be found in a paper prepared by the Middle East Department in 1950 entitled ''Proposals for Influencing Egyptian Public Opinion.'' See also the Research Division's comment on this paper on June 21, 1950, in the same file.

38. Israel State Archive, File 2565/17.

39. See *Ruz al-Yusuf*, February 11, 1952; *al-Ahram*, February 16, 1952; and Israel State Archive, File 3043/5.

# Chapter Six

1. Israel State Archive, File 2848/22/A.

2. Rony E. Gabbay, *A Political Study of the Arab–Jewish Conflict: The Arab Refugee Problem (A Case Study)* (Geneva: Librairie E. Droz, 1958), p. 339.

3. Ibid., pp. 337–40.

4. Walter Laqueur, *The Road to War* (Harmondsworth: Penguin, 1970), p. 23.

5. Maxime Rodinson, *Israel and the Arabs* (New York: Pantheon 1968), p. 40.

6. Fred Khouri, *The Arab–Israeli Dilemma* (Syracuse, N.Y.: Syracuse University Press, 1968).

7. Ibid., pp. 100–101.

8. Malcolm H. Kerr, *The Middle East Conflict*, Headline Series, October 1968, pp. 5–6.

9. Nadav Safran, *From War to War* (New York: Pegasus Books, 1969).

10. Ibid., p. 36.

11. Ibid., pp. 37–38.

12. Ibid., p. 41.

13. Ibid., pp. 43 ff.

14. Books and articles by Sela, Gazit, and Schueftan have already been cited. See also Ilan Pappé, *Britain and the Arab–Israeli Conflict 1948–1951* (London: Macmillan, 1988); Amitzur Ilan, *Bernadotte in Palestine, 1948* (London: Macmillan, 1989); and M. Oren, "Egyptian–Israeli Relations in the Nineteen Fifties" (Ph.D. diss., Princeton University, 1989).

15. Zachary Lockman, "Original Sin," *Middle East Report*, May–June 1988, pp. 57–64.

16. B. Morris, "The New Historiography: Israel Confronts Its Past," *Tikkun*, November–December (1988), pp. 19–23, 99–102.

17. Tom Segev, *1949: The First Israelis* (Jerusalem: Domino Press, 1984) (in Hebrew).

18. Simha Flapan, *The Birth of Israel* (New York: Pantheon, 1987).

19. Avi Shlaim, "Husni Zaim and the Plan to Resettle Palestinian Refugees in Syria," *Middle East Focus*, Fall 1986, pp. 26–31.

20. Avi Shlaim, "Letter to the Editor," *Commentary* 89 (February 1990): 2–9.

21. Shabtai Teveth, "Charging Israel with Original Sin," *Commentary* 88 (September 1989): 24–33.

22. Arieh Shalev, *Co-operation under the Shadow of Conflict—The Israeli–Syrian Armistice Regime, 1949–1955.*

23. Nadhir Fansa, *Days of Husni al-Za'im: 137 Days That Shook Up Syria* (Beirut: Manshurāt Dar el-Āfāq al-Jadida, 1982), p. 129; *New York Times*, August 26, 1949.

24. Yehoshafat Harkabi, *Arab Attitudes To Israel* (New York: Hart, 1972).

25. Khaled al-'Azm, *The Memoirs of Khaled al-'Azm* (Beirut: Al Dar al Muttahida Lil-Nashir, 1973), pt. 1, pp. 380–82 (in Arabic).

# Bibliography

## Documents

State of Israel. *Documents on the Foreign Policy of Israel*. Part 1: May 14–
September 30, 1948. Ed. Yehoshua Freundlich. Jerusalem, 1981.
———. *Documents on the Foreign Policy of Israel*. Part 2: October 1948–
April 1949. Ed. Yehoshua Freundlich. Jerusalem, 1984.
———. *Documents on the Foreign Policy of Israel*. Part 3: Armistice Talks
with the Arab Countries. Ed. Yemima Rosenthal. Jerusalem, 1983.
———. *Documents on the Foreign Policy of Israel*. Part 4: May–December
1949. Ed. Yemima Rosenthal. Jerusalem, 1986.
———. Documents on the Foreign Policy of Israel. Part 5: 1950. Ed.
Yehoshua Freundlich. Jerusalem, 1988.
State of Israel. Ha-Knesset, *Divrey Ha-Knesset* (Minutes of the Knesset),
1949.
United States Government. Foreign Relations of the United States (FRUS):
The Near East, South Asia and Africa. Vol. 6, 1949. Washington,
D.C., 1977.
———. Foreign Relations of the United States: The Near East, South Asia
and Africa. Vol. 5, 1950. Washington, D.C., 1978.

# Archives

Israel: State of Israel, Israel State Archives
England: Public Record Office (PRO), London
United States: National Archives (USNA), Washington, D.C., and
    Maryland
France: Ministère des affaires étrangères (MAE), Paris

# Newspapers

*Al-Ahram*
*Al-Hayat*
*Yedi'ot Aharonot*
*Ruz al-Yusuf*
*New York Times*

# Books

Al-'Azm, Khaled. *The Memoirs of Khaled al-'Azm.* (in Arabic) Beirut: Al
    Dar al Muttahida Lil-Nashir, 1973.
Allon, Yigal. *A Curtain of Sand.* (in Hebrew) Tel Aviv: Hakibbutz Ha-
    meouchad, 1959.
Amitzur, Ilan. *Bernadotte in Palestine, 1948.* London: Macmillan, 1989.
Arslan, Adel. *The Memoirs of Emir Adel Arslan.* 3 vols. (in Hebrew) Beirut:
    Dar al-Taqadumiyya Lil-Nashir, 1983.
Bar Yaacov, N. *The Israeli–Syrian Armistice: Problems of Implementation
    1949–1966.* Jerusalem: Magnes Press, 1967.
Bar Yosef, Uri. *The Best of Enemies: Israel and Transjordan in the War
    of 1948.* London: Frank Cass, 1987.
Ben-Gurion, David. *From Ben-Gurion's Diary—The War of Independence.*
    Ed. G. Rivlin and E. Oren. (in Hebrew) Tel Aviv: Ministry of
    Defence, 1986.

————. *The Restored State of Israel*. (in Hebrew) Tel Aviv: Am Oved, 1969.

————. *The War Diary: The War of Independence, 1948–1949*. 3 vols. (in Hebrew) Tel Aviv: Ministry of Defence, 1982.

Bolitho, Hector. *The Angry Neighbors*. London: Arthur Barker, 1957.

Brecher, Michael. *The Foreign Policy System of Israel*. New Haven, Conn.: Yale University Press, 1972.

Campbell, John. *Defense of the Middle East: Problems of American Policy*. New York: Praeger, 1960.

Claude, Inis, Jr. *Swords into Plowshares*. New York: Random House, 1971.

Cohen, Yeruham. *By Daylight and in Darkness*. (in Hebrew) Tel Aviv: Amikam, 1969.

Copeland, Miles. *The Game of Nations*. London: Weidenfeld & Nicolson, 1969.

————. *The Game Player*. (London: Aurum Press, 1989).

Danin, Ezra. *Unconditional Zionist*. 2 vols. (in Hebrew) Jerusalem: Rivlin, 1987.

Dann, Uriel. *Studies in the History of Transjordan, 1920–1949*. Boulder, Colo.: Westview Press, 1984.

Dayan, Moshe. *The Story of My Life*. (in Hebrew) Jerusalem: Devir House; Tel Aviv: Yedi'ot Aharonot, 1982.

Eban, Abba. *An Autobiography*. London: Weidenfeld & Nicolson, 1977.

Elath, Eliahu. *Zionism and the Arabs*. (in Hebrew) Tel Aviv: Devir, 1974.

Eshed, Haggai. *A One-Man Institution*. (in Hebrew) Tel Aviv: Idanim, 1978.

Eytan, Walter. *The First Ten Years*. New York: Simon & Schuster, 1958.

Fansa, Nadhir. *Days of Husni al-Za'im: 137 Days That Shook Up Syria*. (in Arabic) Beirut: Manshurat Dar al-Afaq al-Jadida, 1988.

Flapan, Simha. *The Birth of Israel: Myths and Realities*. New York: Pantheon, 1987.

Forsythe, David. *United Nations Peacemaking: The Conciliation Commission for Palestine*. Baltimore: Johns Hopkins University Press, 1972.

Gabbay, Rony E. *A Political Study of the Arab–Jewish Conflict: A Case Study*. Geneva: Librairie E. Droz, 1959.

Goren, Asher. *The Arab League, 1945–1954*. (in Hebrew) Tel Aviv: Ayanot, 1954.

Harel, Isser. *Security and Democracy*. (in Hebrew) Tel Aviv: Idanim, Yedi'ot Aharonot, 1989.

Harkabi, Yehoshafat. Arab Attitudes to Israel. New York: Hart, 1972.

Haykal, Yusuf. *Meetings at Raghdan Palace*. (in Arabic) Amman: Dar al-Jalil Lil-Nashir, 1988.

Khouri, Fred. *The Arab–Israeli Dilemma*. Syracuse, N.Y.: Syracuse University Press, 1968.

Ionides, Michael. *Divide and Lose*. London: Geoffrey Bles, 1960.

Kerr, Malcolm. *The Arab Cold War 1958–1954: A Study of Ideology in Politics*. Oxford: Oxford University Press, 1968.

————, ed. *The Elusive Peace in the Middle East*. Albany: State University of New York Press, 1975.

————. *The Middle East Conflict*. Headline Series, October 1968, no. 191.

Kimche, Jon. *Seven Fallen Pillars: The Middle East, 1915–1950*. London: Secker and Warburg, 1950.

————. *Both Sides of the Hill*. London: Secker and Warburg, 1960.

Kirkbride, Alec. *From the Wings*. London: Frank Cass, 1976.

————. *A Crackle of Thorns*. London: John Murray, 1956.

Laquer, Walter. *The Road to War*. Harmondsworth: Penguin, 1970.

Louis, Roger. *The British Empire in the Middle East, 1945–1951*. Oxford: Oxford University Press, 1984.

McGhee, George. *Envoy to the Middle World: Adventures in Diplomacy*. New York: Harper & Row, 1983.

Morris, Benny. *The Birth of a Palestinian Refugee Problem, 1947–1949*. Cambridge: Cambridge University Press, 1988.

Nevo, Yosef. *Abdullah and the Palestinian Arabs*. (in Hebrew) Tel Aviv: Shiloah Institute, Tel Aviv University, 1965.

Pappé, Ilan. *Britain and the Arab–Israeli Conflict, 1948–1951*. London: Macmillan, 1988.

Rafael, Gideon. *Destination Peace*. London: Weidenfeld & Nicolson, 1981.

Rodinson, Maxime. *Israel and the Arabs*. New York: Pantheon, 1968.

Safran, Nadav. *From War to War*. New York: Pegasus Books, 1969.

Sasson, Eliyahu. *On the Road to Peace*. (in Hebrew) Tel Aviv: Am Oved, 1978.

Schueftan, Dan. *The Jordanian Option: Israel, Jordan and the Palestinians*. 2nd ed. (in Hebrew) Tel Aviv: Yad Tabankin, Hakibbutz Hameouchad, 1987.

Seale, Patrick. *The Struggle for Syria*. Oxford: Oxford University Press, 1965.

Segev, Tom. *1949: The First Israelis*. (in Hebrew) Jerusalem: Domino Press, 1984.

Sela, Avraham. *From Contacts to Negotiations: The Relationship of the Jewish Agency and the State of Israel with King Abdullah, 1946–1950*. (in Hebrew) Tel Aviv: Shiloah Institute, Tel Aviv University, 1985.

Shalev, Aryeh. *Cooperation in the Shadow of Conflict*. (in Hebrew) Tel Aviv: Maarachot, Ministry of Defence, 1987.

Sharett, Moshe. *A Personal Diary*. (in Hebrew) Tel-Aviv: Maariv, 1978.

Shlaim, Avi. *Collusion Across the Jordan: King Abdallah, the Zionist Movement, and the Partition of Palestine*. Oxford: Oxford University Press, 1988.

Snow-Ethridge, Willie. *Going to Jerusalem.* New York: Vanguard, 1950.

Teveth, Shabtai. *Ben Gurion: The Burning Ground, 1886–1948.* Boston: Houghton Mifflin, 1987.

———. *Ben Gurion and the Palestinian Arabs.* Oxford: Oxford University Press, 1985.

Vatikiotis, P. J. *The History of Egypt from Muhammad Aly to Sadat.* London: Weidenfeld & Nicolson, 1980.

Zak, Moshe. *Israel and the Soviet Union: A Forty-Year Dialogue.* (in Hebrew) Tel Aviv: Maariv, 1988.

## Articles

Bar-Siman-Tov, Yaacov. "Ben Gurion and Sharett: Conflict Management and Great Power Constraints in Israeli Foreign Policy." *Middle Eastern Studies* 24 (July 1988): 330–56.

Bialer, Uri. "Ben-Gurion and the Question of Israel's International Orientation, 1948–1956." *Cathedra* 43 (1987): 145–72 (in Hebrew).

Dawn, Ernest. "Pan-Arabism and the Failure of Israeli–Jordanian Peace Negotiations, 1950." In Girdhari L. Tikku, ed., *Islam and Its Cultural Divergence.* Champaign–Urbana: University of Illinois Press, 1971, pp. 25–51.

van Dusen, Michael. "Intra- and Inter-Generational Conflict in the Syrian Army." Ph.D. diss., Johns Hopkins University, 1971.

Gazit, Mordechai. "The Israel–Jordan Peace Negotiations (1949–51): King Abdallah's Lonely Effort." *Journal of Contemporary History* 23 (July 1988): 409–23.

Kedourie, Elie. "The Arab–Israeli Conflict." In Elie Kedourie, *Arabic Political Memoirs.* London: Frank Cass, 1974, pp. 218–31.

———. "The Sorceror's Apprentice." In Elie Kedourie, *Arabic Political Memoirs.* London: Frank Cass, 1974, pp. 170–76.

Khoury, Philip. "Divided Loyalties? Syria and the Question of Palestine, 1919–1939." *Middle Eastern Studies,* 21 (July 1985): 324–48.

Little, Douglas. "Cold War and Covert Action: The United States and Syria, 1945–1958." *Middle East Journal,* 44 (Winter 1990): 51–75.

Lockman, Zachary. "Original Sin." *Middle East Report,* May–June 1988, pp. 57–64.

Maddy-Weitzman, Bruce. "The Crystalization of an Arab State System: Inter-Arab Politics, 1945–1954." Ph.D. diss., Tel Aviv University, 1987.

Morris, Benny. "The New Historiography: Israel Confronts Its Past." *Tikkun*, November–December 1988, pp. 19–23, 99–102.

Rabinovich, Itamar. "Inter-Arab Relations Foreshadowed: The Question of the Syrian Throne in the 1920s and 1930s." *Zmanim* no. 3 (Autumn 1980): 92–99 (in Hebrew).

————. "Egypt and the Question of Israel Before and After the July Revolution." *Zmanim*, Winter 1990, pp. 78–87 (in Hebrew).

Rosenthal, Yemima. "Ben-Gurion and Sharett Facing Crucial Decisions in Israel's Foreign Policy." *Skira Hodshit*, December 30, 1988, pp. 15–22 (in Hebrew).

Sela, Avraham. "Syria and the Question of Israel from the Inception of the Arab League till the Armistice Agreement, 1948–1949." *Dapei Elazar* (Tel Aviv University), April–June 1983, pp. 24–42 (in Hebrew).

Shamir, Shimon. "The Arab–Israeli Conflict." In A. L. Udovitch, ed., *The Middle East: Oil, Conflict and Hope*. Lexington, Mass.: Lexington Books, 1976, pp. 195–231.

Sharett, Moshe. "Israel and the Arabs—War and Peace." *Ot*, October 1966, pp. 8–10 (in Hebrew).

Shimoni, Yaacov. "Syria Between Coups." *Hamizrah Hehadash* 1 (1949–50): 7–21 (in Hebrew).

————. "The Jordanian Orientation, the Egyptian Orientation, and the Palestinian Orientation on the Eve of the Establishment of the State and During Its Early Years." (Unpublished paper) (in Hebrew).

Shlaim, Avi. "Conflicting Approaches to Israel's Relations with the Arabs: Ben Gurion and Sharett, 1953–1956." *Middle East Journal*, Spring 1983, pp. 180–202.

————. "Husni Zaim and the Plan to Resettle Palestinian Refugees in Syria." *Middle East Focus*, Fall 1986, pp. 26–31.

Teveth, Shabtai. "The Palestine Arab Refugee Problem and Its Origins." *Middle Eastern Studies* 26 (April 1990): 215–49.

————. "Charging Israel with Original Sin." *Commentary* 88 (September 1989): 24–33.

# Index